FLOWER TYPES

SPIKE RACEME CORYMB PANICLE UMBEL CYME

COROLLA SHAPES

ROTATE CAMPANULATE FUNNELFORM URCEOLATE SALVERFORM

TREE AND SHRUB SHAPES

LOW TRAILING ROUND COMPACT HORIZONTAL SPREADING

ERECT ARCHING UPRIGHT

CONE COLUMN WEEPING GLOBE FASTIGIATE

THE AMERICAN GARDEN GUIDES

oriental
gardening

General Consultants:
Benjamin Chu, Missouri Botanical Garden, St. Louis, Missouri
Roy Forster, VanDusen Gardens, Vancouver, British Columbia
Virginia Hayes, Ganna Walska Lotusland, Santa Barbara, California
Heather O'Hagen, Dr. Sun-Yat-Sen Garden, Vancouver, British Columbia
Henry Painter, Fort Worth-Dallas Botanic Garden
Jerry Parsons, University of California at Berkeley Botanical Garden
Nancy Rose, Minneapolis Landscape Arboretum, Chanhassen, Minnesota

Design Consultants: Holly and Osamu Shimizu
Botany Consultant: Dr. Lucile H. McCook
Enabling Garden Consultant: Eugene Rothert, Chicago Botanic Garden

oriental
gardening

The Japanese Garden Society of Oregon

With Kate Jerome, Writer, Horticulturist

Preface by Maureen Sanchez, Director
Series Editor: Elvin McDonald
Principal Photography by Allan Mandell

Pantheon Books,
Knopf Publishing Group
New York
1996

Acknowledgments
This book was created with the help, expertise, and encouragement of many people. We would like to thank all the consultants who contributed so much to it, and the photographers who provided magnificent photographs. Special thanks to The San Francisco Japanese Tea Garden and The Woodlawn Cemetery for permission to photograph on their grounds and to Lilypons Water Gardens for permission to reproduce their photographs We also appreciate the efforts of Kathy Grasso, Susan Ralston, Anne Messette, Alan Kellock, David Prior, Annie Goh, Serene Lee, Jay Hyams, Ed Mickens, Shirley and Martin Stein, Joey Tomocik, Lainee Cohen, Betty Luber, Chani Yammer, Etti Yammer, Yosef, Tzvi, and Chava Stein, Michelle Stein, and Deena Stein.

Project Director: Lori Stein
Book Design Consultant: Albert Squillace
Editorial Director: Jay Hyams
Associate Art Director: Eric Marshall

Library of Congress Cataloging-in-Publication Data
The Japanese Garden Society of Oregon.
Oriental gardening / by The Japanese Garden Society of Oregon with Kate Jerome.
    p.   cm.   (–The American garden guides)
Includes index.
ISBN 0-679-75861-5
1. Gardens, Oriental–United States.   2. Gardens, Oriental–Canada.
3. Landscape gardening–United States.   4. Landscape gardening–Canada. 5. Plants, Ornamental–Pictorial works.
I. Jerome, Kate.   II. Title.   IV. Series.
SB458.46.S26   1996
635.9–dc20   95-23962
                                    CIP

Manufactured in Singapore

First edition

9   8   7   6   5   4   3   2   1

Opposite: The Japanese Garden of Portland.

contents

3. Garden Design 154

4. Techniques 180

5. Special Conditions 202

the american garden guides

The network of botanical gardens and arboreta in the United States and Canada constitutes a great treasure chest of knowledge about plants and what they need. Some of the most talented, experienced, and dedicated plantspeople in the world work full-time at these institutions; they are the people who actually grow plants, make gardens, and teach others about the process. They are the gardeners who are responsible for the gardens in which millions of visitors exclaim, "Why won't that plant grow that way for me?"

Over thirty of the most respected and beautiful gardens on the continent are participating in the creation of *The American Garden Guides*. The books in the series originate with manuscripts generated by gardeners in one or several of the gardens. Drawing on their decades of experience, these originating gardeners write down the techniques they use in their own gardens, recommend and describe the plants that grow best for them, and discuss their successes and failures. The manuscripts are then passed to several other participating gardens; in each, the specialist in that area adds recommended plants and other suggestions based on regional differences and different opinions.

The series has three major philosophical points carried throughout:

1) Successful gardens are by nature user-friendly toward the gardener and the environment. We advocate water conservation through the precepts of Xeriscaping and garden health care through Integrated Pest Management (IPM). Simply put, one does not set into motion any garden that is going to require undue irrigation during normal levels of rainfall, nor apply any pesticide or other treatment without first assessing its impact on all other life—plant, animal, and soil.

2) Gardening is an inexact science, learned by observation and by doing. Even the most experienced gardeners often develop markedly dissimilar ways of doing the same thing, or have completely divergent views of what any plant requires in order to thrive. Gardeners are an opinionated lot, and we have encouraged all participants to air and share their differences—and so, to make it clear that everyone who gardens will find his or her own way of dealing with plants. Although it is important to know the rules and the most accepted practices, it is also important to recognize that whatever works in the long run for you is the right way.

3) Part of the fun of gardening lies in finding new plants, not necessarily using over and over the same ones in the same old color schemes. In this book and others in the series, we have purposely included some lesser-known or underused plants, some of them native to our vast and wonderful continent. Wherever we can, we call attention to endangered species and suggest ways to nurture them back to their natural state of plenty.

Elvin McDonald
Houston, Texas

director's preface

"The Garden speaks to all our senses not just to the mind alone"

PROFESSOR TAKUMA TONO
DESIGNER, THE JAPANESE GARDEN OF PORTLAND, OREGON

Tranquility lies at the very heart of a Japanese garden. It is more than a feeling; it is palpable. When one enters the world of the Japanese garden one's hope should be to fully realize a sense of peace, harmony, and serenity because it is in this arena that man and gods share equally in the beauty of nature. It is a living reflection of Japanese culture . . . elegant simplicity.

Throughout the centuries, Japanese garden designers, who were both laymen and priests, used three primary elements in every design: stone, the "bones" of the landscape; water, the life-giving force; and plants, the tapestry of four seasons. Secondary elements include pagodas, stone lanterns, water basins, arbors, and bridges.

Gardens are generally asymmetical in design and reflect nature in stylized form. Other important aesthetic concepts include simplicity; *koko,* the importance of age and time; *shizen,* naturalness or the avoidance of the artificial; *yugen*, implying obscurity and darkness (the latter being a metaphor for the mysterious, the profound, the uncertain, or the subtle); and *miegakure,* or the avoidance of full expression. Zen philosophy teaches that the value of suggestion is of utmost importance because in leaving something incomplete, one is privileged to finish the experience according to one's personal imagination. Human scale is maintained throughout the garden so man always feels a part of the environment rather than overpowered by it. These are places of quiet reflection designed to nourish both the heart and soul of man. The main point is that there is always something more in the compositions of stone, water, and plants than meets the eye.

MAUREEN SANCHEZ
THE JAPANESE GARDEN SOCIETY OF OREGON

INTRODUCTION 1

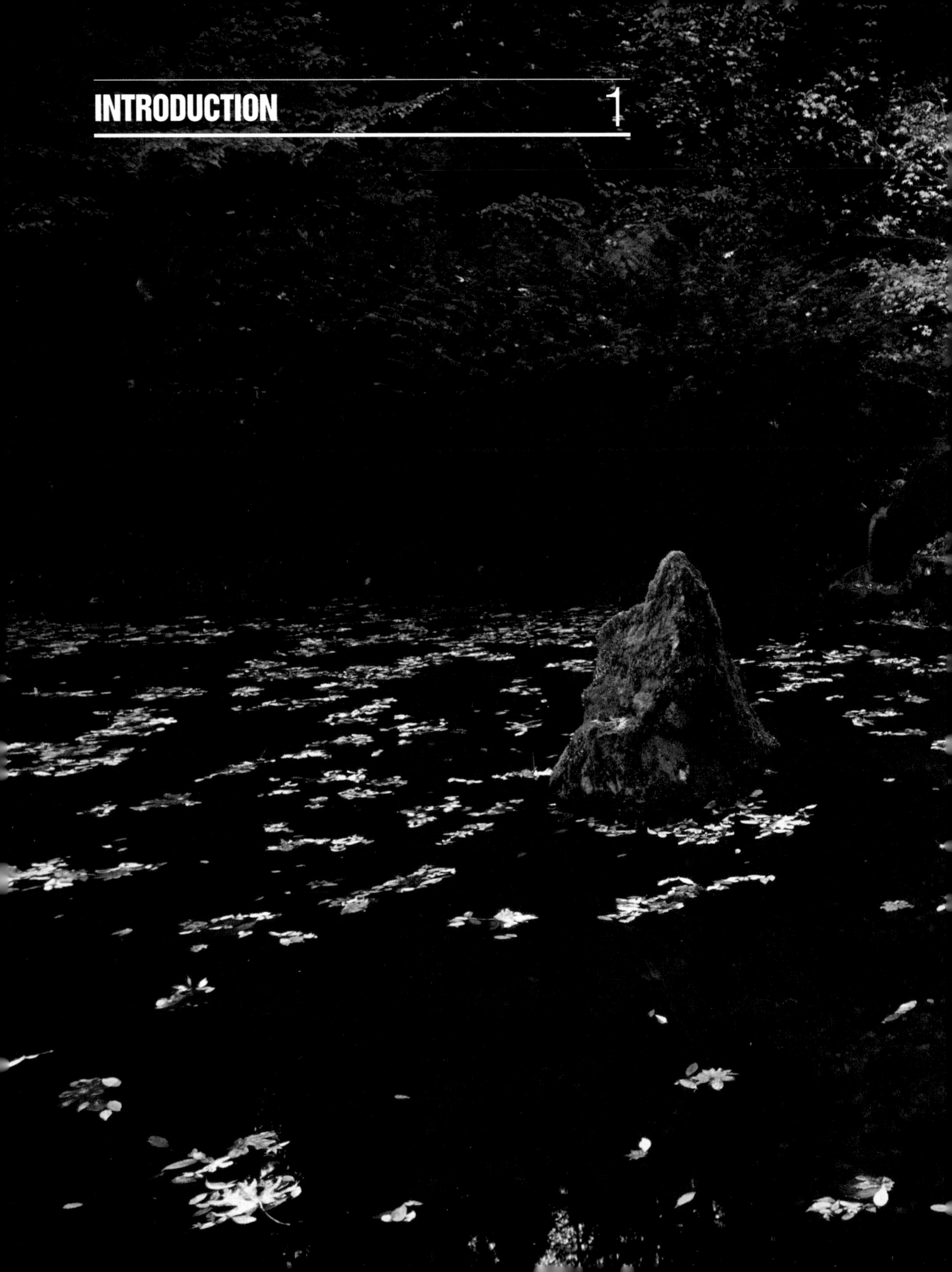

A Western dictionary might describe a garden as a collection of plants; this definition does not apply to oriental gardens. An oriental garden is a place where thoughtful reflection is gently encouraged through the placement and relationships of garden elements. Appealing to the senses, these gardens present contrasts of sunlight, shade, scent, and color. Evocative images—crimson maple leaves scattered on moss, white gravel raked into rippling waves, a red pine branch drooping gracefully over a still pool—form the heart of the garden. The soul of the garden emanates from the moist scent of sprinkled stones, the sweet aroma of flowering plum blossoms, and the sound of rain pattering on banana or bamboo leaves or a splashing waterfall. The essence of the garden exists only in the mind of those who see and appreciate it, for the garden is only complete when it is understood.

Perhaps this can be best explained with a story involving tea master Sen-no-Rikyu (sixteenth century) who built a garden enclosed by a tall hedge that blocked a view of the sea. The client for whom the garden was built was unhappy—until he bent to wash his hands in a water basin. The sea then became visible in a gap between the hedges. As the tea master had hoped, the client realized the intent behind the design as his mind was spurred to make a connection between the water in the basin and the great ocean and thus between himself and the infinite universe.

Below: This garden includes several elements common to oriental gardens—water, lanterns, stones, a pavilion, a bridge. But it is the combination of these elements that is essential, not merely their presence. *Opposite:* The dry garden at The Portland Japanese Garden.

HISTORICAL NOTES

The story of oriental gardens begins in China as early as 200 B.C. with gardens attached to the estates of emperors. Considering their size, these were actually parks; living amid great rivers and densely forested hills, the Chinese saw no need to superimpose designs on nature and sought instead to capture it intact. They filled these spaces with exotic plants and animals and curiously shaped rocks and stones collected from all corners of the immense empire. These early gardens were designed as miniature representations of the world, hills taking the place of mountain ranges, ponds inland seas, and groves of trees standing for trackless forests–a concept of miniaturization later to have great importance in Japan. To the Chinese the world consisted of heaven and earth, and landscapes, with their mountains and water, embodied both. Mountains, both artificial and natural, were of primary importance, first as representations of the Taoist Mystic Isles emerging from the sea and later as the Buddhist holy mountain Sumeru. Rocks, seen as miniature mountains, were avidly collected, particularly those with strange shapes.

The powerful Han emperor Wudi (ruled 140-87 B.C.) took this symbolism a step further and had three small islands made in his park and named for the mythical island homes of the Immortals, legendary personages believed to have achieved immortality through the practice of Taoist doctrine. Hoping to lure the Immortals to him so that he could learn their secrets, Wudi had pavilions and halls built on the islands. Lakes, islands, and mountains thus became primary elements of Chinese gardens. Such lake parks were enjoyed by guests who moved across the shimmering water on various kinds of pleasure craft, accompanied by barges bearing orchestras of concubines.

The emperor Yangdi (569-618) continued this tradition in a great pleasure park, 75 miles in circumference, which was packed with animals and plants and included three islands in the middle of a lake. As part of his active foreign policy, Yangdi opened diplomatic relations with Japan, and so it was that in A.D. 607 Ono no Imoko, first Japanese envoy to the Chinese court, saw Yangdi's park. Four years after the envoy's return to Japan, the first landscape garden, complete with lake and island, was built in Japan's imperial capital.

This garden style, known as the lake-and-island or artificial-hill style, is thus the oldest oriental garden style. Its movement from China to Japan reflects the strong cultural influence of China in Japan from the sixth to eighth centuries, when the Japanese upper classes studied the Chinese language, literature, art, and government, creating their own forms based on Chinese models. Buddhism, which reached China in the first century A.D., was introduced to Japan in 552. In China, Buddhism was applied over traditions from Taoism and Confucianism; in Japan, it joined Shinto, the ancient native religion of Japan with its host of supernatural beings, including divine spirits in trees, mountains, and rocks.

As in China, the first gardens in Japan belonged to rulers and wealthy nobles. During the Asuka (552-646) and Nara (646-794) periods, Japanese gardens, clearly based on Chinese models, were made for the refined pleasures of the nobility and were designed by the noble owners themselves. The design reflected the concept of the garden as miniature representation of the Buddhist cosmos, including artificial hills and ponds. The first reference to a garden in Japanese literature dates to this period, the *Nihonshoki* (721), in which the word used for "garden" is *niwa*, meaning a place purified for worship.

During the Heian period (794-1185), a period of great luxury and

Illustration of "craggy mountains with gnarled trees," from *Mustard Seed Garden Manual of Painting,* a seventeenth-century Chinese book on painting techniques.

elegance among court nobles, the garden was still considered an earthly representation of paradise, but it reached new heights as a pleasure ground, the setting of poetry parties and musical entertainments. The central feature was the pond, but gardens were designed as visual references to sites mentioned in literary works, often Chinese, or as reproductions of famous natural sites in both China and, increasingly, Japan. Garden planning was considered a necessary accomplishment in a gentleman, and gardens were designed to be viewed either from inside a building or from excursion boats floating on the pond. *The Tale of Genji,* a novel from the early eleventh century, includes many vivid descriptions of elaborate gardens. The first known written document on gardening in Japan dates to this period: the *Sakuteiki,* or "Treatise on Gardenmaking," written by a court gentleman, which reveals that the Japanese were no longer copying Chinese gardens and that the Japanese garden, with its mixture of Taoist, Shinto, and Buddhist ideas, was coming into its own. This work deals at great length with the increasingly important topic of rock placement.

Chinese culture in the form of Zen Buddhism had a powerful impact on Japan during the Kamakura period (1185-1392), named for the capital city of Yoritomo, Japan's first shogun. The shoguns and their samurai warriors embraced Zen, which reached its height in Japan during this period and changed gardens from spaces designed for group pleasure to environments meant to facilitate individual meditation. One of the first gardens to demonstrate the important changes introduced by Zen is the temple garden of Tenryu-ji, founded in 1270 in western Kyoto and designed by the Buddhist priest Muso Soseki (1275-1351), the lead-ing figure in medieval Japanese gardening. Soseki also designed the garden of the Saiho-ji temple in Kyoto, commonly known as the Moss Temple (Kokedera) because of its groundcover of many kinds of moss. This garden reflects Zen ideals—it is designed for meditation, reflecting the Zen ideal. These stroll gardens perfected the use of borrowed scenery and hide-and-reveal layouts and changed garden design by bringing the viewer into the garden to stroll through it while contemplating the changing views in the landscape. Most include a body of water with an undulating shoreline as its focal point, and a path that exposes differerent views or perspectives to the strolling visitor. The Katsura Villa, Sento Gosho, and Shugaku-in Villa are particularly famous for their use of borrowed scenery, usually distant mountains.

The Muromachi era (1393-1558), a period of civil war and ongoing unrest, proved one of the most creative in Japan's history. A cultured middle class came into being, and some of the outstanding forms of Japanese culture were refined, including No theater, landscape painting, and the tea ceremony. Gardens were of such importance that the most important periods of Muromachi history are named after the gardens of ruling shoguns. The Kityama period is named for the hills where Yoshimitsu (1358-1408) built the Kinkaku, or Golden Pavilion; the Higashiyama period is named for the hills where Yoshimasa (1436-1490) built the Silver Pavilion. The most famous gardens of this period clearly display the importance of Zen, which was coming to pervade all the arts. Indeed, the outstanding innovation in gardening during the Muromachi period was *karesansui,* the dry landscape garden, the epitome of Zen landscape in which there are no plants or trees and no water, only raked sand and rock groupings. Ryoan-ji in northwest Kyoto and Daisen-in are among the leading examples of the classical Zen garden.

The Momoyama period (1569-1603) continued this trend, as seen in the Sambo-in, the most famous garden from these years. By the late 16th century the *cha-no-yu,* or tea ceremony, had led to important changes in Japanese garden design. Such great tea masters as Sen-no-Rikyu reworked the layout of the garden while elaborating the performance of the tea ceremony.

The tea master Kobori Enshu (1579-1647) marks another important change in the oriental garden: Enshu designed gardens as a professional rather than an accomplished amateur. Garden making was taken over by professionals during the Edo, or Tokugawa, period (1603-1867), with gardeners catering to the increasingly prosperous middle class. As professionals seeking to please patrons, they created a wide range of gardens, including nostalgic evocations of Heian pleasure gardens, versions of the old heavenly paradise gardens, miniature landscapes for meditation, stroll gardens, and in particular gardens made for the tea ceremony.

The years of Tokugawa rule was a period of relative stability for Japan. It was also a period of isolation from the rest of the world. This isolation began to end when Commodore Perry's fleet appeared off Tokyo in 1853. The Meiji Restoration brought an end to Japanese feudalism and began the formation of the modern state of Japan, but it also signaled a turning toward the West in which many traditional arts were left behind or neglected. The "rediscovery" of the traditional oriental garden that has taken place during the past fifty years reflects the application of traditional formulas to modern problems and tastes.

EASTERN RELIGION An understanding of basic oriental gardening principles allows them to be adapted for Western gardens. The traditions of oriental gardens were modified in different countries and during different historical periods; see pages 29-34 for information on how different nations interpreted these philosophies. All these traditions are, however, derived from early teachings of master gardeners, which in turn are intrinsically connected to Eastern religions.

The study and understanding of Eastern religion would take a lifetime; the following brief summary is intended only to serve as a foundation for the gardening principles that are based on them.

In the third century century B.C., Taoism was the main religion and philosophy of China; its main teaching was the search for ideal freedom and simplicity by following Tao (which means "way" in Chinese); it is based on the doctrines of Lao-Tzu. Contemplation of nature, profoundly important to oriental gardening, was already suggested in the teaching of Taoism. Taoists believed that men and women who had achieved perfect harmony lived together on five faraway islands, served by sea turtles and cranes. Islands, sea turtles, and cranes have retained their symbolic significance.

Shinto was the most important religion in ancient Japan until it was modified by Buddhism around A.D. 600. Shintoists worship the elements of nature–its forces and physical representations–believing that they are imbued with divine spirits. Eventually, elements ranging from mountains to single stones–recognized as sacred because of their size, shape, color, or beauty–were deified and considered

Katsura Imperial Villa, Edo period, c. 1620, Kyoto, Japan.

Sento Gosho, a retired emperor's villa, Edo period, c. 1634, Kyoto, Japan.

as shrines. These shrines were roped off or surrounded with stones, creating archetypal oriental gardens. The importance of stone and rocks in oriental gardens–both the stones themselves and their positioning–dates back to Shintoism.

Hinduism, founded in India, has as its essence a belief in a cosmology that sets mountains as the center of the universe, with water and islands as connections. The Hindu religion reached China and Japan mostly in its reformation as Buddhism.

Buddhism, founded by Siddhartha Gautama (Buddha), who was born in Nepal around the fifth century B.C., is probably the most important religious basis of oriental gardening. When he was 35 years old, Buddha achieved enlightenment by meditating under a *Ficus religiosa* tree for 40 days. Buddha taught that there are four truths: that suffering exists; that desire causes suffering; that total transcendance over suffering, called nirvana, can be achieved; and that a path toward nirvana can be found. This "eightfold noble" path requires the right views, resolve, speech, action, livelihood, effort, mindfulness, and concentration. It is found through meditation. For several centuries, Buddhism existed alongside Taoism and Shintoism. In the fifth century A.D., Zen Buddhism, which allowed for "sudden enlightenment," made it more popular.

A constant in these Eastern religions is the importance of nature and the possibility of understanding nature by recreating it and meditating upon it.

PRINCIPLES OF ORIENTAL GARDEN DESIGN Oriental gardens have the beauty of nature as their focus; however, the goal of these gardens is not to simulate nature to but

Much art and effort was needed to achieve this natural look.

to recreate it using human artistry. The work of the human hand is disguised—perfect, contrived, symmetrical landscapes are not desired—and the garden designer strives to sublimate himself in nature. This is one of the paradoxes of the oriental garden: to succeed, a garden must reflect both the randomness of nature and the planned efficiency made possible by the human intervention. The result is an abstraction or idealization of nature, a refinement of its wildness.

A complete and symmetrical space is equated with death; one that is random and unfinished needs a living viewer to appreciate it. For this reason, straight geometrical shapes are rarely used in oriental gardens. When plants or stones are grouped, odd—indivisible—numbers are usually used.

The masters of oriental garden design developed a system of ideas to allow them to recreate nature. In Chapter 3, Garden Design, these ideas are discussed more fully (pages 174-177). The following paragraphs encapsulate them.

Abstraction Natural elements such as mountains, waterfalls, lakes and islands can be presented by symbols. A mountain can be represented by a stone, hills by a patch of contoured land, the sea by a winding stretch of gravel, a great forest by a single tree. Moving water can be a metaphor for life and certain plants symbolize goals and seasons. The peony, for example, symbolizes happiness in Chinese gardens. Empty space represents the rest of the world. Water brings a stillness and peace to the soul of man and thus water plays an important part in all gardens.

Contrast Contrasting shapes and colors stimulate thought and are subjects for meditation. The contrast is often simple and stark: a single red blossom near a field of evergreen trees, white gravel against a deep red Japanese maple, dark gray stones placed near feathery ferns or bamboo.

Simplicity is one of the hallmarks of oriental design; a few carefully chosen and placed plants and stones are used for best effects.

Change and motion Oriental gardens take complete advantage of the beauty of four season. Designers will accentuate all the seasons by choosing plants that undergo seasonal changes. Spring color bursts forth in the blooms of azaleas, dogwoods, plum and cherry trees. Summer's beauty is seen in the contrasting textures and hues of green plants in careful compositions. Japanese maples and chrysanthemums are perhaps the most common and popular plants for fall color. Winter is a time to enjoy the garden rather than a season to withdraw particularly when snow, called *sekka*, the flower of winter, collects along tree branches and trunks, and accentuates the "bones" of the garden.

The easiest way to show movement is with moving water and certainly this is an element element in an oriental garden. Because movement is so important, a way of representing it even when water features cannot be supplied was created: *karesansui,* or dry garden. In these gardens, stones, gravel, or sand are arranged to represent water. (The word *kare* means dry; the term *sansui* refers to paintings of water and mountains.) The gravel or sand could be raked with waves or placed in curved beds to simulate moving or still water; stones could be arranged in paths that represented rivers.

Movement is also seen in features that change each day or each season–petals on a field of moss or sand or shadows flickering over snow-covered lanterns.

Perspective A fundamental principle of almost all oriental garden design is the desire to achieve beauty for the beholder from any point in the garden. Gardens unfold to the viewer and are usually not seen complete in a single glance. To reveal a garden all at once would take away the mystery of discovery and is considered boring. It is the intention that the stroller should pause at any point and see a new panorama or a new aspect of beauty of the garden. This design element

The surrounding landscape is drawn into these gardens with sophisticated design. *Above:* Tall pagodas and raised areas bring in mountains, which are also reflected in the water. *Opposite left:* A pond reflects the outside world. *Opposite bottom:* Black-trunked trees define and trim colorful fall foliage. *Right:* A winding path leads a stroller through a spring garden.

is called *mie gakure* or hide-and-reveal.

Simplicity and quiet The essence of a Japanese garden is simplicity, from plant choices to landscape elements such as rocks, bridges, and lanterns to the overall garden design of flowing curves and varied textures. Architecture in Japanese gardens is always simple, unadorned, and made of naturally occurring unpainted materials. Other than spring bloom, riotous color is avoided in these gardens. Many gardens are filled only with subtle shades and tones of green, making the garden a place for contemplation and reflection. The landscape may merge with the house as rooms open through shoji (paper doors) in the garden. Chinese gardens are somewhat more flamboyant, placing more emphasis on architecture and individual plants, but still refined and reduced to essential ingredients.

Use of plants and their relationship to other garden elements Plants are not the only or even the most important part of an oriental garden; stones, artifacts, bridges, lanterns, water, are all combined in making the garden. Plants are carefully chosen for their ability to blend into the landscape. In some cases, this means they will serve as evergreen backdrops, in other gardens they will be focal points, pruned to accentuate their grace and elegance. The plant's shape and symbolism

are more important than its blossoms. Trees are used as structural elements, pruned to frame a distant view, enhance a weather-sculpted stone, or accentuate a contrast.

Borrowed landscape Oriental gardens freely use the concept of a "borrowed" landscape (*shakkei* in Japanese) in which distant views of a mountain or forest are framed or "trimmed" by using elements in the garden to accentuate them. Walls or hedges may border the garden and screen undesirable views while drawing the eye to the distant focal point. Other elements such as a rock, tree trunks or a stone lantern may gently lead the gaze to a beautiful distant view.

The use of borrowed landscape first began to appear in the gardens of the Heian period (794-1185) and further developed in the Muromachi period (1393-1558). It was popular in China as well and was discussed by Chinese garden designer Li Chi-cheng, who wrote: "There are no particular rules for constructing a garden, but for the borrowing of landscapes there are certain techniques, and they are of the greatest importance in designing a garden with trees. The techniques are of four different types: borrowing from a great distance, borrowing

from nearby, borrowing from a high level, and borrowing from a low level. Any one of these can be used according to the situation and the opportunities available."

The first step in borrowing landscape is choosing a place with good scenery. However, it is not enough for the landscape to be viewable from the garden, it must be captured "alive" in some way. Distant mountains can be brought into focus by building smaller mountains to mirror them. Cherry trees covered with blossoms can pull snow-covered peaks into the garden. The borrowed landscape is often linked to the garden with intermediate objects, such as rocks, flowers, and small trees and shrubs. Scenes glimpsed between tree trunks, under the eaves of buildings, or between stone lanterns remain fixed in the eye of the beholder.

ESSENTIAL ELEMENTS In Western gardens, the main elements are plants. Although garden furniture is often included, it is subordinate to the main ingredients. This is not the case in oriental gardens. The palette of the designer of oriental gardens includes water, stones, paths, waterfalls, bridges, and sculptured ornaments as well as garden plants and trees.

Structural elements other than plants hold as important a place as plants in oriental gardens. They should be chosen to complement the plants and the overall theme of the garden, without overwhelming or overshadowing the basic design. Always keep in mind when choosing non-plant elements that the guiding tenet must be subtlety and integration with the design. Beyond these principles, the garden designer's taste is the only limitation.

Stones are the most important non-plant element in any type of oriental garden and may sometimes even be more important than plants, as in Zen dry gar-

dens. A small oriental garden will often include a Stone of Two Deities, a Guardian Stone, and a flat worshipping stone while some large gardens may have more than a hundred stones, each with a purpose and a name. When choosing stones, consider size, texture, shape, and color. Metamorphic rock is generally prized for its interesting colors and striations and the fact that it doesn't disintegrate. Rocks with many irregularities allow moss to get a foothold, another design element in oriental gardens. Stones may be upright, low and vertical, horizontal and flat, scooped or arching. Buried large stones appear as natural outcrops, and stones set below the water surface give an illusion of depth in a shallow pond.

Water holds almost as important a place in oriental garden design as stones, whether it be a full-sized lake, a small pool, a rushing or trickling waterfall, a dappled stream, or even a dry stream bed. Water has always been so important in oriental design that in formal gardens, galleries are often built to be opened to enjoy the rain. If the designer is lucky enough to have the room to install a lake, the lake should be designed with an irregular, curved shape and planted with trees so that the visitor cannot see all of the shoreline at one time. Lakes usually include one or more islands or rocks, each representing a specific element such as a crane, a tortoise, or clouds. Still water should be sited so it has a feeling of life, exposed to wind, raindrops, and sunlight. Water is always a focal point and still pools should be large enough for reflections.

Streams add coolness and motion to the oriental garden, and even if adding water would be difficult, a dry stream bed gives the illusion of movement. If the garden actually does have a stream, plants and rocks should be placed appropriately to soften and adorn the banks. A particularly attractive feature is to position

Elements of oriental design include use of stone, pathways, seasonal plants, and bridges.

Typical methods of enclosure include bamboo fences and background plantings.

plants and stones to give the illusion that the stream is actually a spring coming out of moss-covered rocks.

Oriental gardens do not traditionally include fountains since the basic premise is to replicate nature. Waterfalls, however, may be a central feature of an oriental garden, and should be placed according to the way nature would place them. Even slight changes in topography can make a creative waterfall, as can a stone basin containing rocks for falling water to splash onto. If an actual waterfall cannot be placed in a garden, then a representation, in the form of a dry waterfall, may be created. Some designers are well known for their dry waterfalls in which they arrange stones with striations that resemble water patterns.

In large gardens, paths are a critical element to draw the visitor through the garden. In courtyard gardens, they are only aesthetic since there is seldom room to walk. Paths should be curved and paved with natural materials such as shredded bark or stone. If cement is necessary to hold small stones in place, it must be placed below soil level so it is not visible. Stepping stones are often used for a central path. The original reason for using stepping stones in a garden was functional, to avoid muddying the feet, but over time, they've become more ritualized by forming a winding, meditative path to the tea ceremony. Stepping stones are essential in a moss garden so the moss will not be trodden and harmed.

For thousands of years, lanterns have symbolized light dispelling darkness,

whether they actually lighted the way to a night tea ceremony or merely gave the illusion of shedding light as a sculptural element in a courtyard garden. The classic oriental lantern is made of a base, a pedestal, a capital, light holder, and headpiece although contemporary lantern makers have taken license with lantern design, and some of these traditional parts may be missing. "Snow" lanterns have two, three, or four legs and a wide top for catching the snow. Some contemporary lanterns are wired for an electric light. Lanterns are made of all types of materials, although stone is still the most popular. Unless the garden is quite large, a small lantern is most desirable since a large lantern will detract from the garden. A flat stone is placed next to the lantern for ease of lighting it and the lantern may be nestled next to a tree with at least one branch partially obscuring it to give a shimmering effect.

Stone basins came into oriental gardens for the ritual cleansing of hands,

A BRIEF LESSON IN BOTANY

Plants are living things and share many traits with animals. Plants are composed of millions of individual cells that are organized into complex organ systems. Plants breathe (take in and expel gases) and extract energy from food; to do this they require water, nutrients, and atmospheric gases. Like animals, plants reproduce sexually, and their offspring inherit characteristics through a genetic code passed along as DNA.

Plants, however, can do one thing that no animal can do. Through a process called photosynthesis, plants can capture energy from the sun and convert that energy into compounds such as proteins, fats, and carbohydrates. These energy-rich compounds are the source of energy for all animal life, including humans.

THE IMPORTANCE OF PLANTS

Because no living animals can produce the energy they need to live, all their energy comes from plants. Like other animals, we eat green plants directly, in the form of fruits, vegetables, and grains (breads and cereals), or we eat animals and animal products that were fed green plants.

The oxygen we need to live on Earth is constantly pumped out of green plants as a byproduct of photosynthesis. Plants prevent the erosion of our precious soils and hinder water loss to the atmosphere.

Plants are also an important source of drugs. Fully one-quarter of all prescriptions contain at least one plant-derived product. Aspirin, one of the most commonly used drugs, was originally isolated from the bark of the willow tree.

THE WHOLE PLANT

Basically, a plant is made up of leaves, stems, and roots; all these parts are connected by a vascular system, much like our circulatory system. The vascular system can be seen in the veins of a leaf, or in the rings in a tree.

LEAVES

Leaves are generally flattened and expanded tissues that are green due to the presence of chlorophyll, the pigment that is necessary for photosynthesis. Most leaves are connected to the stem by a stalk, or petiole, which allows the leaves to alter their position in relation to the sun and capture as much energy as possible.

Leaves come in an astounding variety of shapes, textures, and sizes. Some leaves are composed of a single structure, or blade, and are termed simple. Other leaves are made up of many units, or leaflets, and are called compound (see endpapers).

STEMS

Technically, a stem is the tissue that supports leaves and that connects the leaves with the roots via a vascular system. Stems also bear the flowers on a plant. Therefore, a stem can be identified by the presence of buds, which are the unexpanded leaves, stems, or flowers that will develop later.

A single plant can produce more than one kind of stem; the upright, above-ground stem produces leaves and flowers, while a horizontal, below-ground stem can swell and store food products from photosynthesis. Underground stems can overwinter and produce new plants when conditions are favorable.

The stem of a plant often changes as the plant matures. When a tree is young, its stems are green and soft; as the tree grows and ages, however, the stem develops woody tissues. Wood is composed of hardened cells that provide strength to the stem and that allow water, gases, and nutrients to move both vertically and horizontally through the stem. Concentric circles inside a woody stem are called annual rings. The oldest wood is in the center of the rings, and the youngest wood is in the outer ring. Light-colored rings, or early wood, are composed of cells that were added early in the growing season of each year; these cells are larger and are less densely packed together. Late wood is darker in color because the cells are smaller and packed more closely. Each set of a light and dark ring represents one year in the life of the growing plant stem. When a plant grows under constant environmental conditions, with no changes in tem-

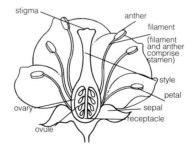

perature or moisture during the year (like in some tropical rain forests), the wood is uniform in color and lacks annual rings.

Bark forms on the outside of woody stems and is made up mostly of dead cells. This corky tissue is very valuable to the stem because it protects the new wood, allows gas exchange into the stem, and lets the stem grow in diameter. All of the bark is not dead tissue, however; the innermost layer is living vascular tissue. If a stem is girdled or the bark is damaged, this vascular tissue, which moves the food products of photosynthesis around in the plant, will be destroyed, and the plant will die.

ROOTS

Although out of sight, roots are extremely important to the life of the plant. Roots anchor a plant in the soil, absorb water and nutrients, and store excess food, such as starches, for the plants' future use. Basically, there are two types of roots: taproots and fibrous roots. Taproots, such as the edible part of a carrot, are thick unbranched roots that grow straight down. A taproot takes advantage of moisture and nutrients far below the soil surface and is a storehouse for carbohydrates. Fibrous roots are fine, branching roots that often form dense mats, making them excellent agents of soil stabilization. Fibrous roots absorb moisture and nutrients from a shallow zone of soil and may be more susceptible to drought. Roots obviously need to come into contact with water, but they also need air in order to work properly. Except for those adapted to aquatic environments, plants require well-drained soils.

VASCULAR SYSTEMS

Plants have a well-developed vascular system that extends throughout the plant body and that allows movement of water and compounds from one part of a plant to another. Roots absorb water and minerals, and the vascular system funnels them to the leaves for use in photosynthesis. Likewise, energy-rich compounds that are produced in the leaves must travel to the stems and roots to provide nutrition for further growth. The vascular system also strengthens plant tissues.

PHOTOSYNTHESIS

A green plant is like a factory that takes raw

materials from the environment and converts them into other forms of energy. In a complex series of energy transfer and chemical conversion events called photosynthesis, plants take energy from the sun, minerals and water from the soil, and gases from the atmosphere; these raw materials are converted into chemical forms of energy that are used for plant growth. These same energy-rich compounds (proteins, sugars and starches, fats and oils) can be utilized by animals as a source of food and nutrition. All this is possible because of a green pigment, chlorophyll.

Photosynthesis is an extremely complex series of reactions that takes place in the cells of leaves, the byproducts of which are connected to other reactions throughout the cell. The most basic reactions of photosynthesis occurs like this: Energy from the sun strikes the leaf surface, and electrons in the chlorophyll molecule become "excited" and are boosted to a higher energy level. Excited electrons are routed through a chain of reactions that extracts and stores energy in the form of sugars. As a byproduct of electron loss, water molecules are split; hydrogen moves in to replenish the electrons lost from chlorophyll, and oxygen is released, finding its way into our atmosphere. In another photosynthetic reaction, carbon dioxide from the atmosphere is "fixed," or converted into organic compounds within the plant cell. These first chemical compounds are the building blocks for more complex reactions and are the precursors for the formation of many elaborate chemical compounds.

PLANT NUTRITION

Plants require mineral nutrients from the soil, water, and the atmosphere in order to maintain healthy growth and reproduction. Macronutrients, those nutrients needed in large amounts, include hydrogen, oxygen, and carbon–all of which are abundant in our atmosphere. Other macronutrients are nitrogen, phosphorus, potassium, sulfur, and calcium. If macronutrients are in limited supply, growth and development in the plant will be strongly curtailed. Nitrogen is an important component of chlorophyll, DNA, and proteins and is therefore an essential element for leaf growth and photosynthesis. Adding nitrogen to garden soil will generally result in greener, more lush plant growth. But beware of too much of a good thing; too

much nitrogen can burn tender plants. Or, you may have large and lovely azalea leaves, but with no flowers! Phosphorus is also used in building DNA and is important in cell development. Phosphorus is necessary for flowering and fruiting and is often added to garden soil. Potassium is important in the development of tubers, roots, and other storage organs.

LIFE CYCLE

Higher plants (except for ferns) begin life as a seed. Given the right set of conditions (temperature, moisture, light), a seed will germinate and develop its first roots and leaves using food stored in the seed (humans and other animals take advantage of the high-quality food in seeds when they eat wheat and corn, just to name a few). Because of the presence of chlorophyll in the leaves, the small plant is soon able to produce its own food, which is used immediately for further growth and development. As the seedling grows, it also grows in complexity. The first, simple root gives way to a complex root system that may include underground storage organs. The stem is transformed into an intricate system of vascular tissue that moves water from the ground up into the leafy part of the plant, while other tissues transport energy-rich compounds made in the leaves downward to be stored in stem and root systems.

Once the plant reaches maturity, flower initiation begins. Flowers hold the sexual apparatus for the plant; their brilliant colors and glorious odors are advertisements to attract pollinators such as insects or birds. In a basic, complete flower, there are four different parts, given below. However, many plants have incomplete flowers with one or more of these parts missing, or the parts may be highly modified.

1. Sepals. The outermost part of the flower, sepals cover the young floral buds. Although they are often green, they may be variously colored.

2. Petals. The next layer of parts in the flower, petals, are often colorful and play an important role in attracting pollinators.

3. Stamens. Stamens are located next to the petals, or may even be basally fused to the petals. The stamens are the male reproductive parts of the flower; they produce the pollen. Pollen grains are fine, dust-like particles that will divide to form sperm cells. The tissue at the end of the stamen that holds

pollen is called the anther.

4. Pistil. The innermost part of the flower holds the plant's female reproductive apparatus. The stigma, located at the tip of the pistil, is often covered with a sticky substance and is the site where pollen is deposited. The stigma is held by a floral tube, call the style. At the base of the style, the ovary holds one to many ovules, which contain eggs that represent undeveloped seeds.

Pollination is the transfer of pollen from an anther to a stigma and is the first step in the production of seeds. Pollen can be transferred by an insect visiting the flower, by the wind, or even by the splashing of raindrops. After being deposited on a compatible stigma, the pollen grains grow into tubes that travel from the stigma, down the floral tube into the ovary, depositing sperm cells to the ovules. If all goes well, sperm cells unite with the eggs inside the ovules, and fertilization takes place.

After fertilization, the entire floral structure is transformed into a fruit. Fruit can be fleshy, like an apple, or dry like a pea pod. Within each fruit, fertilized eggs develop into seeds, complete with a cache of storage tissue and a seed coat.

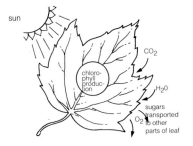

sun

CO_2

H_2O

chlorophyll production

sugars transported to other parts of leaf

O_2

mouth, and heart before the tea ceremony and have remained as an essential design element, even if not actually used. Some basins are made of bronze, but the traditional basin is a hollowed out stone with a hole in the middle. Tall basins are used when standing, such as at the door to a house, and low basins are used when kneeling, usually placed in a tea garden. The stones that accompany the basin include a stone for a hot-water bucket, a lamp stone, and several front stones. Together, these become one design element. The basin may be filled with fresh water from a portable container or may have water splashing into it continually from a bamboo spout connected to a water source.

The Japanese feel that koi represent strength, wisdom, and courage, and these carp have been cultivated for use in pools and lakes for 2,000 years. Koi are classified by color, pattern, and body shape, and the most prized is the *nishiki koi,* or brocaded koi. The flash of golds and reds is a beautiful addition to the garden, and koi can be trained to come to the surface for feeding. Some gardeners even like to discuss the individual personalities of their fish.

Adding koi to an oriental garden is a serious commitment since the fish can live up to 50 years. They must have clean water, and if the lake or pool is not spring fed, it is important to install an aeration and filtration system. The ideal temperature for healthy fish is 65-75° F although they will survive low temperatures for very short times. In cold climates, it is necessary to bring them indoors during the winter, and it is a difficult task to keep them thriving. Mature koi are very hardy and may survive in ponds that have completely frozen over if water is at least 20 inches deep.

This stroll garden unfolds, leading the viewer into new visions at every turn.

Other elements such as fences, gates, walls, towers, trellises and arbors may be used in the oriental garden, as long as the guiding principles for good design are followed. They should always be constructed of natural materials and not painted but left to weather naturally.

Bridges of stone, earth, or wood are intended to be lingered upon to see different garden views. They seldom have handrails to avoid any separation of nature and man. Zigzag bridges make the stroller take many turns so that he forgets the constraints of space and time. Use of the zigzagging *yatsuhashi* (eight bridges) with irises dates back to Ise and Ariwara Narihira, who admired irises growing along the eight channels of the Azuma River, each with its own bridge.

DIFFERENCES AND SIMILARITIES BETWEEN ORIENTAL GARDENS Gardens in China, Japan, and other areas in Asia developed from similar religions and philosophies (as opposed to Indian and Persian gardens which are more closely connected to Western gardens). Within each country, the principles were used in somewhat different ways.

Japanese gardens Japanese gardens evolved over the centuries into several forms, including the strolling garden, the tea garden, the dry garden, and the courtyard garden. Each of these contemporary types includes elements of an old garden style called the hill and pond garden. However defined, each broad category has within it many nuances.

The strolling garden is a place that beckons the visitor to move about and explore the beautiful elements and views. Although the garden may seem a natural occurrence, a close look will reveal its careful orchestration. The garden's stones represent mountains and the pools represent the ocean. The garden provides stone paths that curve, slowly revealing hidden areas but never revealing its entirety from one vantage point. Walking through the garden also exposes the variety of elevations on which stroll gardens are usually built.

Tea gardens assist the visitor in preparation for the formal tea ceremony. They are participatory gardens which induce an introspective, meditative state of mind and do not use the grand vistas of borrowed landscapes. As a visitor strolls along the *roji*, "dewy path," the garden elicits a calmness and detachment from the world. Stepping stones are often placed strategically to slow the pace and induce meditation. No flowers are used and striking foliage contrasts are avoided in order not to startle the participant out of introspection. The garden may include a quiet stream, but never a splashing waterfall. The sunlight is filtered and stones are set with only a small portion showing above the ground. All is designed to reflect restraint and quietude. A tea garden always includes ritual elements such as lanterns for lighting the path, a stone water basin for washing the hands and rinsing the mouth, and stepping stones through the garden to keep the feet clean and to slow the pace. Once inside the tea house, however, the doors are closed and the garden is not viewed from within. At this point, the tea ceremony is of utmost importance.

Dry gardens, introduced centuries ago by Buddhist monks, may be large in scale or quite small and intimate. The expanse of smooth sand or gravel is intended for viewing from a raised platform beside the garden. The white sand or gravel of a Zen garden represents water, and low plants or rocks placed strategically represent islands. The gravel or sand is carefully raked into ridges around the rocks to represent waves breaking on the shore. Buddhist monks are taught early how to

Some gardeners use only oriental plants, like false cypress and Japanese umbrella pines. Others use American counterparts, like the ferns and deciduous trees above.

rake the gravel to precipitate the meditative process and put them in tune with nature. Austerity is the driving force, and the gardens may include dry waterfalls and rock stream beds. Often the only green in the garden is moss.

Courtyard gardens are meant to be viewed from within the house. They are not miniatures but are intimate in scale and spare in adornment. The garden not only gives pleasure, but also lighting and ventilation for the home. Many contain elements of the Zen dry garden such as gravel or sand and low, unobtrusive plants or stones. The intimacy of the courtyard garden is often accentuated with bonsai, some of which may be family heirlooms, as are penjing in Chinese gardens.

Chinese gardens Chinese garden design builds on nature, but instead of abstracting it, as in Japan, it is exaggerated almost to the point of being whimsical. The rockwork in particular may be abundant, in steep involuted forms. Where Japanese gardens reduce nature's scale, Chinese gardens are more robust. Their open-air pavilions put the visitor into the garden in all seasons. The gardens are for contemplation and continual use and families entertain in their gardens as well as using them for solitude, meditation, and worship.

A Chinese garden must have water to be complete, and the Chinese created the concept of the borrowed landscape by borrowing the sky in reflecting pools. Chinese gardens are more highly ornamented than Japanese gardens, and are often colorful. This is particularly true of the Northern style, in which the architecture is painted in bright colors. The Southern style is more restrained, influenced by the scholarly and artistic traditions of the Yangtze delta. Many gardens have splashing waterfalls to accompany still pools. These pools need not be sparkling and clear; the jade green opaque water resulting from algae growth is appropriate to the naturalism of the Chinese garden. Everything in Chinese gar-

Above: The Korean pavilion at VanDusen Botanical Garden.
Left: Pavilion at Sun Yat Sen Chinese Garden.

Although oriental gardens are not known for bright color, spring usually brings abundant blossoms, as in the garden at right. The garden below is shown in summer, when the bloom on the prunus shrub has faded and the glossy foliage remains attractive.

dens is named, and many gardens have plaques throughout with names and poems or words of wisdom to inspire the garden visitor.

Private gardens are often limited in space, so the design concept of constructing many garden rooms makes the garden seem larger. Each room is a little different than the last. Walls and screens figure heavily in Chinese gardening, to set apart these garden rooms and courtyards. They are often embellished with grilles or lattice for ornamentation and to prevent a claustrophobic feeling. Seeing another garden room through an iron grille tempts the visitor to explore further. The concept of yin-yang is critical to garden design and contrasts of dark/light, closed/open, solid/void, hard/soft, rough/fine, straight/crooked, and static/dynamic punctuate the garden room style. Gardens will often become more complex as the visitor wanders, inviting a slow stroll to see everything. The larger gardens always have many buildings and pavilions, as if to indicate that man and his works are an immutable part of nature and the garden. Chinese garden architecture, in contrast to austere Japanese architecture, is complex and playful. This is most evident in the whimsical upturned corners of their pavilions.

Other oriental gardens Thai and Burmese gardens evolved along the same philosophical lines as Chinese and Japanese gardens, but their tropical climate produced a different use of plants. Formal gardens may contain elaborate gardens with rockeries, grottos, winding paths, rustic bridges, and arbors, all adorned with lush tropical foliage and flowers.

Formal Thai gardens often feature immense clipped lawns surrounded by trees and shrubs which contrast strongly with the almost uncontrollable encroaching jungle. The lawns are decorated with tables that hold scenes in pots that include tiny rocks, trees, and lakes in shallow dishes. Contemporary gardens incorporate lattice arbors hung with potted orchids and other flowering, scented plants that are used for cutting for religious offerings.

Southeast Asian gardens are designed to keep the lush jungle at bay rather than taking great care to plant and maintain special varieties. The jungle provides multitudes of flowering plants that are used as the natural focus of the garden.

Plants that yield flavorings and scents are an integral part of these gardens.

Indian and Persian gardens also make great use of tropical flowers. Water is critical to the design of both types, with the classic Persian courtyard pool being the most familiar water feature. The pools are often raised and in symmetrical shapes, sometimes long and canallike with a cross axis. Potted flowers and scented plants adorn the sides of the pools. This courtyard is essentially another room of the house that happens to be open to the sky. Gardens outside the courtyard are filled with flowering trees, roses, and orchards of fruits and almonds.

FAMOUS GARDENS China The city of Suchou in China is one of the oldest cities in the Yangtze delta, and has two well-preserved old gardens. One is called the Garden of the Stupid Official and includes such elements as a Pavilion of the Perfumed Snow (named for the plum tree that blooms while there is snow on the ground), the Land of Perfumes, the Loquat Garden, and the Hall of the Fragrance That

This garden is enclosed by tall trees, a mid-height wooden gate, and a low bamboo fence.

Above: **The antique gate at The Portland Japanese Garden.**

Paintings, and the Pavilion of the Moon Arriving and the Coming Breeze. These gardens and pavilions leave no doubt as to their finest attributes or what one should do when there.

Peking contains probably the most famous collection of gardens, not only in the city but also in the surrounding countryside. One of the most famous is the Garden of Earthly Repose which includes elaborate carved marble balustrades, rockeries and paths, and buildings all brightly painted. The best example of an authentic classical Chinese garden in North America is the Sun Yat Sen Classical Chinese Garden in Vancouver, Canada.

Japan The monastery at Ryoan-ji in Kyoto has the most famous Japanese dry garden. It was constructed in 1500 and is still maintained today. The garden is small and rectangular and is surrounded by an earthen wall. The surface of the garden is covered with white sand, and it contains only 15 stones, arranged so that one stone is always hidden when viewed from any point on the viewing platform. No one enters the garden except a monk to refresh the patterns raked in the sand. There are no plants except moss on the stones and a few trees as a background to the garden.

one enters the garden except a monk to refresh the patterns raked in the sand. There are no plants except moss on the stones and a few trees as a background to the garden.

The Katsura Detached Palace or Imperial Katsura Palace is a well-known strolling garden in Kyoto which has influenced the design of many contemporary gardens. The garden is large with many tea houses, each of which has a private tea garden. The tea gardens, all of different design, are situated around a large lake and connected by a path.

The Shugaku-in Palace is a good example of a garden based on the principle of borrowed scenery. Its gardens and lakes frame a spectacular backdrop of distant mountains.

ADAPTING EASTERN TRADITIONS TO WESTERN GARDENS The design of a formal oriental garden is fairly prescriptive in either the Japanese or Chinese tradition. Most Western gardeners, however, will choose a few, carefully selected oriental components for their gardens rather than designing the entire garden to conform to a single garden type or style. The decisions are a matter of personal taste, and a clear understanding of the basic types of oriental gardens will you help choose elements that suit your style.

One of the most important criteria for choosing a garden type is the amount of space available for the garden. If the garden has plenty of room for wandering about, a garden resembling a tea garden or strolling garden would be most appropriate. In this garden type, stone, gravel, or bark paths wind through a heavily planted garden. Both types also usually involve changes in elevation, such as low ridges and swales. Either type of garden must have enough room for curving paths to hide parts of the garden from view and to beckon the visitor to explore. To make a true hill and pond strolling garden, it is necessary to study natural elements carefully and place stones to represent mountains.

If the garden site naturally provides grand vistas, by all means, "borrow" these vistas to make an impressive stroll-type garden. A tea garden uses more intimate space, so if vistas are lacking, an introspective tea garden might be appropriate.

If the space is limited, it is more efficient to choose a Zen dry garden or a courtyard garden. The Zen garden can be as large or small as the designer wishes, but they tend to be no larger than one can see in one glance. This allows the gardens to be easily used for their primary focus of meditation. You can even capture the essence of an intimate Zen garden with one stone and a small amount of sand.

Many homes have an ideal spot for an intimate, simple courtyard garden as an extension of a living or family room. Since this type of garden is a discrete garden enclosed by walls and not influenced by any other part of the landscape, the garden outside the courtyard can be any style desired.

If you're fortunate to have naturally occurring water features, by all means use them to your advantage. Streams, waterfalls, or pools are key features of strolling and tea gardens. A strolling garden can take beautiful advantage of a waterfall or merrily splashing stream. A tea garden, on the other hand, makes good use of a quiet stream or still pool, both of which are a calming influence for meditation. If your plans include adding a pond, select the sunniest spot possible. A pond needs maintenance and that maintenance requirement increases if the pond is in shade.

THE JAPANESE GARDEN OF PORTLAND

The Japanese Garden of Portland is run by the Japanese Garden Society of Oregon. Plans for the Garden began in 1961 and the Garden opened to the public in 1967. Designed by the renowned Japanese designer Dr. Takuma P. Tono, The Japanese Garden of Portland is considered the most authentic and extensive Japanese garden outside Japan.

Five separate but interconnected gardens comprise The Japanese Garden of Portland. The Flat Garden (*Hiraniwa*) is a simple, irregularly shaped garden of white sand, moss, grass, and evergreen plantings; it contains circle and gourd shapes, symbolizing enlightenment and happiness. The Strolling Pond Garden (*Chisen-Kaiyu-Skiki*) is a combination of two large ponds connected by a stream; this rock and water garden is highlighted by the wooden Japanese bridge arching over the upper pond, and is especially pleasing because it offers views from many perspectives. The Tea Garden (*Rojiniwa*), includes the ceremonial tea house; symbolic placement of stepping stones, stone lanterns, and traditional stone water basins are arranged with the utmost authenticity. The Natural Garden (*Shukeiyen*), is a series of cascading waterfalls. Finally, the Sand and Stone Garden (*Seki Tei*), surrounded by a wall and capped with beautiful Gifu tile, uses sand in the manner of the *Ryoan-ji* Garden is Japan. In all, The Garden makes up five-and-one-half acres that change with every season and are beautiful throughout the year.

In this volume, plants are arranged in the following order:
• Needle evergreens (shrubs and trees); including *Abies* (fir); *Cedrus* (cedar) *Chamaecyparis* (falsecypress); *Picea* (spruce); Pinus (pine); *Taxus* (yew); *Thuja* (arborvitae); *Tsuga* (hemlock) and others.
• Broadleaf evergreens (shrubs and trees; including *Camellia; Citrus; Ilex* (holly); evergreen magnolias; *Pieris*; evergreen rhododendron; roses.
• Deciduous trees; including *Acer* (maple); *Betula* (birch); *Cercidiphyllum* (katsura tree); *Cercis* (redbud); *Cornus* (dogwood); deciduous magnolias; *Malus* (crabapple); *Prunus* (cherry, plum); *Salix* (willow).
• Deciduous shrubs; including *Berberis* (barberry); *Chaenomeles* (quince); deciduous rhododendrons; *Syringa* (lilac)
• Vines and groundcovers, including *Clematis; Thymus* (thyme); *Wisteria*; mosses
• Flowering herbaceous plants; including astilbes; hostas; lilies; meconopsis.
• Foliage herbaceous plants, including ornamental grasses.
• Ferns
• Bamboos
See index for a complete list of plants.

SELECTING PLANTS FOR THE ORIENTAL GARDEN

Selecting the plants for an oriental garden is critical and can be intimidating. Always keep in mind what you are trying to accomplish with each plant. When choosing plants for focal points, select those with beauty in all seasons. Textures of foliage and branching patterns are as important in oriental gardens as the color of flowers. In a tea garden, subtlety is the guiding element, so select plants without bright flowers or striking foliage contrasts.

If you have unlimited time to spend maintaining the garden, you might opt for plants that need intensive pruning and care. Otherwise, be aware of the maintenance each plant requires, and choose accordingly. A somewhat naturalistic garden with oriental elements is beautiful in a different way as a formal garden in which everything is severely pruned and trained.

Once the structural plants of the garden are in place, you can certainly experiment. Remember that seldom is a garden static. It will change often as it grows, and if something doesn't please you where it was placed, don't hesitate to move it to make the overall garden more pleasing.

There are only a few keys to successful gardening; choosing the right plant is among them. If a well-tended plant refuses to thrive or succumbs to disease, it probably doesn't belong in its present site. Before deciding on a plant, you need to understand the special conditions of your own garden. Is it sunny, shady, or a combination of both? Is rainfall abundant, or nearly nonexistent? Is the soil sandy, loamy, heavy? How much organic matter does it contain? Does it drain well? What is your soil's natural pH? Information on how to answer these questions is located in Chapter 4; your local nursery, botanical garden, or agricultural extension service can also help. But don't forget that your site is unique, with a microclimate of its own created by the contours of the landscape, shade, and natural barriers; it may be different from those next door, let alone at a nursery ten miles down the road.

To help match plant and gardener, each plant portrait includes information on the following:

Sun and shade Some plants that thrive in full sun in cool climates need some shade in warm climates; in the tropics, most plants benefit from a least a bit of shade from brightest afternoon sun. But there are plants that will thrive in every conditions, from brutal sun to deep shade. Shade-loving plants include hostas, astilbes, ferns, and groundcovers such as pachysandra.

Soil You make minor adjustments in your soil so that the plants can establish itself or survive an unusual drought. But don't try to grow a plant that thrives on nutrients in poor, dry soil; you'll spend the rest of your life pampering it and it will never do as well as a more practical choice.

Water There are plenty of plants that thrive in dry climates and are suitable for the oriental garden. Notations throughout this chapter point out plants that are adapted to dry climates. Because water supplies everywhere are becoming more scarce, all gardeners would do well to heed the basic principles of xeriscaping: proper garden design, maintenance, and especially plant selection.

Hardiness Consider your area's general climate, but keep in mind too that planting in a protected area might allow you to gain one warmer zone–if you don't mind the risk of perhaps, in some years, experiencing winter damage. Courtyard gardens are usually protected and can include some tender plants. If you plant tender species in containers, the container can be taken indoors for winter. See page 212 for information on gardening in cooler climates. In the West, climate zones are not as important as summer highs and rainfall.

Pests and diseases We've noted problems that are common to particular plants; if these pests or diseases are rampant in your area, avoid the plants in question. See pages 200-201 for more information on pests and diseases.

Plants are only one of the elements you'll be choosing for your oriental garden; non-plant elements–stones, gravel, bridges, walkways and pathways, pavilions, fences–should be chosen with similar care. Some materials are more suitable for very cold climates, others will withstand brutal sun. Remember that most of the large stones you place will be more or less permanent; try to position them so that they do not intefere with plantings.

Plants may not be the only or the most important element in your oriental garden–but they must be chosen carefully and combined properly with other elements to provide the effect you desire.

The map below was created by the United States Department of Agriculture. It divides the United States and Canada into climate zones. Most nurseries (and this book) use these classifications to advise where plants will be hardy. Although this is a useful system, it is not foolproof; it is based on average minimum temperature, and a particularly cold winter might destroy some plants that are listed as hardy in your climate zone. More often, you will be able to grow plants that are not listed as hardy in your zone, particularly if they are in a sheltered area.

There are other climate-zone classifications; the Arnold Arboretum's is also used quite often. The climate zones referred to in this volume are those of the USDA.

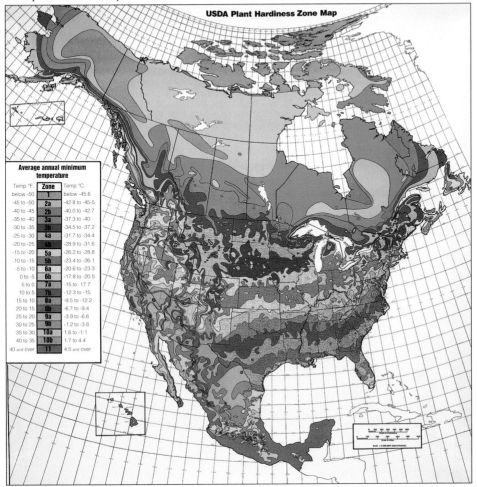

USDA Plant Hardiness Zone Map

Average annual minimum temperature		
Temp °F.	Zone	Temp °C.
below -50	1	below -45.6
-45 to -50	2a	-42.8 to -45-5
-40 to -45	2b	-40.0 to -42.7
-35 to -40	3a	-37.3 to -40
-30 to -35	3b	-34.5 to -37.2
-25 to -30	4a	-31.7 to -34.4
-20 to -25	4b	-28.9 to -31.6
-15 to -20	5a	-26.2 to -28.8
-10 to -15	5b	-23.4 to -26.1
-5 to -10	6a	-20.6 to -23.3
0 to -5	6b	-17.8 to -20.5
5 to 0	7a	-15 to -17.7
10 to 5	7b	-12.3 to -15
15 to 10	8a	-9.5 to -12.2
20 to 15	8b	-6.7 to -9.4
25 to 20	9a	-3.9 to -6.6
30 to 25	9b	-1.2 to -3.8
35 to 30	10a	1.6 to -1.1
40 to 35	10b	1.7 to 4.4
40 and over	11	4.5 and over

EVERGREENS

Evergreen trees and shrubs serve a multitude of purposes in the oriental garden. They often serve as screens, blocking out unpleasant views; the view outside the garden is considered to be an important part of it, so if it does not add to the garden it should be covered. Background evergreens are often reflected in the water that is usually present in an oriental garden–part of the "borrowed landscape" principle developed by early Japanese garden. Tall evergreens can be used to frame distant vistas, another way of borrowing landscape. And, because they are green all year, evergreens provide interest through the winter and are especially attractive when covered with snow or ice. In summer, their many shades of green blend with greens of other plants.

Probably the most important single evergreen plant is the pine; many species are used, including black pines, Japanese black pines, Japanese red pines, Austrian pines, and mugo pines. Some of these tower above the garden, others are kept as low shrubs or hedges. Complex procedures for training these adaptable trees have been developed (see page 200); often a tree is trained to overhang a body of water. However, pines are not the only evergreens worthy of consideration. The following pages list useful evergreens, such as hinoki falsecypress, low-growing Chinese juniper, and the graceful Japanese umbrella tree and oriental arborvitae.

Many evergreen plants are conifers, or cone-bearing plants. Conifers often have needlelike or scalelike foliage, and are also known as needle evergreens (even when their foliage is not needlelike). A section on broad-leaved evergreens follows the one on needle evergreens.

Above and below: **Evergreens and others.** *Opposite:* **Cedars flank a waterfall.**

NEEDLE EVERGREENS
ABIES FIR *Pinaceae*

The pyramidal firs are native to cool, mountainous regions of the northern temperate zone. They have flattened needles of green to blue-green, and the needles are attached directly to the branchlets rather than on tiny pegs as with spruce. Young plants have smooth bark, and the branches and trunk have small resin blisters. Their cones are held erect and vary from purple to green. The scales are shed while the cone is still held upright on the branch.

Firs are extremely coldhardy and will not thrive in hot, dry, or polluted areas. Provide firs with good drainage and moist, acid soil; rocky or sandy soil is ideal. Firs work well as the basic structural element in oriental gardens, and because of their stature, only one is needed for most gardens. Transplant only as a balled-and-burlapped plant in early spring. Pruning is generally unnecessary. Fertilize infrequently and provide plenty of moisture, especially on drier soils. Propagate by cold-stratified seed; cuttings generally give very poor yields.

SELECTIONS *Abies firma* (Japanese fir, Momi fir) native to Japan; grows to 150 feet in the wild but only 90 feet in cultivation; thick spreading branches; gray corky bark; cones are 5 inches long and yellow-green; hardy to Zone 6.
A. homolepis (Nikko fir) has stiff horizontal branches that accept heavy pruning.
A. mariesii (Maries fir) native to the mountains of Japan; grows 75-90 feet; smooth gray bark; blue-green needles and purple 3½-inch cones; ascending upper branches, descending lower branches; hardy to Zone 6.

CEDRUS CEDAR *Pinaceae*

A cedar grown in an appropriate site is among the most attractive of conifers. Its branches are well spaced and dense, its color is vivid, and it imparts a distinct, but not overpowering, fragrance to the air. Their soft foliage provides excellent contrast to rocks used in oriental gardens. Cedars are not particularly coldhardy; most are hardy only in Zones 6 or 7. They need moderately moist, fertile soil and full sun and should not be exposed to drying winds. Most cedars do not tolerate wet soils.

Most cedars are not easy to transplant. Transplant containerized or balled-and-burlapped trees in spring. *C. deodara* often needs to be staked for the first year or two. Provide enough water to keep soil evenly moist, but don't leave them in wet soil. Do not overfeed, or soft growth that promotes disease will occur. Prune cedars when young to establish a single leader. Once the basic shape is established, pruning becomes unnecessary. Propagate by seeds sown in fall, grafting in the spring, or cuttings taken in summer. Cedars need lots of room to grow and are not at their best when crowded by other trees, but a well-grown specimen cedar is unbeatable.

Cedrus atlantica (atlas cedar) grows in a pyramidal form for several years, then branches out horizontally, eventually reaching a height of 120 feet; Zones 6-9. The cultivars **'Argentea'** and **'Glauca'** have bluish needles. **'Glauca Pendula'** has drooping branches. This species is somewhat difficult to transplant and should be purchased containerized. Although it prefers moist, deep loam, atlas cedar will

ABIES NORDMANNIANA (NORDMAN FIR) 20 feet tall at 20 years, 50-55 feet at 50 years. Dark green, shiny needles to 1 inch long. Full sun or light shade, cool, moist climate, slightly acidic well-drained soil. Tolerates heat better than most firs. Zones 4-7.

CEDRUS DEODARA (DEODAR CEDAR) 20-25 feet tall at 20 years, 50-60 feet at 50 years. Pyramidal form, graceful, pendulous branches. Moderately moist, fertile soil, full sun; do not expose to drying winds. Zones 6-8.

CHAMAECYPARIS OBTUSA CV. (HINOKI FALSECYPRESS) 15 feet tall at 10 years, 30-35 feet tall at 50 years. Narrow pyramid with dark green drooping branches, leaves in form of flattened fans. Moist, well-drained soil, full sun. Zones 4-9.

CHAMAECYPARIS PISIFERA 'FILIFERA' (JAPANESE FALSECYPRESS) To 8 feet tall. Loose, airy habit with fine-textured foliage, drooping branches. Moist, well-drained soil, full sun. Zones 4-9.

plant selector

accept sandy or clay soils; it will not, however, thrive with wet feet.

C. deodara grows to 150 feet and is hardy only to Zone 7. It has a natural pyrami-dal form and pendulous branches that are particularly graceful. The cultivar **'Limelight'** has attractive yellow-green foliage. **'Shalimar'** and **'Kingsville'** are hardier than the species, with silvery foliage; reliably hardy to Zone 6. This species trans-plants more easily than other cedars, especially if root pruned and planted in a sunny, dry site.

C. libani (cedar of Lebanon) is the tree that was used to build Solomon's temple. It has a stiff, conical form and grows to 150 feet.

CHAMAECYPARIS FALSECYPRESS *Cuppressaceae*

Falsecypresses are widespread across North America and Asia, and some grow to 100 feet or more in the wild. They vary from pyramidal to columnar shaped with flattened needles and branches. The branchlets gently droop, setting them apart from arborvitae, which they closely resemble. Their small cones are rounded with distinct coarse scales. Chamaecyparis lend not only winter color to the oriental landscape, but also a somewhat formal look.

Provide falsecypress with moist, well-drained soil and full sun. Some species are found naturally in swampy areas and along stream banks, indicating their

Falsecypress (upper left), juniper, top-iary boxwood, and flowering cherry trees are combined at the San Francisco Tea Garden.

need for moisture and tolerance of less than well drained soil. Their needles may brown in areas exposed to winter winds and sun so site them away from a west exposure. Transplant in fall or spring only as balled-and-burlapped plants. Pruning is not generally necessary, but falsecypresses can be sheared for an extremely formal look. Otherwise, prune only to remove damaged limbs or branch tips. Fertilize infrequently. Propagate by softwood or hardwood cuttings; seed propagation is seldom successful.

SELECTIONS *Chamaecyparis obtusa* (hinoki falsecypress) is native to Japan; grown commercially for its wood; grows 50-75 feet in a narrow pyramid with dark green drooping branchlets; orange-brown cones when mature; hardy Zones 5-8.

C. o. **'Nana'** (dwarf hinoki falsecypress) is only 3 feet tall; an extremely slow-growing cultivar; perfect for use in a rock garden; lends itself well to the intimate oriental garden.

C. pisifera (Japanese falsecypress) is a commonly grown landscape plant, native to Japan; grows to about 50-70 feet in cultivation; airy, loose form with slightly drooping branchlets—a graceful addition to the garden. Many cultivars are used in oriental gardens; hardy Zones 3-8 (avoid areas of extreme exposure).

C. p. **'Filifera'** is a fine-textured plant that grows 6-8 feet in height; drooping branches. *C. p.* **'Filifera Aurea'** is a yellow-leaved version.

C. p. **'Plumosa'** has feathery branches and branchlets.

CRYPTOMERIA JAPONICA JAPANESE CEDAR *Taxodiaceae*

This genus includes only one species; it is grown commercially for wood and use in the landscape. It will grow to 100 feet in ideal conditions, but only reaches 50-60 feet in the landscape. Its wide-spreading branches make a formal pyramidal shape with graceful drooping tips. Its blue-green needles turn somewhat bronze in winter, and it has tiny dark brown cones. This is another formal addition to the oriental garden although its formality is somewhat softened by the drooping branch tips. Japanese cedar is often used as background or screen; it is used that way at the Sanzen-In Temple near Kyoto, built 1648-1654, as well at the Japanese Garden of Portland.

Cryptomeria grows best in moist soils of average fertility and does not tolerate polluted air. Provide a sunny, open site that is somewhat protected from winds. It is hardy in Zones 5-9 provided it is sited well. Provide average moisture, supplementing rainfall only when severely lacking. Fertilize only every few years and prune only if needed to shape. Seed propagation is not usually successful, so propagate by softwood or hardwood cuttings. Rooting will take several months.

CUNNINGHAMIA CHINAFIR *Taxodiaceae*

Native to eastern Asia, these evergreen trees grow to 75 feet in the landscape in a pyramidal shape with dramatically drooping branches. Their wood is highly valued in China for all types of woodworking. Chinafirs have spirally arranged, sharply pointed dark green needles with broad white bands on the undersides. The male flowers cluster at the branch tips, and the female cones are solitary.

Golden-leaved *Chamaecyparis obtusa* 'Cripsii'.

Low-growing *J. chinensis* var. *procumbens* {*Juniperus procumbens*} thrives in dappled sunlight under *Chamaecyparis pisifera.*

Plant balled-and-burlapped plants when very young. Provide moist, well-drained, somewhat acid soil. Chinafir tolerates shade and grows quite well in open areas under the protection of other trees, away from windy sites. Fertilize infrequently and provide steady moisture. Propagate by semihardwood cuttings taken in November. Chinafirs exhibit topophysis–cuttings taken from lateral branches will grow laterally; cuttings taken from upright branches will grow upright.

SELECTIONS *Cunninghamia lanceolata* (common chinafir) grows to around 75 feet; it closely resembles *Cryptomeria japonica* so it can be used for the same effect in the oriental landscape. Native to China; hardy Zones 7-9. *C. l. 'Glauca'* has blue-green foliage.

CUPRESSUS CYPRESS *Cuppressaceae*

These evergreen trees and shrubs are widely spread across temperate areas of North America, Euope, and Asia. They have very small scales for leaves and red-brown flaky bark. Their cones are quite small. The plants are closely related to falsecypress, which are generally hardier. Cypresses are most often used as focal points in the oriental gardens of warm climates, although they function well as a backdrop when used in groups. At the garden of the Entsu-ji in Kyoto, cypresses and Japanese cedars planted in the middle ground of the garden, "draw" the neighboring Mount Hiei into the landscape. Their large size necessitates ample space.

Most cypresses perform well in hot, dry areas, and several species thrive on alkaline soils. Plant young container-grown plants in early spring or late summer. They seldom need pruning; do not fertilize. Provide moisture during the first year to establish, but irrigation is seldom needed beyond the first year. Propagate by fresh seed.

SELECTIONS *Cupressus duclouxiana* (Yunan cypress) grows to 150 feet in the wild (much less in cultivation) with a distinctly pyramidal, almost columnar shape. Brown bark and drooping branchlets with blue-green needles. Native to southwestern China; hardy to Zone 9.

C. funebris (mourning cypress) grows to around 45 feet in cultivation; drooping branches with flattened branchlets and light green needles. Native to China; hardy to Zone 8.

JUNIPERUS JUNIPER *Cuppressaceae*

Juniper species and cultivars range from low shrubs to tall trees. They are spread all across the northern hemisphere, extending into the Arctic. Their needles may be sharp and pointed or rounded and scalelike, and colors range from yellow to deep blue green. The male cones are small and yellow and the female cones are glaucous blue or green and berrylike. Juniper berries are used for medicine, varnish, and to flavor gin. The uses for junipers in the oriental landscape are as varied as the shapes of the shrubs, from groundcovers to hedges to specimens to screens. They are valuable particularly for their blue-green winter color.

Junipers are infinitely adaptable as to their culture, but particularly thrive

CRYPTOMERIA JAPONICA (JAPANESE CEDAR) 18 feet at 20 years, 40-45 feet at 50 years. Pyramidal tree with spreading branches, shredding reddish brown bark. Full sun on coast, some shade inland, light, well-drained, moist acidic soil. Zones 6-9.

CUNNINGHAMIA LANCEOLATA 'GLAUCA' (BLUE CHINA FIR) 10 feet at 10 years, 50-55 feet at 50 years. Pyramidal shape with drooping branches and pointed blue-green needles. Full sun or partial shade, well-drained, slightly acidic soil, warm climates. Zones 7-9, Zone 6 with protection.

X CUPRESSOCYPARIS LEYLANDII (LEYLAND CYPRESS) 15 feet at 10 years. 60-65 feet at 50 years. Columnar to pyramidal habit, blue-green needles. Full sun, well-drained, slightly acidic soil, warm climates. Zones 6-9.

JUNIPERUS CHINENSIS CV. (CHINESE JUNIPER) Can grow to 60 feet, but many cultivars can be kept smaller through training and cutting back. Full sun, well-drained soil. Zones 6-9.

plant selector

in full sun and well-drained soil. They can fill a niche on impoverished, dry soils and do quite well in containers because of their tolerance of poor conditions. They should be watered from the bottom and planted with plenty of space for good air circulation to avoid fungal disease problems. They respond well to hand-pruning once a year to maintain a soft, feathery appearance. Some varieties can be sheared, although they do not put on new growth as vigorously as other evergreens, such as arborvitae or falsecypress. Plant as balled-and-burlapped plants in spring or early fall. Junipers seldom need fertilization, and their drought tolerance precludes much supplemental watering. To propagate by seed, scarify the seeds in acid and then cold-stratify for about four months. Cuttings will root well if taken during winter after plant has been exposed to freezing temperatures.

SELECTIONS *Juniperus chinensis* (Chinese juniper) The species grows to 60 feet, but there are countless cultivars with every shape and size imaginable, from low and spreading to short and shrubby to tall and pyramidal. Native to temperate eastern Asia; hardy to Zone 4.

J. chinensis var. *procumbens* [*Juniperus procumbens* (Japgarden juniper) is 12-24 inches high; blue-green sharp foliage; makes excellent, softly mounded groundcover. Performs well in alkaline soils. Native to the mountains of Japan; hardy Zones 4-9. *J. c.* var. *procumbens* 'Nana' [*Juniperus procumbens* 'Nana'] (dwarf Japgarden juniper) has the same appearance as the species but grows only in a 12-inch-high mat.

Junipers and pines at Dr. Sun Yat-Sen Classical Chinese Garden. Complex tapestries of plants make the area appear larger than it is.

J. horizontalis (creeping juniper) grows 1-2 feet high; widely spreading prostrate branches and branchlets that point upward. Many cultivars available with varying textures and colors ranging from blue to silver. The species and most cultivars turn purplish-brown in winter. Native to the northern United States and Canada; hardy Zones 3-9.

PICEA SPRUCE *Pinaceae*

Symmetrical, conical spruce trees are a staple in northern gardens. Spruces are among the most dependable of conifers, holding their needles densely even in extreme conditions and developing evenly and uniformly into tall trees. Like most conifers, spruce trees like cool climates, moist, rich, slightly acidic soil, and full sun. They do not appreciate heat or pollution, but will accept heavy soils.

Picea abies 'Diffusa'.

Spruces have shallow but spreading roots; look for balled-and-burlapped or container plants. Spring planting is best. Mulching with organic matter helps keep soil moist and rich. Pruning is rarely needed, except to cut away dying lower branches. If healthy branches need pruning, midsummer to fall is best (to avoid excessive bleeding of pitch). A spruce grown under proper conditions will resist pests and diseases. Heat, drought, and city pollution will cause stress that leaves the tree open to attack. Mites, spruce gall aphids, and bagworms are the most frequent pests, but a host of others is possible; *Cytospora* canker sometimes kills the lower branches of Colorado blue spruce. Spruces can be propagated easily by seeds sown in fall, cuttings taken in winter, and grafts made in late winter and early spring.

SELECTIONS *P. abies* (Norway spruce) is a fast-grower for northern gardens (to 30 feet in 20 years). **'Acrocona'** grows at half the rate of the species and bears purplish red spring cones on branch tips. **'Cupressina'** is narrow with ascending branches. Zones 2-6(7).

P. glauca (white spruce) is a popular Christmas tree in the North and Midwest, with aromatic foliage; it grows to 25 feet in 20 years, eventually reaching 50 feet tall and 20 feet wide. **'Conica'** (dwarf Alberta spruce) requires a cool, moist spot; it reaches 7 feet at 20 years and eventually grows to 15 feet and 5 feet wide with a perfect conical shape. Zones 2-(6)7.

P. likiangensis (Likiang spruce) from China has bright purplish red young cones and is no stranger to heat and drought; grows 20 feet in 20 years and eventually 50 feet tall and 25 feet wide. *P. l. var. purpurea* has violet purple cones. Zones 5-7.

P. omorika (Serbian spruce) has beautiful arching branches and cascading bicolor foliage. Pyramidal when young, it becomes spirelike with maturity. To 20 feet in 20 years, eventually to 60 feet tall, 15 feet wide. Zones 4-7.

P. orientalis (Oriental spruce) is elegantly clothed in tiny, deep green needles and bears small bright red cones in spring. It grows to 18 feet in 20 years and eventually to 80 feet tall and 20 feet wide.

PINUS PINE *Pinaceae*

Pines are native to the entire northern hemisphere and range widely in size and shape, depending on species and age. They may be distinctly pyramidal or shrubby when young and round-topped or flat-topped in old age. Pine needles are of varying lengths and are borne in bundles of two, three, or five, a feature

PICEA ORIENTALIS (ORIENTAL SPRUCE) 18 feet at 20 years, 40-50 feet at 50 years. Pyramidal shape, glossy dark green needles (smaller than most other spruces), brown cones in fall through winter. Full sun, moist, rich soil, cool climates. Zones 4-8.

PINUS CONTORTA (SHORE PINE) 15-25 feet tall. Round-topped tree with dense, deep foliage. Full sun, moist, rich soil, cool climates. Zones 4-8.

PINUS DENSIFLORA (JAPANESE RED PINE) 20 feet at 20 years, 40-60 feet at 50 years. Horizontal branches covered in blue-green needles, 3-5 inches long. Full sun, moist, rich soil, cool climates. Zones 4-8.

PINUS MUGO VAR. MUGO (MUGO PINE) Grows to 8 feet tall if unpruned; usually kept smaller. Multiple trunks, 2- to 3-inch-long medium green needles. Full sun, moist, rich soil, cool climates. Zones 3-7.

used for classifying them. Pine cones are also of varying sizes and composed of hard scales that enclose and protect papery seeds. Cones take one to three years to mature. Pines are used extensively for timber and paper manufacturing, and one species provides food in the form of pine nuts. Oriental gardens make much use of pines, with particular care to coax them into old age. The bark of many old pines is particularly beautiful. Old pines are often propped up with bamboo supports when growing at odd angles, and designers often train pine branches to hang out over a pool. Sometimes they are even planted at an angle over the water and then tied and propped (props are considered artistic elements in the garden). "Character pines" may be trained into shapes that draw the eye toward beautiful spots in the garden.

Most pines thrive in full sun although a few will tolerate partial shade. They are adaptable to many situations, but for best performance, plant balled-and-burlapped plants into well-drained soil that is low in organic material,

Above: Mugo pine, coast pine. *Left:* Carefully tended pines are an important element in the oriental landscape.

Right: An Austrian pine being trained at The Portland Japanese Garden. Training devices are considered ornamental. See page 200 for more information about training.

with plenty of room for the plant to reach its mature size. Pines rarely need pruning except for artistic design in oriental gardens. If pruning is necessary to maintain shape and size, the only method that maintains the attractive qualities of the plant is to pinch out up to half of the "candles," or new growth (see Chapter 4, Techniques). Pines naturally shade out and lose their lower branches, adding to their artistic qualities. Transplant as balled-and-burlapped plants in spring or early fall. Provide plenty of water in fall since they do not go completely dormant and continue to transpire. Fertilize only every few years. Propagate by stratified seed only (stratifying requirements vary according to species). Some pines can be successfully grafted onto seedling pines.

SELECTIONS *Pinus bungeana* (lacebark pine) grows 30-50 feet and becomes flat-topped with age. May grow to 75 feet, but usually somewhat bushy and often multistemmed in colder areas; used particularly for its flaking bark that reveals a mosaic of moss green, white, and cinnamon. Two- to 4-inch needles in bundles of three; light to medium green. Very adaptable to alkaline soils. Native to China; hardy Zones 4-8.

P. densiflora (Japanese red pine) can grow to 100 feet or more, but usually stays at 40-60 feet in the landscape. Broad, flat-topped crown when mature, open and loose throughout life; 5-inch-long slightly twisted needles in bundles of two; bright blue-green. Native to Japan, Korea, and China; hardy Zones 3-7, but may be damaged in extreme exposures. *P. d. 'Umbraculifera'* (Tanyosho pine) is a dwarf cultivar that grows to only 9 feet with an umbrellalike crown and dense branching; remarkable-looking specimen plant.

P. koraiensis (Korean pine) may grow to 100 feet in the wild, but usually 30-40 feet in the landscape. Loose habit with branches to the ground; gray-green needles in bundles of five; native to Japan and Korea; hardy Zones 3-7 but may be damaged in extreme exposures.

Below: Training yields gnarled branches and complex shapes. Often, trees are trained to overhang lakes and ponds.

Arashimay, white with snow
Almost seems to be
Engulfed in clouds of flowers
Pine trees by a magic touch
Transfigured into cherry trees.
MUSO SOSEKI, 1464

P. massoniana grows 75-80 feet with 8-inch-long dark green needles; light green cones. Large spreading crown. Native to China where it is used as a timber tree; hardy to Zones 7-8.

Pinus mugo var. mugo (mugo pine) is a low-growing variety of the species; it grows to about 8 feet if not pruned. Multiple trunks give it a somewhat mounded appearance; stubby cones and 2- to 3-inch-long medium green needles. One of the best shrubby pines for use in the garden. Native to mountains of central and southern Europe; hardy Zones 2-7.

P. parviflora (Japanese white pine) is a small pine that grows 25-50 feet; short blue-green needles in bundles of five, forming tufts at ends of branches which give it unusual character with fine-textured appearance. Native to Japan; hardy Zones 4-7.

P. tabuliformis (Chinese red pine) grows to 80 feet or more with 6-inch-long stiff needles and small cones; pyramidal crown becoming broad and flat-topped with age. Native to China; hardy to Zone 5.

P. thunbergiana (Japanese black pine) is a towering pine to 150 feet or more in the wild, it reaches only 20-40 feet in cultivation; irregular shape from youth; shiny bright green medium to long needles in bundles of two. Native of Japan; hardy Zones 5-7.

PODOCARPUS *Podocarpaceae*

These dioecious conifers have flat yewlike leaves and attractive male and female cones. The leaves are very dark green, giving almost a tropical look to the plants. Some podocarpus are grown for lumber, and others are grown for ornament. In oriental gardens, they complement pines with similar form but different foliage.

Transplant balled and burlapped in early spring. Provide well-drained rich soil and full sun or partial shade. These will not tolerate wet soils or cold weather. No pruning is needed; fertilize infrequently and provide plenty of moisture as long as the soil is well drained. Propagate by hardwood cuttings.

SELECTIONS *Podocarpus macrophyllus* **var. maki** (Chinese podocarpus, Buddhist pine) grows to 25-30 feet; formal columnar shape; red to purple attractive fruits; native to central and southwestern Japan; hardy Zones 8-10.

SCIADOPITYS VERTICILLATA JAPANESE UMBRELLA PINE

Taxodiaceae

This genus has only one species and is native to central and southern Japan. It may grow to 100 feet or more in ideal situations, but is extremely slow growing and usually only reaches 20-30 feet in cultivation. It grows as a compact pyramid when young, rounding with age. It has two types of needles, one a tiny scale type that occurs tightly pressed to stems and clustered at the ends, and the other a more typical flat dark green needle that can be 3-5 inches long and occurs in whorls along the branches. These whorls looks like umbrellas, giving its common name.

Umbrella pine performs well in moist, fertile, protected sites. Provide full sun and good air circulation. It is a striking focal point in the landscape, par-

PINUS NIGRA (AUSTRIAN PINE) 25 feet at 20 years, 35-60 feet at 50 years. Dense pyramidal shape with dark green 3- to 6-inch-long needles. Full sun, moist, rich soil, cool climates. Zones 4-8.

PINUS THUNBERGIANA (JAPANESE BLACK PINE) 25 feet at 20 years, 35 feet at 50 years. Irregular shape, shiny bright green needles, medium to long, in bundles of two. Full sun, moist, rich soil, cool climates. Zones 5-7.

PODOCARPUS GRACILIOR (AFRICAN FERN PINE) 25-30 feet tall if unpruned, can be kept to 8 feet. Rich, well-drained soil, full sun to partial shade. Zones 8-10.

SCIADOPITYS VERTICILLATA (JAPANESE UMBRELLA PINE) 10 feet at 20 years, 20-30 feet at 50 years. Symmetrical conical habit, dense, lustrous dark green needles with yellow markings; mature trees produce 5-inch cones. Full sun, slightly acidic soil. Zones 5-8.

ticularly because of its unusual texture. Transplant balled and burlapped in spring into a suitable spot. Fertilize every few years and provide plenty of moisture all season. Pruning is seldom needed; a pruned plant will take a long time to recover because of its extremely slow growth. Propagate by either warm- or cold-stratified seed or by hardwood cuttings taken in late winter; hardy Zones 5-8.

TAXUS YEW *Taxaceae*

Yews are native to many parts of the northern hemisphere and have become ubiquitous parts of the American landscape. There are eight species from which many cultivars are derived. and size ranges from 50-foot trees to 1-foot shrubs, depending on the cultivar. Yews have dark glossy green needles in two ranks with a lighter underside and are dioecious, meaning that male and female flowers appear on different plants. Female plants produce attractive fruits that are bright red with a black exposed center seed. The aril is edible, but the seeds and foliage are poisonous. The twigs of the current season's growth are pale green, and the new needles in spring are pale green as they emerge. Older yews have exfoliating cinnamon-red bark, an attractive addition to the oriental garden.

Yews tend to be popular plants for most landscapes because of their ability to thrive in shade and their tolerance of pruning and shearing. They are used for formal foundation plantings and hedges or may be left feathery as a focal point. Yews will not tolerate wet soil, and certain species have a tendency to turn brown if planted in sites where they are exposed to winter wind and sun. Avoid south and western exposures and any soil that is not perfectly drained. Transplant balled and burlapped or as container-grown plants in spring or early fall. Provide plenty of moisture in fall to help compensate for the water loss from transpiring through winter. Propagate by semi-hardwood cuttings taken in fall.

SELECTIONS *Taxus cuspidata* (Japanese yew) grows 20-40 feet in a pyramidal or spreading form, depending on the seed source. Beautiful brown peeling bark on older plants. Can be sheared to resemble formal "cone" or left natural for soft pyramidal shape. Native to Japan and Korea; hardy Zones 4-7. *T. c.* **'Nana'** (dwarf Japanese yew) is very slow growing and horizontally-spreading; needles are arranged in spirals, giving a bottlebrush effect; maintains natural globe shape without pruning; females have excellent fruit display.

THUJA ARBORVITAE, WHITECEDAR *Cupressaceae*

Native to North America and eastern Asia, arborvitae are most often columnar or pyramidal evergreen trees although shrubby cultivars have been developed for use in the landscape. The leaves are scalelike, medium green to yellow green to blue-green and closely pressed to the branchlets. The sprays of branchlets are flattened, giving a formal, neat appearance. Some species of arborvitae turn off-color in winter, making them appear somewhat ragged. However, there are cultivars that were developed to remain green the entire winter.

Japanese umbrella pine has a symmetrical, pleasing natural shape. It can be trained to a more complex form, as seen opposite.

TAXUS CUSPIDATA (JAPANESE YEW) 10 feet at 20 years, 20-40 feet at 50 years. Irregular, multistemmed habit; can be trained as shrub or tree. Dark green leaves with yellow undersides, attractive bark. Full sun or partial shade; slightly acidic, well-drained soil. Zones 4-7.

THUJA PLICATA (WESTERN REDCEDAR, GIANT ARBORVITAE) 25-30 feet at 20 years, 60-70 feet at 50 years. Narrow pyramidal form, lustrous scalelike needles. Full sun or light shade, slightly acidic to alkaline well-drained soil, cool climates. Zones 5-9.

PLATYCLADUS ORIENTALIS 'ELEGANTISSIMA' (ORIENTAL ARBORVITAE) 6 feet at 20 years, 14 feet at 50 years. Vertical, multistemmed tree with reddish bark and fernlike bright green foliage. Tolerates heat and humidity; slightly acid, and alkaline, moist, well-drained soil; sun or light shade. Zones 6-9.

TSUGA CANADENSIS 'PENDULA' (CANADIAN HEMLOCK) 6 feet at 20 years, 20 feet at 50 years. Squat form with pendulous branches covered densely with dark green needles; small oval cones. Full sun or partial shade, slightly acidic or alkaline soil, cool climates. Zones 3-8.

Planting is a favorite means of screening undesirable views, and very often the amateur gardener immediately thinks of evergreen conifers and the ubiquitous Leyland cypress, which is a very dull, short-lived spcies whose only useful attribute is that it grows fast. Instead of these, try a number of other evergreens, such as thuja, ligustrum, chamaecyparis, or bambo, which give a better effect and can be planted at a large size if a more immediate screen is desired.

PHILIP CAVE,
CREATING JAPANESE GARDENS

Arborvitae will grow in partial shade although their best growth is in full sun. They have shallow roots, making them quite tolerant of wet areas, and they are adaptable to high pH. Provide plenty of moisture to avoid stress. They tolerate shearing well although their slow growth keeps them naturally compact. They are useful as hedges or for massing and screening. Transplant as container-grown plants or balled and burlapped in early spring or early fall. Fertilize infrequently and propagate by semihardwood cuttings or seed (which need not be stratified).

SELECTIONS *Thuja occidentalis* (American arborvitae) grows 40-60 feet and usually only spreads about 10 feet at maturity. Usually has only one trunk although multiples can occur; dark green leaves that turn somewhat brownish in winter; horizontal branch sprays. Cultivars have been bred to avoid this color change; other cultivars quite narrow or dwarf in form. Native to eastern North America; hardy Zones 2-8.

T. plicata (Western redcedar) has lustrous scalelike leaves and thrives in most areas of the Pacific Northwest.

Platycladus orientalis (Oriental arborvitae) originally named *Thuja orientalis*, this arborvitae differs from American arborvitae in that its branch sprays are distinctly vertical and it is multi-stemmed, making it much more bushy. Not as tolerant of cold and harsh winters, so more useful in southern climates. Native to China and Korea; hardy Zones 6-9.

TSUGA HEMLOCK *Pinaceae*

Hemlocks are widespread woodland understory plants in the temperate areas of North America and eastern Asia. The species all have a characteristic pyramidal habit and graceful, wispy branchlets, although cultivars have been developed that are weeping, ground-hugging, or columnar. They have small, medium green soft needles with white bands on the undersides. Their cones are small, brown, and profuse and their red-orange bark is particularly appealing in the winter oriental landscape.

Hemlocks perform well in sun but will not tolerate hot, dry sites. Ideally, provide a partially shaded spot and some protection from extreme winds. Plant in moist, rich cool soil that is well drained and somewhat acidic for the best performance. Since they naturally grow in the woods, imitating these conditions as best you can will provide a beautiful landscape specimen. Pruning is seldom necessary, although hemlocks will tolerate shearing. Fertilization is unnecessary. Propagate by cold-stratified seed. Most cultivars are grafted.

SELECTIONS *Tsuga canadensis* (Canadian hemlock) grows 40-60 feet in cultivation; widely used as a landscape plant; slow growing and extremely graceful; shears well for use as a hedge; provide some protection. Native to eastern North America; hardy Zones 3-7.

Tsuga sieboldii (Japanese hemlock) grows to 100 feet; cones to 1¼ inches; white bands on needles are very slender. Native to Japan; hardy to Zone 6.

BROADLEAF EVERGREENS

As with conifers, broadleaf evergreens provide interest through the winter; in addition, some like rhododendron and camellia, also provide color through abundant flowers. Many broadleaf evergreens, like box, holly, and euonymus, accept shearing very well; these are the plants often used in topiary in Oriental Gardens. Other broadleaf evergreens serve as groundcovers, screens, backdrops, or hedges. They assort well with each other.

Among the broad-leaved evergreens mentioned in the writings of the Japanese master gardeners (as discussed in *Secret Teachings in the Art of Japanese Gardens* by David A. Slawson) are camellias ("while there is no fixed places for using camellias in the landscape garden, you will do well to plant it in association with pines so as to create a scenic effect . . . these two must be planted in perfect harmyony"); citrus ("Plant citrus trees so as to capture in a single scenic ambience the impression of a village bordering on hills and fields. Keep in mind that the pattern of a formal wooden fence extending out from the eaves can serve to recall this image.") and azaleas ("Azaleas are woody plants that make hills and fields their principal home. Nevertheless, there is general agreement that it is good to plant azaleas as the undergrowth in deep mountains. They are fascinating when hidden away among rocky crags or when planted on the banks above a pond. They make both *yin* and *yang* mountains their principal home."

Left: Camellias, holly, pieris, and aucuba at The Sun Yat Sen Classical Chinese Garden.

Aucuba japonica is available in several cultivars with strikingly variegated foliage.

ARDISIA *Myrsinaceae*

These natives of warm temperate and tropical areas are shrubs or trees with small leathery leaves and small white flowers. They have red berries that remain on the plant for a long time. Use them in oriental gardens as a focal point, for contrast with needled evergreens or for groundcover. They also perform well when grown in containers.

Transplant as container-grown plant in spring. Grow in partial to full shade in moist, organic soil. Provide some protection from winter winds and sun and provide constant moisture (as long as the soil is well drained). Prune almost to the ground in early spring for lush, fresh growth, and fertilize annually after the plant is well established. Propagate by seed or semihardwood cuttings.

SELECTIONS *Ardisia crenata* (coralberry) grows to 6 feet; wavy leaf margins; white or pink flowers; usually grown for its attractive long-lasting coral-red berries. Native to Japan and northern India; hardy to Zone 7.

A. crispa grows 2-4 feet; similar in appearance to *A. crenata*; flowers pink. Hardy to Zone 7.

A. japonica (marlberry, Japanese ardisia) grows to 8-12 inches; bold foliage; bright red berries; makes superb woodland groundcover. Native to Japan and China; hardy Zones 6-9.

AUCUBA *Cornaceae*

This group of evergreen shrubs is grown for its highly ornamental foliage and fruits. The glossy leaves, purple flowers, and orange to red fruits make an attractive statement in the landscape. Cultivars have variegated foliage, a pleasing focal point in an oriental landscape. The green leafed varieties look especially attractive under large deciduous trees.

Provide some shade as leaves will blacken in the sun in extremely hot climates. Plant in moist, well-drained soil with ample organic material. Transplant container-grown plants into soil amended with abundant organic material. Fertilize every couple of years, and provide average moisture in addition to a naturally moist site. Pruning is seldom necessary except to remove damaged branches. Propagate by soft, semihardwood or hardwood cuttings.

SELECTIONS *Aucuba japonica* (Japanese aucuba, Japanese laurel) grows 6-10 feet; well-groomed arching branches and attractive red fruits; many cultivars have multicolored leaves. Native to Himalayas and Japan; hardy Zones 8

BUXUS BOX, BOXWOOD *Buxaceae*

This group of evergreen trees and shrubs includes widespread natives of Europe, the Mediterranean, temperate east Asia, and Central America. Boxwoods have tiny leathery leaves on slender stems, making them ideal for shearing into tight shapes. Leaf color is medium green, with some species turning brownish in winter. They are used all over the world for hedges, formal gardens and topiary. Boxwood flowers are inconspicuous with their light green color, but they bloom with an intense fragrance in early spring. They also attract a multitude of bees and wasps when blooming.

Boxwoods perform well in full sun or partial shade and well-drained soil.

ARDISIA CRENATA (CORALBERRY) Plant to 6 feet tall; medium green leaves with wavy leaf margins; white or pink flowers; long-lasting coral red berries. Partial to full shade, well-drained, moist, organic soil. Zones 7-10.

AUCUBA JAPONICA CV. (JAPANESE AUCUBA, JAPANESE LAUREL) 6- to 10-foot-tall shrub with arching branches, red fruits. Rich, moist, well-drained soil; light to partial shade. Zones 8-10.

BUXUS SEMPERVIRENS (COMMON BOX) 6- to 15-foot-tall plant with 1½-inch leaves that are lustrous, rich green above and yellow-green below. Full sun or partial shade; well-drained soil. Zones 5-9.

CAMELLIA JAPONICA 'FREEDOM BELL' (JAPANESE CAMELLIA) 10-15 feet tall. Glossy green foliage, single rose pink flowers, 3-5 inches across. Partial shade, well-drained, slightly acid soil. Zones 7-9.

CAMELLIA JAPONICA 'NUCIO'S GEM' (JAPANESE CAMELLIA) 10-15 feet tall. Glossy green foliage, single rose pink flowers, 3-5 inches across. Partial shade, well-drained, slightly acid soil. Zones 7-9.

CITRUS x 'CALOMONDINE' [C. RETICULATA x FORTUNELLA SP.] (CALOMONDINE ORANGE) Columnar tree, 8-10 feet tall produces abundant small (½- to 1½-inch) sour oranges. Full sun, fertile, well-drained soil with generous moisture. Zones 9-10.

COCOS NUCIFERA (COCONUT PALM) Single-trunked palm to 80 feet tall with large, pinnate arching fronds, up to 20 feet long. Full sun; tolerant of a wide range of soil conditions and salt. Zone 10.

CYCAS REVOLUTA (SAGO PALM) 6-10 feet tall, long, shiny, overlapping yellow-green leaves. Full sun to partial shade (some shade in dry climates), well-drained soil. Zones 9-10.

They may suffer some winter dieback under extreme winter sun and winds, so choose a site with some protection such as an east side of a building. They withstand hot summers better if their shallow roots are mulched to keep them cool. Boxwoods are available as balled and burlapped or container-grown plants, both of which transplant easily in spring or fall. Boxwoods have a naturally compact shape, so do quite well without pruning. They also tolerate shearing to give the look of a very formal hedge or topiary. Propagate by softwood, semi-hardwood or hardwood cuttings. Seed propagation is tedious.

SELECTIONS Buxus sinica var. insularis (littleleaf box) grows only 3-4 feet; medium green foliage turning yellow-green in winter. Native to Japan; hardy Zones 6-9 (some cultivars are hardy to Zone 4).

B. sempervirens (common box) This tree grows 6-15 feet high and has larger leaves that are lustrous, rich green above and yellow-green below. Doesn't turn off-color in winter. Its wood is used commercially. Performs best in climates without extremes. Native to Europe, northern Africa and western Asia; hardy Zones 5-9.

CAMELLIA *Theaceae*

The genus *Camellia* contains about 80 species of shrubs and small trees native to eastern Asia. This important genus provides us with tea, seed oils, and for the landcape, spectacular blossoms. The foliage is rich, glossy green. There are cultivars that provide single, semi-double, and double flowers in shades of red, white, pink, and salmon. They are best suited as a tall hedge plant or for a focal point in the oriental garden.

Camellias bloom well in partial shade and may languish in full sun. Provide them with well drained, slightly acid rich soil and mulch over their shallow roots. Temperatures of 0° F will kill flower buds. Camellias are usually grown in containers and transplant quite easily. Pruning for shape should be done after flowering. Fertilize every couple of years and provide ample water throughout the season, particularly in dry times. Propagate by planting seed immediately after harvesting, or by softwood or semi-hardwood cuttings.

SELECTIONS Camellia japonica (Japanese camellia) may grow 10-15 feet; this is the most common camellia grown for beautiful flowers; thousands of cultivars. Single or double flowers range from 3-5 inches across. Plants are pyramidal shaped. Native to the coasts of Japan, south Korea and Taiwan; hardy in Zones 7-9.

C. sasanqua (sasanqua camellia) grows only to 6-10 feet and flowers in fall and winter. Smaller flowers than *C. japonica*; range from white to rose, with cultivars expanding these colors to red and lavender. Native to Japan; hardy Zones 7-9.

CITRUS *Rutaceae*

The *Citrus* genus contains many species commercially grown for their familiar lemons, limes, oranges and grapefruit. All citrus have beautiful glossy leaves, often dotted with glands that give off a pungent odor when rubbed. Their waxy white to purple flowers can easily fill a room with their sweet fragrance.

Camellias were a symbol of happiness in ancient Japan (except to the samurai, who regarded the fleeting life of the flowers as suspicious). Camellia japonica is known in Japan as tsubaki, "the tree with shining leaves." It was worshipped in the Shinto religion as the residence inhabited by gods during their earthly transformation. Camellias were brought to the western world in 1694 by German naturalist Engelbert Kaemper; he had to sneak this (and other plants) out of the country because local shoguns were not cooperative. Camellias were first brought to America in 1820 and became an important part of horticulture in the South. *Above: Camellia japonica* 'Rosea'.

Palms and cycads are often used in oriental gardens in tropical or subtropical climates, like the one above at Ganna Walska Lotusland in Santa Barbara.

Citrus fruits vary in size from the tiny calamondin orange to the large grapefruit. Most citrus fruits remain green until absolutely ripe, when they turn shades of orange, yellow and pink. The rinds of the fruits also contain the glands, making them aromatic in themselves. The ornamental citrus often have flowers, green and ripe fruit on them at the same time, making them showpieces in the garden. They are well-adapted to container culture, so in climates where they are not hardy, they can be grown in tubs and moved indoors for the winter.

Transplant as a and burlapped or container-grown plant into moist, organic soil. They need full sun to produce fruit. They will tolerate a range of soils, but provide plenty of moisture while establishing, and irrigate in dry times in subsequent years. Citrus must have a dry, dormant period during the winter to flower, so hold back somewhat on water in the winter. Fertilize annually and prune in late winter as needed to restrict size. Citrus will tolerate clipping into formal shapes, but their natural shapes are quite attractive. Propagate by fresh seed and grafting. Seeds from commercial oranges or lemons will grow into trees, but will seldom produce the same type of fruit since citrus readily cross-pollinate.

SELECTIONS *Citrus aurantium* (sour orange) grows to 25 feet with rounded crown. Dark, lush leaves have wings on the petioles; white flowers are quite large and intensely fragrant. Fruits are bright orange tinged with red. The bitter fruits are grown for oil and use in marmalade. Native to southeast Asia, hardy to Zone 9.

C. nobilis (tangor) small tree that grows to 12 feet and suckers. Flowers hang in racemes; fruits have thin peel in yellow, green and orange. The commercial orange **'Temple'** is a cultivar of this species. Native to Vietnam, hardy to Zone 9.

COCOS NUCIFERA COCONUT PALM *Arecaceae*

This genus contains only one species. Its nativity is questionable, but it is widely cultivated in all tropical areas. This is the familiar single-stemmed palm that grows to 80 feet, usually leaning at a graceful angle, and is topped by pinnate leaves up to 20 feet long. It is monoecious, meaning that male and female flowers are different structures on the same plant. The fruit, coconuts, are widely used commercially for their oil, milk and fibrous outer husk. The coconut palm adds an instant tropical look to any garden. In colder climates, coconut palms can be grown in tubs and brought indoors for the winter. Many cultivars are available; hardy to Zone 10.

Although coconut palm is tolerant of a wide range of conditions, it must have well-drained soil. It is tolerant of salt but will not tolerate drought. Water well throughout its life to produce an attractive plant. Pruning and fertilization are not necessary. Propagate by seed.

CYCAS CYCAD PALM, BREAD PALM *Cycadaceae*

This genus contains about 20 species of palms native to Old World tropics. They are ancient in origin (Mesozoic Era) and are thus quite primitive seed plants. Their form is like that of typical palms, with a strong trunk of 10-20 feet and a rosette of 8- to10-foot leaves. The leaves are divided into many stiff leaflets. The plants are dioecious and both male and female plants produce conelike structures. Cycad palms have a strong place as a focal point in oriental gardens of warm climates. They are easily grown in tubs to be brought indoors in harsher climates.

Depending on the species, some cycads thrive in full sun and dry soil while others must have moist, shady conditions. Provide grainy, loose soil and excellent drainage. They are extremely slow-growing and do not require any pruning except to remove spent leaves. Do not fertilize. Propagate by removing basal suckers or by fresh seed.

SELECTIONS *Cycas revoluta* (sago palm) grows 6-10 feet, erect at first and then becoming procumbent as it ages; long shiny leaves of yellow-green that overlap. Often used for bonsai; will withstand short periods of exposure to frost as long as crown is protected with straw or other material. Native to southern Japan and the Ryukyu islands. Zone 9.

Cycas revoluta's feathery fronds contrast with a smooth mossy groundcover and a stone sculpture.

DAPHNE *Thymelaeaceae*

Native to Europe and Asia, these shrubs may be evergreen or deciduous. They are grown in the landscape for their attractive glossy foliage and fragrant white or purple flowers.

Well-drained, light soil is essential to keep daphnes performing well. Poorly drained soil will contribute to a quick demise. Grow in full sun or partial shade. Evergreen types should have some protection in extreme climates. Traditionally grown as a container plant. Plant where the plant will remain since they do not respond well to transplanting, and only in spring or very early fall. Provide plenty of water as long as the soil is well-drained. Fertilize every couple of years, and prune right after flowering if necessary for shaping. Propagate by cold stratified seed or by semi-hardwood cuttings.

SELECTIONS *Daphne cneorum* (rose daphne, garland flower) grows to only 1 foot; abundant rose pink to white fragrant flowers in spring and early fall; native to the mountains of Europe; hardy Zones 4-7.

D. odora (fragrant daphne, winter daphne) is an evergreen shrub of 4-6 feet; white to rose-purple extremely fragrant flowers in late winter to early spring; grows well in shade. Native to China; hardy Zones 7-9.

ERIOBOTRYA JAPONICA LOQUAT *Rosaceae*

Loquat is grown in tropical areas not only for its attractive evergreen foliage, but also for its tasty fruit. These plants, native to China and Japan, have holly-like leaves that are deeply wrinkled and dark, glossy green on top and covered with rusty hairs on underside. The fragrant white flowers are borne upright on the ends of branches in winter, and are covered with rusty brown hairs. The fruits are yellow, applelike and sweet. These are borne in spring and summer. This outstanding, tough evergreen makes a beautiful hedge; hardy Zones 8-10.

Loquat is fairly tolerant of most soil conditions, although it thrives in deep, moist soil. These plants have pleasing shapes naturally, but they tolerate shearing and can be made into a formal hedge. They transplant easily as balled and burlapped or container-grown plants. Plant in full sun for the best fruit production, although the plants will tolerate partial shade. Do not fertilize and water only in extremely dry times—they will tolerate dry conditions. Propagate by seed or cuttings.

EUONYMUS SPINDLE TREE *Celastraceae*

This genus contains every type of plant—from deciduous to evergreen, from tree to shrub to vine. Most species have angled stems that remain green at least during their first year, if not several years beyond. The flowers are inconspicuous, and the seeds are enclosed in orange or red arils which are in turn enclosed in a yellow or tan capsule. The capsule splits to reveal the arils—most striking on heavily fruiting plants. Evergreen varieties are often used as hedge plants in oriental gardens. Generally the fruit display is merely a secondary attraction.

Most euonymus will tolerate average to poor soil, alkaline soil, and full sun

DAPHNE ODORA 'CAROL MACKIE' (FRAGRANT DAPHNE, WINTER DAPHNE) 2-4 feet tall; fragrant pink and white flowers; small green leaves banded in white. Full sun or partial shade, tolerates shade well. Zones 7-9.

ERIOBOTRYA JAPONICA (LOQUAT) 6-8 feet tall, wrinkled, dark green leaves, fragrant white flowers, edible yellow fruit. Full sun and deep, moist soil are best, adapts to other conditions. covered with rusty brown hairs. Zones 8-10.

EUONYMUS JAPONICUS (JAPANESE EUONYMUS) Dense shrub to 10 feet tall; waxy dark green leaves. Full sun to partial (or even deep) shade; well-drained, moist, rather poor soil. Zones 7-9.

FATSIA JAPONICA (JAPANESE FATSIA) 6-10 feet tall, very large palmate leaves with seven to eleven lobes. Partial shade; moist, rich soil. Zones 8-10.

Above: Ficus religiosa (also called the bo, peepul, or Bodhi tree), under which the Buddha is said to have attained enlightenment. One such tree, at Anuradhapura in Sri Lanka is considered the world's oldest historical tree, having been brought there from India as a seedling in 288 B.C. and its life recorded ever since.

or partial shade. Some evergreen varieties will easily tolerate full shade. Transplant as container-grown plant in early spring or fall in soil that hasn't been amended. Provide average supplemental water through the season, providing the soil is well-drained. Fertilize infrequently and prune as needed for shaping. Propagate by cold-stratified seed or by softwood cuttings. Evergreen euonymus exhibit topophysis–cuttings taken from lateral branches will grow laterally; cuttings taken from upright branches will grow upright.

SELECTIONS *Euonymus japonicus* (Japanese euonymus) is a dense evergreen shrub that grows to 10 feet; waxy dark green leaves and pink and orange fruits. Native to Japan; hardy Zones 7-9.

FATSIA JAPONICA JAPANESE FATSIA *Araliaceae*

This genus contains only one species of evergreen shrubs. It is native to Japan and has very large palmate leaves with seven to eleven lobes. It grows to 6-10 feet high and its foliage makes a bold statement in the landscape. There are several cultivars that are more compact than the species; hardy Zones 8-10.

Grow fatsia in full shade if possible. It will tolerate most types of soils, but performs best in organic, moist soil. In colder areas, provide winter protection. Transplant from containers into soil amended with organic matter. Provide plenty of water through the season–it will tolerate very wet conditions. Fertilize yearly for maximum growth and prune as needed to shape. Propagate by semihardwood cuttings.

FICUS BENGHALENSIS BANYAN TREE *Moraceae*

The figs are in a genus of great variety that has been used for many years in the home and conservatory. The banyan tree reaches about 90 feet in height and sends aerial roots down to the ground to support the crown. This makes the tree spread wide; in fact, an old tree may spread over several acres. The leaves are like miniature versions of the rubber tree, also in the *Ficus* genus. The banyan has inconspicuous flowers and orange-red fruits. It is native to India and Pakistan where it is considered sacred; hardy to Zone 10b. This massive tree should be used with discretion, particularly because of the room its aerial roots will take.

Transplant as a balled and burlapped plant into well-drained, moist soil. Although tolerant of most conditions, banyans will drop their leaves when over- or under-watered. Organic soil will help keep the moisture levels consistent. Prune only as needed for shaping (when cut, the leaves and stems exude a milky sap that can be a skin irritant). Propagate by seed, layering or softwood cuttings.

ILEX HOLLY *Aquifoliaceae*

Hollies are native to temperate and tropical North America, South America and Asia. There are deciduous and evergreen types, most of which are grown for their attractive red or black fruits. Hollies are dioecious, so a planting must have at least one male to produce fruits on the females. Evergreen hollies make superb hedges and are often tightly pruned to resemble stones in oriental gardens.

FICUS BENGHALENSIS (BANYAN TREE) Large, spreading tree to 90 feet in height, covered in aerial roots; small dark green leaves. Full sun, well-drained moist soil. Zone 10b.

ILEX AQUIFOLIUM 'GOLDEN QUEEN' (ENGLISH HOLLY) Tree 8-10 feet at 20 years, 20-25 feet at 50 years. Pyramidal form with densely packed branches, small yellow berries. Full sun to half shade, moist, acid, fertile soils. Zones 5-8.

ILEX CRENATA (JAPANESE HOLLY, BOX-LEAVED HOLLY) Dense, twiggy shrub to about 10 feet tall; leathery shiny leaves; black fruits. Full sun to half shade, moist, acid, fertile soils. Zones 5-7.

ILEX CRENATA 'CONVEXA' (JAPANESE HOLLY, BOX-LEAVED HOLLY) Dense, twiggy shrub to about 6 feet tall; convex, leathery shiny leaves; black fruits. Full sun to half shade, moist, acid, fertile soils. Zones 5-7.

Meserve hollies, like 'Blue Princess', above, have pointed blue-green leaves and produce abundant bright green berries. *Ilex cornuta,* Chinese holly, also bears attractive deep green lobed leaves with prominent spines; it grows 10-15 feet tall. Useful cultivars inlcude 'Burfordii' with glossy dark green convex leaves and 'Burfordii Nana', which grows to only 5 feet tall.

Provide hollies with fertile, well-drained soil. Evergreen hollies need extra moisture before winter in northern climates to assure their survival. To avoid winter damage, evergreen hollies should also be sited out of the winter sun and wind, preferably on an east or south side. Transplant balled and burlapped or container-grown plants into soil amended with organic matter. Prune after new growth is full-sized as needed to shape, and fertilize with acid fertilizer once a year if the soil is alkaline. Propagate by softwood, semi-hardwood or hardwood cuttings. Seed propagation is complicated and lengthy.

SELECTIONS *Ilex crenata* (Japanese holly, box-leaved holly) is a dense, twiggy shrub to about 10 feet; leathery shiny leaves; black fruits that are hidden by the leaves; many cultivars; used often in Japan for hedges and bonsai subjects. Native to Japan; hardy Zones 5-7.

Ilex integra (mochi tree) grows 10-25 feet; oval dark glossy green leaves; creamy yellow flowers; red fruits. Native to Japan; hardy Zones 7-8.

I. x *meserveae* [*I. rugosa* x *I. aquifolium*] (meserve holly) cultivars grow 7-8 feet with leathery, spiny leaves; grown for its attractive red fruits. Fruit size and leaf shape are dependent on cultivar. Most common cultivars are **'China Girl'**, **'China Boy'**, **'Blue Angel'**, **'Blue Prince'** and **'Blue Princess'**; hardy Zones 3-7.

I. rotunda (Kurogane holly) grows to 60 feet; red fruits; native to Japan, China, Korea, Taiwan and Vietnam; hardy to Zone 7.

LIGUSTRUM JAPONICUM JAPANESE PRIVET, WAXLEAF PRIVET
Oleaceae

These evergeen shrubs and trees are most commonly used as hedge plants, although they do make attractive specimens as well. They have dark green glossy opposite leaves and clusters of creamy white flowers followed by small black fruits. They are native to Japan and Korea and hardy in Zones 7-10.

Privets will grow in most types of soil with little care. They are tolerant of dry soils but may not perform well in extremely wet soils. Plant in full sun or partial shade. They prune extremely well into formal hedges, but are also attractive in their natural state. Privets transplant well as container-grown, balled and burlapped or bare root plants. Provide average amounts of water through the season and prune only as needed. Fertilize infrequently. Propagate by softwood cuttings or cold-stratified seed.

LITCHI CHINENSIS LYCHEE *Sapindaceae*

This genus contains only one species, native to southern China, that grows to about 40 feet. Although it is grown most often for its fruit, it is a beautiful ornamental tree that seems a natural choice for the oriental garden. It is round-topped in form with coppery red young leaves and rosy-colored fruits. The fruits are composed of a succulent aril surrounding a hard seed; they are considered delicacies whether eaten fresh, dried or preserved in syrup; hardy to Zone 9.

Transplant in early spring as a balled and burlapped plant into moist, acid, organic soil and mulch immediately to preserve moisture. If growing specifically for fruit production, site the tree to provide some shelter. Lychees will

LIGUSTRUM JAPONICUM (JAPANESE PRIVET, WAXLEAF PRIVET) To 10 feet tall; dark green glossy opposite leaves, clusters of creamy white flowers, small black fruits. Full sun to partial shade, average to dry soil. Zones 7-10.

LITCHI CHINENSIS (LYCHEE) 40-foot-tall, round-topped tree with coppery red young leaves and rosy-colored fruits. Full sun, moist, acid, organic soil. Zones 9-10.

MAGNOLIA GRANDIFLORA (EVERGREEN MAGNOLIA, SOUTHERN MAGNOLIA, BULL MAGNOLIA) Large tree, to 100 feet tall; very large dark green glossy leaves, 10-inch fragrant creamy white flowers. Full sun or partial shade, rich, well-drained soil. Zones 6-10.

MAHONIA AQUIFOLIUM (OREGON GRAPE) 3-6 feet tall; leaves open bronze, turn dark green in summer, bronze-green in fall; bright yellow flowers in mid spring, clusters of deep blue berries in early fall. Acid soil, full sun to part shade. Zones 4-8.

My definition of a successful combination is one that creates an aesthetically pleasing and attractive scene. Compositions that fit these criteria for me are beautiful, well-placed stones in combination with boxwoods, yews, and azaleas.
BENJAMIN CHU, MISSOURI BOTANICAL GARDEN

We have had great success combining plants with rocks and stones. Some combinations that have worked well are ferns around the base of a stone basin or lantern; lilyturf rising out of the gravel on a path near, but not in, the planting bed; bamboo almost at the edge of a path that makes you feel as if you were in the grove.
VIRGINIA HAYES, GANNA WALSKA LOTUSLAND, SANTA BARBARA

We've had success with Japanese iris planted along a stream, wooly thyme used as a groundcover in hot and dry locations, and legally collected Ponderosa pines (*Pinus ponderosa*).
JIM HENRICH, DENVER BOTANIC GARDENS

One of our best combinations combines dwarf burford holly, dwarf Chinese holly, dwarf yaupon, junipers, and mondo grasss. Another consists of aralia (*Fatsia japonica*), cast iron plant (*Aspidistra* sp.), holly fern, and mondo grass.
HENRY PAINTER,
FORT WORTH BOTANIC GARDEN

Opposite: Osmanthus, pieris, and camellia surround a moss-covered stone water basin.

grow on alkaline soil, but must be treated annually with chelated iron in order to avoid iron chlorosis. Provide ample moisture throughout the growing season, and cut back on watering during the fall and winter. Lychees must have a dry dormant, cool (45-55° F) period through the winter to produce flowers and fruits the following spring. Fertilize annually and prune as needed for shaping. Propagate by softwood cuttings or fresh seed. Most commercially produced cultivars are grafted.

MAGNOLIA *Magnoliaceae*

Magnolias have been used as focal points in Chinese and Japanese gardens for many years. There are many species to choose from, and magnolias are surprisingly hardy and easy to care for. They reward us with extraordinary flowers and rich, leathery foliage. The evergreen magnolia lends a tropical look with its long glossy leaves and huge fragrant flowers. Magnolia leaves, bark and even roots have a distinct spicy smell. Magnolias vary in size and shape, and there are many cultivars available to suit every taste. In the oriental garden, they not only make superb focal points, but they can also function well as shade trees and as a backdrop for flowering or evergreen shrubs.

Magnolias do not transplant easily, so balled and burlapped plants should be transplanted only in spring before growth starts. They have very fleshy roots that are easily damaged. Rich, well-drained moist soil will best support a magnolia, but they are fairly tolerant of more adverse conditions. Water abundantly during the first year of establishment so the plant can replenish its root system. In subsequent years, water whenever rainfall is inadequate to provide an inch a week. Plant in full sun or partial shade. Fertilize only every two or three years, and prune as needed to shape (after flowering). Propagate by cold-stratified seed.

SELECTIONS *Magnolia grandiflora* (evergreen magnolia, southern magnolia, bull magnolia) is the familiar large tree of southern areas; grows to 100 feet. Very large dark green glossy leaves with 10-inch fragrant creamy white flowers. Performs best in partial shade and somewhat protected from winter winds and sun. Many cultivars available. Native to southeastern U.S; hardy Zones 6-10.

MAHONIA OREGON GRAPE, HOLLY GRAPE *Berberidaceae*

These evergreen shrubs are native to eastern Asia, and north and central America. They have pointed, thornless compound leaves, yellow panicles of flowers and waxy blue-black berries. Some are less than a foot high and make superb groundcovers, while others are shrubby and upright, making excellent foundation or specimen plants.

Provide mahonia with a protected spot in more northern climates since they may tend to brown somewhat on exposed sites in winter, and don't easily tolerate the heat of summer. They perform best in acid soil, and grow well in shade. Transplant container-grown plants into soil amended with organic matter. Fertilize once a year with acid fertilizer on alkaline soils. Pruning is seldom necessary except to remove winter damage. Provide average amounts of water. Propagate by cold-stratified seed or softwood or hardwood cuttings.

Nandina domestica closely resembles bamboo and can be used to achieve its effect. Shown above with a low-growing juniper.

SELECTIONS Mahonia aquifolium (Oregon grape) grows 3-6 feet with bronzy leaves in spring turning to dark glossy green in summer; turns bronze-purple in fall. Native to northwestern North America; hardy Zones 4-8.
M. bealei (leatherleaf mahonia) grows 10-12 feet; gray-green leaves with pale yellow green on the undersides; fragrant yellow flowers on 4-inch upright racemes. Native to China; hardy Zones 6-8.
M. japonica grows to 6 feet; similar in appearance to *M. bealei* except the flower clusters hang down and may be up to 10 inches long. Native to China; hardy to Zone 6.

NANDINA DOMESTICA HEAVENLY BAMBOO, SACRED BAMBOO
Berberidaceae
Only one species occurs in this genus. It closely resembles bamboo, hence the common name. It is a native evergreen from India to eastern Asia with narrow, straplike leaves that turn red in the fall and back to green in spring. The species grows 6-8 feet high, and there are cultivars that grow to only 4 feet. Its flowers are white, followed by clusters of bright red berries, making it quite ornamental. Nandina provides the look of bamboo, so important in the oriental landscape, but also provides color in its leaves, flowers and berries.

Nandina is extremely hardy and survives well in containers and low light. It thrives in full sun as long as it receives plenty of water. The species must be carefully pruned to make it branch well and stay compact. Transplant container-grown plants into average soil and provide plenty of water through the season. Fertilize infrequently. Renewal prune older stems every year, and cut tips of other stems back to make plant compact and dense. Propagate by semi-hardwood or hardwood cuttings. Seed propagation is slow and tedious. It is root hardy to Zone 6, but will only remain evergreen in Zones 7-9.

OSMANTHUS DEVILWEED *Oleaceae*
Osmanthus species are evergreen holly-types of plants, with deep green to olive leathery leaves that are may be pointed like holly or rounded. All *Osmanthus* species have clusters of tiny creamy white flowers. The flowers are not spectacular in show, but their fragrance is almost overpowering in its sweetness. These make good natural hedge plants without pruning, and are often planted just for the fragrance.

For best performance, plant in rich, moist, somewhat acid soil. Most species, however, are somewhat adaptable. Pruning is usually unnecessary unless using them in a hedge. Transplant container-grown plants into amended soil and provide average water through the season. Fertilize infrequently. Propagate by semi-hardwood cuttings.
SELECTIONS Osmanthus heterophyllus (Chinese holly, false-holly) usually grows 8-10 feet but can reach up to 20 feet; flowers are white and quite fragrant; native to Japan and Taiwan; hardy Zones 7-9.
O. fragrans (sweetolive) grows to 30 feet; creamy white flowers used to flavor Chinese tea. Native to eastern Asia; hardy to Zone 8.

NANDINA DOMESTICA CV. (HEAVENLY BAMBOO, SACRED BAMBOO) 4 feet tall, narrow, straplike leaves that turn red in the fall and back to green in spring, white flowers, clusters of bright red berries. Full sun, moist soil. Zones (6)7-9.

PHOTINIA GLABRA (JAPANESE PHOTINIA) 10-12 feet tall, red foliage, white clusters of flowers, red fruits that ripen to black. Full sun to partial shade, any soil that is not extremely wet. Zones 7-8.

PIERIS JAPONICA (JAPANESE PIERIS) 9- to 12-foot-tall shrub or small tree; simple, glossy leathery leaves; long racemes of creamy white fragrant flowers. Moist, acid soil rich in organic matter, partial shade. Zones 5-8.

PITTOSPORUM TOBIRA 'VARIEGATA' (JAPANESE PITTOSPORUM) 18 feet tall; alternate, dark glossy green leaves, banded in white; clusters of fragrant white to pale yellow flowers. Acid or alkaline, sandy, dry soils, full sun or heavy shade. Zones 8-9.

Rhododendrons often the only bright color in oriental gardens. In some gardens, such color is not desired, and flowerbuds are removed. The evergreen shrubs (some species are deciduous) are valued for their neat rounded shape and glossy foliage. *Above: Rhododendron macrantha* 'Rosea', an evergreen azalea.

PHOTINIA GLABRA JAPANESE PHOTINIA *Rosaceae*

Japanese photinia grows to 10-12 feet and is native to Japan. Photinias are grown for their striking foliage, white clusters of flowers and abundant red fruits that ripen to black. They have a coarse texture which can be useful for contrast in the landscape, and their size makes them work well for screening. The flower and fruit display add to the impact. They are hardy in Zones 7-8.

Photinias are very tolerant of most soils and transplant easily. They will not thrive in extremely wet soils. Provide full sun to partial shade. Transplant balled and burlapped or as container-grown plants into average soil. Provide average moisture through the season and prune as needed to keep the plant thick. Pruning may take some practice since the plant does not branch easily at cuts. Fertilize to produce abundant growth if desired, and watch for nitrogen deficiency. Propagate by semi-hardwood cuttings.

PIERIS JAPONICA JAPANESE PIERIS *Ericaceae*

Native to Japan, Japanese pieris grow 9-12 feet as a shrub or small tree. They have simple, glossy leathery leaves and graceful long racemes of creamy white fragrant flowers that hang like tiny bells from a slender stem, resembling lily-of-the valley. They combine well with other ericaceous plants such as rhododendron and azalea since they have the same cultural requirements. The delicate, subtle flowers are a nice contrast to bold-colored rhododendron flowers. There are many cultivars available with pink or reddish flowers. Hardy in Zones 5-8.

Provide Japanese pieris with moist, acid soil rich in organic matter and partial shade. They perform well in full sun or partial shade and are more tolerant of alkaline soils than many of the other ericaceous plants. They benefit from shelter from strong winter winds. Transplant container-grown or balled and burlapped plants into well-amended soil. Fertilize with acid fertilizer on alkaline soils and provide ample moisture through the season. Prune after blooming. Propagate by seed immediately after harvesting or by softwood or semi-hardwood cuttings.

PITTOSPORUM TOBIRA JAPANESE PITTOSPORUM *Pittosporaceae*

Native to China and Japan, this evergreen tree grows to 18 feet. Its leaves are alternate and dark glossy green. The flowers are white to pale yellow borne in clusters. Japanese pittosporum is sometimes called house mock orange because of the intensely fragrant flowers. Pittosporums are used frequently as hedge plants in southern climates and for seaside plantings along the coast. Hardy Zones 8-9.

Pittosporums are used extensively because of their adaptability. They thrive in hot climates and sandy, dry soils. They perform well in acid or alkaline soils, full sun or heavy shade, and tolerate heavy pruning. They are also pollution and salt tolerant, adding to their appeal for urban gardens. Transplant container-grown plants into average soil and provide average moisture as the plant is establishing its roots. After that, supplemental water is generally unnecessary. Fertilize infrequently and prune in late spring.

RHAPIS LADY PALM *Arecaceae*

The name *rhapis* is derived from the Greek word for needle; lady palm's leaves are pointed and somewhat needlelike. These low-growing plants have unusual leaf sheaths and leaves that grow like the fingers of a hand. Short clusters of flowers appear several times a year. Lady palms are excellent backgrounds to oriental gardens, blending and adding texture.

Lady palms are fairly easy to grow. They require moist, fertile soil and partial to even deep shade. Mulch to keep roots moist. They are easily propagated by division in spring.

SELECTIONS *R. excelsa* has puckered leaved and grows to 15 feet tall. *R. humilis* is lower and more compact.

RHODODENDRON AZALEA, RHODODENDRON *Ericaceae* [see also entry under deciduous shrubs]

The genus *Rhododendron* includes over 900 species and thousands of cultivars, not only the evergreen rhododendron but semievergreen and deciduous plants as well. The distinctions between rhododendron and azalea are somewhat arbitrary, depending on which gardener is consulted; all azaleas are rhododendrons, but not all rhododendrons are azaleas. Generally, azaleas are deciduous and have funnel-shaped flowers, and rhododendrons are evergreen or semievergreen with more bell-shaped flowers, although there are certainly exceptions. In oriental gardens, tightly pruned azaleas are often used to represent stones, or as western gardeners use boxwood. In either case, they are severely pruned to keep their shape at the expense of blooms. In other instances, they are used as a focal plant because of their flowers. Most bloom in spring.

The one necessity to keep rhododendrons healthy is acid soil. Provide them

Many oriental gardeners grow rhododendrons for their neat, mounded shape instead of for their showy flowers.

RHAPIS EXCELSA 'VARIEGATA' (LADY PALM) 15-foot-tall palm with pointed, puckered leaves. Partial to deep shade; moist, fertile soil. Zones 9-10.

RHODODENDRON 'HINO CRIMSON' (KURUME AZALEA) 4- to 6-foot-tall shrub with glossy dark green leaves and clusters of crimson flowers, 1½ inch across. Full sun to partial shade, moist, acid soil. Zones 7-9.

RHODODENDRON CATAWBIENSE (CATAWBA RHODODENDRON) 8- to 15-foot-tall shrub with large leaves and 3-inch magenta-lilac flowers in mid-late spring. Full sun to partial shade, moist, acid soil. Zones 4-7.

ROSA CHINENSIS 'SLATER'S CRIMSON' (CHINA ROSE) 3- to 4-foot-tall shrub with double red flowers, touched with white at the base; light tea scent. Full sun, moist, rich soil. Zones 7-9.

with peat-based, rich soil with plenty of moisture and they will thrive. They perform best in a somewhat protected sunny spot, but will tolerate semi-shade. Large-leaved rhododendrons may burn from winter sun and wind, so the ideal planting site is with protection from larger deciduous trees. Using rhododendrons or azaleas in partial shade may mean reduction in the number of flowers. Transplant container-grown or balled-and-burlapped plants into well-amended soil. Fertilize after flowering with acid fertilizer (on alkaline soils). The only pruning usually needed is to remove flowers after they fade. Propagate by non-stratified seed or by cuttings. The time to take cuttings varies with species.

SELECTIONS *Rhododendron* **Kurume hybrids** (Kurume azaleas) [*R. kaempferi* x *R. kiusianum*] are usually 3 feet tall, with white, scarlet, purple, speckled or striped flowers. Zones 7-9.

Rhododendron indicum (macranthum azaleas) grow to 6 feet and have flowers of rose to scarlet. Native to Japan; Zones 5-6.

Rhododendron linearifolium (spider azaleas) grow to 4 feet tall with pink to lilac flowers. Native to Japan. Zones 6-7.

Rhododendron obtusum (Kirishima azaleas, Hiryu azaleas) are semievergreen to evergreen shrubs of 3 feet with leaves up to 1¼ inch long; rose to purple flowers shaped like funnels. Native to Japan. Zones 6-7.

ROSA ROSE *Rosaceae*

This large genus consists of over 100 species of thorny deciduous and evergreen shrubs and trailers. Roses are grown for their highly ornamental white, pink, red, salmon, and yellow flowers. Flowers will vary from single forms to semi-double and full double. Shrub and climbing roses are used in oriental gardens for focal points and fragrance, and the climbing or long-caned types are used to adorn trellises and arbors. A garden of hybrid tea roses, however, is not appropriate for the subtlety of an oriental garden.

Provide roses with full sun and well-drained soil that is high in organic matter. Most species roses need no winter protection in cold climates. Selecting resistant varieties will avoid the high maintenance of treating for disease and insect problems. Transplant container-grown, balled-and-burlapped or bare-root plants into amended soil. Water well while the plant is establishing roots and then only as needed to provide an inch of water a week. Fertilize species roses infrequently; hybrid roses should be fertilized monthly during the growing season. Prune after new growth begins to emerge, cutting off damaged or dead branches and shaping. Propagate by cold stratification, softwood or hardwood cuttings.

SELECTIONS *Rosa banksiae* (Lady Banks' rose) grows to 20 feet and is evergreen. Its stems are nearly thornless, its flowers white or yellow and single. It is a rampant grower. Native to China. Zone 7.

Rosa chinensis (China rose, Bengal rose) is a low growing evergreen shrub; flowers pale pink to white to scarlet or crimson. Native to China. Zone 7.

Along with teas and silks, European traders of the late 1700s and early 1800s brought another treasure home with them: *R. chinensis*, the China rose, which the Chinese had cultivated for centuries, creating many hybrids from their native wild roses. These hybrids possessed a special characteristic unknown to European roses–they were everblooming, putting out new flowers all through the growing season. Breeders immediately seized on this attribute, crossing the repeat-blooming Chinas with the hardier but once-blooming Western roses and revolutionizing rose growing in the process. The Chinas (and the related Teas) became the ancestors of all modern roses.

Above: Maple and lacebark elms begin to dress in fall colors, marking the change in seasons.

DECIDUOUS TREES

Despite the importance of pines and other evergreen trees, an oriental garden can hardly be considered complete without some deciduous plants. It is these plants that transform the garden from season to season, marking the change that is so important a part of oriental gardening. In summer, their leaves, usually larger than those of the evergreens, blend with other greens and provide shade and texture. Autumn many be the showiest season for deciduous trees, as they turn spectacular shades of red, orange, gold, brown, and purple. In winter, bare, their architecture becomes visible and often fascinating. In spring, their new green leaves, and in some cases masses of flowers, spread an aura of rebirth throughout the garden.

Japanese maples are the quintessential deciduous trees for oriental gardens. Any of the wide range of trees and shrubs, from low-growing threadleaf maples to bright red five-lobed cultivars, has a place in any garden; indeed, most designers include at least one in every garden. But there is no reason to stop with maples. For a showstopping display of blossoms in spring, try cherry, almond, or pear trees, which have long been used by oriental gardeners. As pointed out by David Slawson in Secret Teachings in the Art of Japanese Gardens, the cherry "may be planted in any location without difficulty," so long as you plant one specimen in the cherry's home environment. The following pages describe many deciduous trees that are useful in oriental gardens, but many more are available and are becoming useful not only in oriental gardens, but in Western ones as well. The lacebark elm (*Ulmus parvifolia*), for example, is now a popular substitute for the American elm. Properly chosen and sited, deciduous trees will provide beauty through many years.

Acer griseum, paperbark maple, has an exquisite peeling bark.

ACER MAPLE *Aceraceae*

Maples, or *momiji*, are a mainstay of oriental gardens, not only because of their stateliness as trees, but for their beautiful form, bark, and fall color. Maples are native to temperate regions all over the world, and are a very common component of residential and commercial landscapes. They vary in form from upright and narrow to wide-spreading and rounded to small-sized shrubby trees to short shrubs, giving us a maple for just about all landscape situations. Maple leaves vary from a typical three- to five-lobed maple leaf to finely dissected leaves of threadleaf maples. Leaves vary from bright green to bronze to maroon, and fall color ranges from red to orange to yellow. Maples are monoecious, with female and male flowers appearing on the same tree. Although the flowers are small, they can be quite showy in reds and yellows, particularly because they bloom fairly early. Maple fruits, samaras, are usually two winged in the familiar coat-hanger shape. Some fruits are brightly colored, adding an attractive element. Maple wood is prized for cabinetry, and the sugar maple provides us with maple syrup, made from its sap. The oriental garden is an ideal setting for maples, especially the smaller trees. The Japanese maple is perhaps the most widely used maple in oriental gardens, prized for its beautiful shape, elegant leaves, and rich colors.

Although some maples are tough enough to withstand transplanting by almost any method, others are peculiar in their need for planting in spring only. They transplant well as container-grown or balled-and-burlapped plants. Some maples do not tolerate alkaline or heavy clay soils, becoming chlorotic because of an inability to take up manganese; red maples, for example, do not perform well in the Chicago area. Rather than attempting to treat the condition, it's advisable to select a different tree. Maples also vary in their cultural requirements which will be addressed in the entries below. Most require well-drained, average soil and full sun to partial shade. Maples should be fertilized with a general fertilizer the second year after they are planted. After that, every two or three years is adequate. If pruning is needed, prune only in mid-summer or late fall to avoid "bleeding.". Propagate by seeds or cuttings.

SELECTIONS *A. buergeranum* (trident maple) has a rounded crown with a height and spread of 20-30 feet, to 50 feet in ideal conditions. Distinct three-lobed leaves of dark green with white on the underside, turning orange and red in fall. Performs well in containers; plant balled-and-burlapped in spring in full sun and well-drained soil. Native to China. Zones 4-8.

A. ginnala (amur maple) is known as the hardiest of all the maples, a shrubby tree that grows to 30 feet. Unusual, asymmetrical shape as plant matures and often loses lower branches. It can be pruned to accentuate this shape. Transplant in fall or spring as balled-and-burlapped plant; full sun or partial shade; not fussy about soil. Small three-lobed leaves; fragrant yellow-white flowers; attractive red fruits during summer—nice contrast to deep green foliage. Fall color red to yellow—purchase in fall to be sure of fall color. Makes an attractive hedge; grows well in containers. Native to China, Mongolia, Manchuria, Korea, Japan. Zones 2-7.

A. griseum (paperbark maple) is grown for its cinnamon-brown papery, peeling

ACER BUERGERANUM (TRIDENT MAPLE) 10-15 feet at 20 years, 20-30 feet at 50 years. Rounded crown, tree-lobed leaves dark green on top, white underneath. Full sun, well-drained soil. Zones 4-8.

ACER CIRCINATUM (VINE MAPLE) 15 feet at 20 years, 25-30 feet at 50 years. Dense green lobed leaves turning red or orange in fall, ornamental purplish and white flowers, widespreading habit. Full sun or up to half shade, any fertile soil. Zones 6-9.

ACER PALMATUM (JAPANESE MAPLE) 15 feet at 20 years, 30 feet at 50 years. Shrubby, mounded habit. Dense, deeply lobed green or red foliage, turns bright red in fall. Full sun (some tolerate partial shade), any fertile soil, not drought tolerant. Zones 5-8.

ACER SACCHARUM 'GREEN MOUNTAIN' (SUGAR MAPLE)
Deciduous. 20-25 feet at 20 years: 50-60 feet at 50 years. Wide, rounded crown. Dense foliage, bright green in summer turns orange and gold in autumn. Moderately fertile, well-drained, loamy soil on the acidic side; full sun to half shade in the North and ¾-¼ sun in the South. Zones 3-8.

Acer ginnala with chrysanthemums.

bark. It grows 15-30 feet tall and is shrubby and rounded in outline, with compound leaves with three leaflets of medium matte blue-green, turning brilliant red-orange in fall. Performs well in high pH soils if well-drained. Transplant balled-and-burlapped in spring. Native to China. Zones 4-8.

A. japonicum (fullmoon maple) is a shrub or small tree that grows 20-30 feet with a rounded form that can become irregular as it ages. Palmately lobed leaves of seven to 13 lobes are rich green in summer, turning yellow and red in fall; attractive purple-red flowers; horizontal samaras; many cultivars. Good substitute for *A. palmatum* if soil is somewhat heavy or alkaline. Performs best in partial shade and well-drained soil. Native to Japan. Zone 5.

A. mandshuricum (Manchurian maple) is a shrub or small tree that grows to 20-30 feet. It bears compound leaves with three leaflets and produces crimson fall color earlier than other maples. Fruits form right angles. Performs best in acid, well-drained soil. Native to Manchuria and Korea. Zones 4-7.

A. palmatum (Japanese maple) grows 20-30 feet and bears green, bronze, or purple leaves with deeply cut lobes; scarlet fall color; leaves held late in fall. The **'Dissectum'** group of cultivars have fernlike foliage. Hundreds of cultivars, including variegated and golden leaves. Performs best in partial shade and well-drained soil; somewhat adaptable to high pH. In northern reaches of Zone 5 it should be planted in a protected spot since it is susceptible to spring frost damage. Pruning can enhance shape as focal point. Does well in containers and for bonsai. Used extensively in oriental garden design. Native to Korea, China and Japan. Zones 5-8 (hardiness varies considerably depending upon the cultivar).

Acer palmatum 'Bloodgood'.

Acer palmatum 'Everred'.

Acer palmatum 'Atropurpureum'.

Acer palmatum 'Bloodgood'.

Acer palmatum 'Tsukubane'.

Acer japonicum 'Maiki jaku'.

A. rubrum (red maple, swamp maple) is a stately tree to 100 feet in ideal situations with an oval to rounded crown and striking silvery bark; leaves three lobed, medium green with bright white undersides; turn yellow to brilliant scarlet in fall. Pick out plant in fall to be assured of fall color—seedling trees will vary in color. Male and female flowers may be on separate trees; flowers are usually red and striking in early spring. Attractive red fruits emerge early in spring before the leaves. Plant in somewhat acid soil—has chlorosis problem on alkaline soils. Needs plenty of moisture and will tolerate swampy sites. Plant balled-and-burlapped in spring. Many cultivars available. Native to northeastern and central U.S. Zones 3-9.

A. triflorum (three-flowered maple) is a single-stemmed tree that grows 20-40 feet; rounded crown. Striking, peeling tan bark. Compound medium gray-green leaves with three leaflets, yellow to red fall color. Transplant balled-and-burlapped in spring into moist, acid soil; can become chlorotic in alkaline soil. Native to Manchuria and Korea. Hardy to Zone 5.

A. truncatum (shantung maple) is a medium-sized tree that grows 50-75 feet. Its glossy deep green leaves with five to seven lobes emerge bronze in spring and turn golden to orange in fall. Plant balled-and-burlapped in spring or fall; tolerant of most soils; no pruning required. Native to east central Asia. Zones 5-8.

AESCULUS TURBINATA JAPANESE HORSECHESTNUT

Hippocastanaceae

Japanese horsechestnut, native to Japan, can grow to a height of 75-95 feet. Its palmate leaves are dark glossy green with five to seven leaflets, and its lovely flowers are creamy white with a red spot and borne in erect clusters up to 10 inches long. Japanese horsechestnut blooms in summer and the fragrance is a welcome addition to the oriental garden. Such a large tree should be given a place of prominence, usually some distance from the house. Its palmate leaves provide very dense shade that usually precludes grass from thriving beneath it, so plan to use a shade-tolerant groundcover to skirt it. Hardy to Zone 6.

Horsechestnuts thrive in most situations except those that are constantly dry. Transplant as a balled-and-burlapped plant into moist soil. Provide plenty of moisture throughout the season, especially during the first year while the plant is becoming established. Prune only as necessary for shaping, and fertilize only every three years. Propagate by cold-stratified seed or grafting.

AMELANCHIER SERVICEBERRY, JUNEBERRY *Rosaceae*

Amelanchiers are commonly found throughout the temperate zone, as woods' edge and understory trees, and in landscapes across the world. Their form will vary according to species. Often planted for their showy early spring blooms, they also offer interest in the other three seasons. Their small oval blue-green leaves emerge bronze with some species having soft hairs along the edges and on the back sides. The white flowers are typically shaped as other members of the rose family, and they are borne in showy racemes. Depending upon the species, the flowers may emerge before or with the leaves. The plant produces red to blue fruits that are sweet and enjoyed by birds and people alike. Some

AESCULUS GLABRA (OHIO BUCKEYE) 20 feet at 20 years, 30-35 feet at 50 years. Rounded crown. Large green compound leaves turn bright orange in fall; yellow flowers, not very showy. Ordinary, well-drained soil, full sun. Zones 3-8.

AMELANCHIER CANADENSIS (SHADBLOW) 10 feet at 20 years, 20 feet at 50 years. Small, pointed oval leaves turn yellow to gold in fall; white flowers in spring, bluish fruit, attractive silvery bark. Full sun or partial shade, moist well- drained soil, acid to neutral. Zones 3-7.

BETULA PAPYRIFERA (PAPER BIRCH, WHITE BIRCH) 35 feet at 20 years, 55 feet at 50 years. Very white, chalky peeling bark, small bright green leaves, open habit. Stony to loamy soil, full sun; does not tolerate shade, heat, or pollution. Zones 2-6.

CASTANEA CRENATA (JAPANESE CHESTNUT) 30 feet at 20 years, 50-60 feet at 50 years. Very wide spreading crown, deep green, deeply toothed leaves. Full sun, somewhat acid, well-drained soil, tolerates dry conditions after establishment. Zones 6-9.

Betula albo-sinensis (Chinese paper birch) was introduced in the United States in 1910 by Earl Wilson, who called it the best birch for home gardens.

species of amelanchier are grown specifically for their large, abundant fruit. Leaves turn rosy pink to red to orange in fall, and in winter the silvery, striated bark is a beautiful accent. Amelanchiers make a particularly nice focal point when backed by evergreens which make the colors of all the seasons stand out dramatically. Their airy, graceful habit is an elegant addition to the oriental garden.

Amelanchiers are tolerant of most types of soil, being particularly adaptable to high pH. Transplant balled-and-burlapped in spring or fall and provide plenty of water to help the plant become well established. These will perform best if planted in full sun or partial shade. They perform well when used as an understory plant, although in heavier shade, they will not flower as dramatically. Pruning is seldom needed except for suckers on some species. Suckers can be controlled most successfully by pruning in mid-summer when growth has slowed. Fertilize only every two or three years. Propagate by cold-stratified seed or by digging suckers. Cuttings are not usually successful.

A. asiatica (Asian serviceberry) is a shrub or multistemmed tree to 35 feet tall with a graceful habit, dark green leaves, and red-orange fall color; dense clusters of flowers followed by blue-black fruits. Native to Japan, China, Korea. Zone 5.

A. canadensis (shadblow) is an upright shrub to about 20 feet; it suckers from its base so it can form thicket; blooms appear with the leaves. Naturally found in swampy areas. Zones 3-7.

BETULA PLATYPHYLLA VAR. JAPONICA JAPANESE BIRCH

Betulaceae

Japanese birch has become almost a standard in Japanese gardens if for no other reason than its striking white bark. These natives of Japan and China are upright, usually multistemmed trees that grow to about 60 feet. The young bark is maroon-brown with prominent white lenticels, and gradually peels to reveal the clear white bark so prized in the landscape. These birches have glossy medium green heart-shaped leaves that turn golden yellow in fall. The plants are monoecious, meaning that male and female flowers are in separate structures on the same tree. The male catkins, which are borne on the branch tips through the winter, expand to 6 inches in spring and shed their pollen to the female flowers which are borne upright along the branches. The female flowers then produce small conelike structures which bear the tiny winged seeds. A white-barked birch against a backdrop of evergreen and other deciduous trees is a magnificent focal point, particularly when reflected in a still pond. Hardy to Zone 4.

Transplant birches as balled-and-burlapped plants only in spring into moist, well-drained soil. They will tolerate wet soils, but will not grow as large. Provide plenty of water throughout the year and mulch the roots immediately upon planting. Cool roots and moist soil will help avoid the stresses that make birches susceptible to insect and disease problems. Prune birches only in mid-summer or late fall to avoid the "bleeding" that occurs when the sap is rising in spring. The bleeding does not harm the plants, but makes a mess and is quite unsightly. It also tends to draw insects. Fertilize every two or three years and propagate by cold-stratified seed or semi-hardwood cuttings.

CASTANEA CRENATA JAPANESE CHESTNUT *Fagaceae*

Japanese chestnut is prized not only for its beautiful appearance, but also for its tasty nuts and its resistance to chestnut blight, a remarkable combination for a chestnut. Its deeply toothed leaves are deep green and up to 6 inches long. The tree's crown spreads widely with branches that begin quite low to the ground; it grows 50-60 feet high with a spread almost twice that. Japanese chestnut needs a place of prominence with plenty of room to spread to its natural size. It's a marvelous shade tree, providing dense shade, but place it so that the chestnuts do not become a litter problem. It is native to Japan and thus hardy to Zone 6.

Plant in somewhat acid, well-drained soil. Transplant as a balled-and-burlapped plant when young to assure establishment. Provide plenty of moisture the first year as long as the soil is well-drained. In years following, supplemental irrigation is probably not necessary since chestnuts are very tolerant of dry soils. Fertilize yearly after the first year to produce nuts quickly (they will often bear chestnuts two to three years after planting). Pruning is seldom needed. Propagate by cold-stratified seed or by cuttings taken from very young trees.

CATALPA OVATA CHINESE CATALPA *Bignoniaceae*

This broad-spreading tree is native to China, but has escaped cultivation and is now widely spread in the northeastern U.S. It grows to 30 feet or more with at

Catalpa bignonioides is a large, spreading tree that lends a soft, peaceful look to this Japanese garden.

A study in contrasts: a gently spreading and sloping katsura tree with a rigidly upright trained ginkgo.

least the same spread. The large heart-shaped leaves grow up to 10 inches long. The showy flowers are borne on the ends of the branches and are yellow-white with orange and violet, somewhat reminiscent of an orchid flower and their fragrance fills the warm evening air. The beanlike fruits are 8- to 12-inch-long pods. Although not as towering a tree as some of the larger ones mentioned, Chinese catalpa makes a distinct statement in the landscape because of its coarse texture. It is best used at a distance because this coarseness tends to overwhelm anything near it. Hardy to Zone 4.

Transplant into almost any soil as a balled-and burlapped-young plant. Spring planting will bring assured establishment. Catalpas are well-known for their adaptability to soil types and moisture levels. They tolerate drought as well as acid or alkaline soils. Fertilization is unnecessary as is pruning except for shaping and to remove occasional dead branches. Easily propagated from seed or root cuttings. Seed-grown plants flower quite young.

CEDRELA SINENSIS CHINESE TOON *Meliaceae*

This large tree, to 60 feet, has been grown in oriental countries for many years for its beautiful pendulous flowers. The tree is upright with a broad oval crown and may be single or multiple stemmed. The compound leaves are large, giving the plant a substantial, coarse texture. They emerge bronze and turn to medium green. The young leaves smell like onions, and the shoots are boiled and eaten by the Chinese. Its light brown bark peels, giving effective texture to the oriental garden. The white fragrant flowers bloom in 12-inch clusters that hang below the leaves in early summer. The size and coarse texture of the tree indicate its use at a distance where the fragrance of the flowers will gently waft over the entire garden. Zones 6-8.

Transplant as balled-and-burlapped tree into a fertile, loamy soil. Chinese toons will tolerate most types of soil and are particularly adaptable to alkalinity, a definite reason for planting in the Midwest. The tree suckers, so it will need to have suckers pruned out annually unless a colony is the desired look. Fertilization is generally unnecessary, and supplementary watering is seldom needed except in extremely dry times.

CERCIDIPHYLLUM JAPONICUM KATSURA TREE *Cercidiphyllaceae*

Katsura tree is a large, extraordinarily beautiful tree, growing to 100 feet in the wild. Although usually single-trunked, the branches may begin close to the ground, giving it a multiple-stemmed look. The crown is symmetrical and oval. Its small, tidy heart-shaped leaves emerge bronze-red, deep blue-green in summer, and yellow to apricot-orange in fall, a beautiful accompaniment to the reds and oranges of maples. The trees are dioecious, with male and female flowers emerging before the leaves. The flowers are small, but give the trees a pleasant haze of reddish green. A mature katsura tree adds serenity and elegance to the oriental garden with its symmetry and tidy appearance. Hardy Zones 4-8.

Transplant as a balled-and-burlapped plant only in early spring–they can be somewhat difficult to establish. Plant in moist, rich soil that is well-drained.

CEDRELA SINENSIS (CHINESE TOON TREE) 20 feet at 20 years, 35-40 feet at 50 years. Compound leaves, small white flowers in foot-long panicles. Moist alkaline soil, full sun but adapts to shade. Zones 5-9.

CERCIDIPHYLLUM JAPONICUM (KATSURA TREE) 20 feet at 20 years, 45-50 feet at 50 years. Heart-shaped gray-green leaves (spring growth is pink to purple); tree develops horizontal plates of foliage. Full sun, moist, rich, well-drained soil. Zones 5-9.

CERCIS CHINENSIS (CHINESE REDBUD) 10 foot multistemmed shrub. Small purple-pink pea-shaped flowers. Moderate shade or sun, prefers rich soil, but tolerates a wide range of soils, humidity, drought, and heat. Zones 6-9.

CHIONANTHUS RETUSAS (CHINESE FRINGETREE) Small tree, to 20 feet, with oval crown. Abundant white flowers in spring, blue-black fruit, gold foliage in fall. Full sun or partial shade, moist, rich soil. Zones 5-8.

A kousa dogwood flowers profusely in back of this pond at the Asian garden of the University of British Columbia Botanic Garden.

Katsuras adapt well to acid or alkaline soil, but they languish on heavy clay soil that does not drain well. If the tree becomes chlorotic, the soil is probably not well drained enough. Plant in full sun and provide copious amounts of water during the first year. Consequently, provide water whenever rainfall is insufficient. Pruning is seldom necessary since the plant has a near-perfect form naturally. Propagate by non-stratified seed or softwood cuttings from young trees.

CERCIS REDBUD *Fabaceae*

Native to the temperate areas of North America, southern Europe and Asia, redbuds are small-scale trees, seldom growing taller than 25 feet. They are vase-shaped when young and open to a wide, flat-topped crown as they mature. Although often grown specifically for their abundant pea-like fuchsia flowers, the trees are perhaps most spectacular in summer when clothed with verdant heart-shaped leaves. The leaves emerge bronze in spring and turn to golden yellow in fall. Their brown, flaking bark rivals crabapples in its beauty. The redbud is an excellent tree for use in a small garden as a central focal point or to soften the corner of a building.

Transplant balled-and-burlapped in spring or fall into rich, well-drained moist soil. Redbuds will adapt to alkaline or acid soil, but will not withstand soil that is permanently wet. Water well when first planted in order to establish a healthy root system. Subsequently, water as necessary during dry times. Fertilize annually after the first year and prune as necessary to remove dead or damaged branches. Redbuds have problems with cankers and verticillium wilt, both of which will cause limbs to die. This can be prevented to a certain extent by keeping the tree as healthy and vigorous as possible. Propagate by scarified and cold-stratified seed or by softwood cuttings. When purchasing a redbud, make certain that its seed source is local, particularly in northern locations. Southern-grown trees will seldom survive the cold temperatures in the north.

SELECTIONS *C. canadensis* (eastern redbud) grows 20-25 feet tall and bears fuchsia or white flowers. Native to eastern U.S. Zones 4-9.

C. chinensis (Chinese redbud) grows to 10 feet and is a multistemmed shrub with larger flowers than *C. canadensis.* Native to China. Hardy to Zone 6.

CHIONANTHUS RETUSAS CHINESE FRINGETREE *Oleaceae*

Chinese fringetree is a handsome small-scale tree that performs beautifully as a focal point in the oriental garden. Native to China, it grows to about 20 feet high, with an oval, symmetrical crown. The plants is naturally multiple-stemmed, but is often grown on a single stem in the landscape. When grown with multiple stems, the overall shape is much more rounded and wide spreading. The leaves are medium green in summer, and as they are expanding, the plant produces clouds of white flowers, borne in clusters on the ends of the branches. The plant is dioecious, so female plants develop blue-black fruits. Hardy Zones 5-8.

Fringetrees grow well in wet areas, so provide moist, rich, slightly acid soil. Transplant as a balled-and-burlapped plant in spring only. Grow in full sun or light shade. Fringetrees seldom need pruning except to remove damaged limbs. If pruning is necessary, prune after the plant flowers since it flowers on buds formed the preceding summer. Fertilize annually after the first year and provide plenty of moisture while it is becoming established and in dry times subsequently. Propagate by warm and cold stratified seed.

CORNUS DOGWOOD *Cornaceae*

Dogwoods are ubiquitous in the landscape, particularly because there are so many species and cultivars. They range from small shrubs to large trees, and have all varieties of flowers and fruits. They are native to temperate areas of North America, Asia and Europe. In the oriental garden, dogwoods are traditional as focal points, particularly the flowering and kousa dogwoods.

Dogwoods will grow in most soils, but best performance is in well-drained, rich soil. Some dogwoods adapt well to very wet situations. The tree types should be transplanted as balled-and-burlapped plants while quite young in order to assure establishment. Provide sun or partial shade. Some species of dogwood must be renewal pruned every year to keep the shrub in bounds and to produce juvenile wood that is brightly colored. The tree species rarely need pruning except to shape. Fertilize every two to three years. Propagation varies by species.

Above: Dogwood blossoms bring color and softness to the evergreens featured in this Japanese garden.
Left: A kousa dogwood and a live oak show markedly different textures and colors.

CORNUS KOUSA (KOUSA DOGWOOD) 15 feet at 20 years, 20-30 feet at 50 years. Creamy white floral bracts, attractive strawberrylike fruits Full sun or partial shade, acid soil. Zones 5-8.

CORNUS FLORIDA (FLOWERING DOGWOOD) 20 feet at 20 years, 40 feet at 50 years. Rounded to wide-spreading crown, abundant white or pink bracts, red fruits, checkered bark. Moist, acid soil, partial shade; Zone 5.

COTINUS OBOVATUS (AMERICAN SMOKETREE) 15 feet at 10 years, 20 feet at 50 years. Spreading or rounded habit, excellent fall color. Full sun, adapts to many soils, including dry and rocky. Zones 5-8.

DAVIDIA INVOLUCRATA 'VILMORINIANA' (DOVE TREE) 15 feet at 20 years, 35 feet at 50 years. Broadly pyramidal, especially when young; flowers with very large creamy white bracts. Light shade, deep rich moist but well-drained soil. Zones 6-8.

Cornus controversa (giant dogwood) grows to 60 feet in the wild but only 35-40 in cultivation; horizontally-branched. Performs best on moist, somewhat acid soil; grow in full sun or partial shade. White clusters of flowers followed by blue-black fruits. Propagate by warm followed by cold stratification. Native to China and Japan. Zones 5-7.

Cornus florida (flowering dogwood) grows to 40 feet; rounded to wide-spreading crown. Grown for its beautiful white or pink bracts that surround tiny flowers. Attractive scarlet-red fruits and checkered bark. Grow in moist, acid soil in protected location with partial shade; they seldom survive in heavy clay soils or drought conditions. Even though listed as hardy to zone 5, they must have ideal conditions in northern areas to flower well. Propagate by cold-stratified seed or softwood cuttings. Native to eastern U.S. Hardy to Zone 5.

Cornus kousa (kousa dogwood) grows 20-30 feet; horizontally branched; creamy white floral bracts (true flowers are inconspicuous); attractive strawberry-like fruits that are edible. Drought resistant but requires acid soil. Grow in full sun or partial shade. Propagate by cold-stratified seed or softwood cuttings. Native to Japan, Korea and China. Zones 5-8.

Cornus kousa var. ***chinensis*** (Chinese dogwood) grows to about 30 feet with larger flowers and wider spreading branches than *C. kousa*.

COTINUS COGGYGRIA SMOKETREE *Anacardiaceae*

Native to southern Europe and Asia, smoketrees grow to about 15 feet in the wild. They are often considered large shrubs since their natural form is multiple-stemmed. The oval leaves are matte blue or gray-green, turning red or yellow in fall. There are several purple-leafed cultivars. Although smoketrees are beautiful in leaf, they are most often selected for their unusual striking inflorescences. Although the flowers are fairly inconspicuous, they leave behind panicles of softly drooping, fuzzy wands which are actually the pedicels covered with hairs. They are pink to purplish, and from summer into fall, the shrub looks as if it has a haze of smoke draped about it. Smoketrees make attractive accent plants, particularly the purple-leafed varieties, or companions to other white-flowered focal plants such as spirea or flowering dogwood. Hardy Zones 5-8.

When planning to use a smoketree, be certain to allow enough room for it to grow to its natural shape. Pruning destroys this shape and makes the tree look messy. Smoketrees transplant easily as balled-and-burlapped plants in spring or fall. They grow best in full sun although will survive in partial shade where their shapes will be more open and loose. Plant in average, well-drained soil and water well to establish. In subsequent years, water only in times of extreme drought. Smoketrees are tolerant of drought conditions and high or low pH. Fertilization is generally unnecessary. Propagate by scarified and stratified seed or softwood cuttings.

COTONEASTER MULTIFLORUS MANYFLOWERED COTONEASTER
Rosaceae

This small tree, native to western China, is an excellent change from traditional crabapples. It grows only 10-12 feet tall and spreads up to 15 feet. A

Many cotoneasters (like rockspray cotoneaster, above) are prostrate and can be used as groundcovers. In fall, most produce ornamental berries.

mature plant will have a very wide, flat-topped crown and branches very low to the ground. Its small leaves are matte blue-green, and as the leaves are emerging, the tree blooms with hundreds of small white flowers up and down the branches. These flowers are followed by abundant small red apples in late summer through the fall. A spectacular plant in flower and fruit, this small tree makes a beautiful specimen in the oriental garden. Zones 3-7.

Transplant as a balled-and-burlapped or container-grown plant in spring. As with all cotoneasters, plant in very well-drained, loose soil in full sun. Cotoneasters are infinitely adaptable to any situation except permanently wet soil and have few maintenance requirements. Prune only as necessary to shape. Supplemental water is necessary only when the plant is establishing itself in the first year. After that, they are quite tolerant of whatever the weather might provide. The easiest method of propagation is by softwood cuttings taken in summer. Seeds must be scarified in acid and then cold-stratified to germinate.

DAVIDIA INVOLUCRATA DOVE TREE *Nyssaceae*

The dove tree, native to western China, grows 50-60 feet in the wild. This exquisite tree performs well as a shade tree with its large leaves and coarse branches, although it's so beautiful in flower that it's an unmistakable focal point of the garden. Its wide crown is somewhat pyramidal in shape. Although the flowers are pleasant themselves, the showier "doves" are actually creamy-white bracts poised in the branches. These bracts can be as large as 10 inches. Hardy Zones 6-8.

Dove trees transplant well as balled-and-burlapped plants in spring. Plant into moist, well-drained soil that is rich in organic matter. If you do not have this soil naturally, consider using another type of tree since amending the soil seldom works for a tree this size (see section on Planting in Chapter 4, Techniques). Water well for the entire season while becoming established, and subsequently when rainfall is lacking. Dove trees do not tolerate drought. Pruning is seldom needed because of the naturally symmetrical form. Fertilize every two or three years. Propagate by warm and cold-stratified seed or leaf-bud cuttings.

FIRMIANA SIMPLEX CHINESE PARASOL TREE *Sterculiaceae*

This native of eastern Asia grows to 60 feet and has large, lush maplelike leaves. Its bark is smooth gray-brown, and the yellow-green flowers hang in long racemes. Although it has interesting flowers and fruits, it is generally used as a shade or street tree. Its rich appearance lends a tropical look to the oriental garden. Zones 7-9.

Transplant balled-and-burlapped plants into well-drained, moist soil. Provide ample water throughout its life–it will not tolerate drought well. Prune only as necessary and do not fertilize. Propagate by fresh seed.

GINKGO BILOBA MAIDENHAIR TREE *Ginkgoaceae*

Ginkgos hold the honor of being one of the oldest trees on earth, over 150 million years old. They have been grown in their native southeastern China for years not only as beautiful 50- to 80-foot shade trees, but also for their edible fruits and for their medicinal properties. Their "nuts" or seeds are prized by the Chinese. Gingkos are dioecious, meaning that male and female flowers appear on separate trees. In the landscape industry today, ginkgos are grown from cuttings taken from male trees in order to avoid the fruit production of the female trees. The fruits have a smell of rancid butter when they fall and begin to decompose. The ginkgo is a gymnosperm, meaning that it is more closely related to the pine family than any of the deciduous shade trees. This classification is made according the fruit. Ginkgos have a bilobed fan-shaped leaf that is fresh lime green in summer and turns a remarkable golden in fall. Zones 3-8.

Ginkgos are well known for their toughness. They are drought and pollution tolerant and will grow well in almost any kind of soil. Transplant balled and burlapped as a young plant and provide abundant water through the first year. In subsequent years, add supplemental water only in extremely dry times. Pruning and fertilization are not needed, two more reasons for adding this beautiful tree to the garden. Propagate by cold-stratified seeds or softwood cuttings.

GLEDITSIA TRIACANTHOS VAR. INERMIS HONEYLOCUST

Fabaceae

Honeylocusts, natives of the eastern U.S., have been planted in landscapes almost to the point of overkill because of their resistance to disease and their ease of care. These large trees can grow to 70-80 feet in the home landscape and naturally have irregular, sprawling crowns. The species has long, vicious

Ginkgo biloba usually exhibits a spreading habit with lush foliage (top); it can also be trained to a rigid columnar form, as above.

spines, but this naturally occurring variety is thornless. Honeylocusts have large compound leaves with tiny leaflets, giving the tree an extremely fine texture. The yellow-green flowers appear in early summer, and although they are not showy, their fragrance is delightful. The female flowers produce 8- to 10-inch-long wavy pods that can pose a litter problem when they fall. Most of the cultivars available (and there are many) are virtually seedless. Honeylocusts are desirable additions to the oriental garden because of their open, airy appearance, their ability to filter light into the garden and make patterns on the ground, and their irregular, interesting branching habit. Zones 3-9.

Transplant honeylocusts as balled-and-burlapped plants in spring or fall. They tolerate almost any type of soil and are drought and pollution tolerant. They are native to swampy areas and bottom lands, so are able to withstand flooding and fairly compacted soil. Provide supplemental water while establishing, but in subsequent years, irrigation is seldom needed. Plant in full sun. Prune only as desired to open and shape crown, keeping in mind that it will always be irregular and without a central leader. Do not fertilize—members of the pea family have the ability to "fix" atmospheric nitrogen and thus provide their own food source. Propagate by scarified seed.

KOELREUTERIA PANICULATA GOLDEN RAINTREE, VARNISH TREE *Sapindaceae*

Golden raintree is native to China and Korea and can grow to 45 feet. Its large compound leaves (up to 18 inches long) are dissected into many leaflets, giving the tree a finer texture than one would assume, given their size. The leaves emerge bronze-red in spring and turn to bright medium green for summer and yellow in fall. The tree is usually grown as a specimen for its huge panicles of bright yellow flowers in mid to late summer. When in flower, it truly looks as if it is raining gold. The flowers are followed by brown papery fruits in autumn. The golden raintree performs well not only as a specimen, but as a shading tree for a south or west side of the house. It has few branches, so lets in a flood of sunlight when the leaves fall in autumn. Hardy Zones 5-9.

Golden raintrees are considerably hardier than their reputation would suggest. They transplant easily as small balled-and-burlapped plants in spring or fall and will adapt to most any kind of soil. Water well for the first year, but supplemental water isn't usually necessary after that. Do not fertilize; pruning is seldom needed. Propagate by scarified and cold-stratified seed.

MAGNOLIA *Magnoliaceae*

Magnolias have been used as focal points in Chinese and Japanese gardens for many years. There are many species to choose from, and magnolias are surprisingly hardy and easy to care for. They reward us with extraordinary flowers and rich, leathery foliage. The evergreen magnolia lends a tropical look with its long glossy leaves and huge fragrant flowers. Magnolia leaves, bark, and even roots have a distinct spicy smell. Magnolias vary in size and shape, and there are many cultivars available to suit every taste. In the oriental garden, they not only make superb focal points, but they can also function well as shade trees and as a backdrop for flowering or evergreen shrubs.

FIRMIANA SIMPLEX (CHINESE PARASOL TREE) To 60 feet tall. Large maplelike leaves, smooth gray-brown bark, yellow-green flowers in long racemes. Well-drained, moist soil. Full sun or partial shade. Zones 7-9.

GINKGO BILOBA (MAIDENHAIR TREE) 15 feet at 20 years, 50-80 feet at 50 years. Lime green fan-shaped leaves turn gold in fall. Any soil, full sun or light shade. Tolerates drought. Zones 3-8.

GLEDITSIA TRIACANTHOS VAR. INERMIS (HONEYLOCUST) 25 feet at 20 years, 70-80 feet at 50 years. Tall tree with irregular spreading head, compound leaves with tiny leaflets. Any soil, full sun. Zones 3-9.

KOELREUTERIA PANICULATA (GOLDEN RAINTREE, VARNISH TREE) 20 feet at 20 years, 45 feet at 50 years. Compound leaves, up to 18 inches long, dissected into many leaflets; huge panicles of bright yellow flowers. Any soil, full sun or partial shade. Zones 5-9.

Magnolias do not transplant easily, so balled-and-burlapped plants should be transplanted only in spring before growth starts. They have very fleshy roots that are easily damaged. Rich, well-drained moist soil will best support a magnolia, but they are fairly tolerant of more adverse conditions. Water abundantly during the first year of establishment so the plant can replenish its root system. In subsequent years, water whenever rainfall is inadequate to provide an inch a week. Plant in full sun or partial shade, and to avoid losing flower-buds to frost, plant in an exposed, cold location to keep flower buds dormant as long as possible. Fertilize only every two or three years, and prune as needed to shape (after flowering). Propagate by cold-stratified seed.

SELECTIONS *M. heptapeta* (Yulan magnolia) grows to 40 feet and bears 7-inch-long glossy leaves and large fragrant erect white flowers very early in spring (they are often nipped by frost). Native to China. Zone 5.

M. kobus (Kobus magnolia) grows to 40 feet; large dark green leaves; white flowers with a pink tinge; very early. Native to Japan; hardy to Zone 4.

M. x loebneri 'Merrill' (Merrill magnolia) grows 25-30 feet; many-petaled white flowers make splendid display. Propagate by softwood cuttings. Zone 3.

M. quinquepeta (lily magnolia) is a shrubby magnolia that grows only to about 12 feet. Flowers are pink-purple on outside, white on inside. Native to China. Zones 5-8.

M. stellata (star magnolia), a small magnolia, grows to 20 feet; flat-topped crown at maturity. Small matte gray-green leaves that turn amber in fall. Many-petaled clear white fragrant flowers in spring, can be damaged by frost. Native to Japan. Zones 3-8.

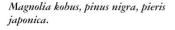

Magnolia kobus, pinus nigra, pieris japonica.

MAGNOLIA STELLATA (STAR MAGNOLIA) To 20 feet tall. Small matte gray-green leaves, many-petaled clear white fragrant flowers. Full sun to partial shade, moist, rich well-drained soil is best. Zones 3-8.

MALUS FLORIBUNDA (SHOWY CRABAPPLE) To 25 feet. Wide-spreading round crown. Pink buds open to white flowers, followed by small, yellow or red fruits. Full sun, well-drained average soil is best. Zone 5.

PRUNUS MUME (JAPANESE APRICOT) To 25 feet. White to deep red flowers, small yellow bitter fruits. Full sun, any well-drained soil. Zone 6.

PRUNUS X YEDOENSIS (YOSHINO CHERRY) To 40 feet tall. Single pink flowers that fade to white. Full sun, any well-drained soil. Zones 5-8.

*Above: **Malus hupehensis** with rhodo-dendrons.*
*Opposite top: **Prunus subhirtella***
'Pendula' with 'PJM' rhododendron.
*Opposite bottom: **Prunus yedoensis**.*

MALUS CRABAPPLE *Rosaceae*

There are hundreds of cultivars of crabapple to choose from, and one should never be limited to only the species crabapples. Crabapples come in all sizes and shapes from very low and shrubby to upright with a narrow crown. Most have medium green leaves, some of which may be lobed. Fall color ranges from gold to salmon. Some cultivars have purple to maroon leaves. Flower color varies from white to pink to rose to deep red, and the applelike fruits range from pale red to yellow to orange to almost black. Crabapples are best chosen not only for flower and fruit color, but for disease-resistance and fruit retention. Some of the species and older cultivars are highly susceptible to apple scab, often losing their leaves by August and making an unsightly statement in the landscape. New cultivars have fewer problems with disease, flower well before the leaves, and retain their tiny fruits through the winter, often only dropping them as new leaves emerge in spring. Crabapples are definite focal points, wherever they are planted, and make a beautiful addition to the oriental garden. Hardiness varies according to species and cultivar, although most are hardy into Zone 4.

Crabapples are some of our toughest trees, being tolerant of most types of soil except permanently wet. They will survive in partial shade, but full sun will produce the most beautiful shape and flower display. Transplant balled-and-burlapped plants in spring or fall into well-drained, average soil. Fertilize every couple of years after the first, and water well the first year. After the plant is established, supplemental irrigation will only be necessary in times of drought. Prune only as needed, immediately after blooming. Some crabapples sucker profusely, so prune suckers and watersprouts in mid-summer when growth has slowed. Purchase crabapples from a reliable nursery to ensure receiving the correct cultivar–they are often mixed up in the trade. Crabapples are usually propagated by budding, grafting, or softwood cuttings. The selections listed below are only a sampling of the species available.

SELECTIONS *M. floribunda* (showy crabapple) a true oriental type that has been around for many years. Grows to 25 feet; wide-spreading round crown. Reliable blooming and fruit set. Pink buds open to white flowers, followed by small, yellow or red fruits. Fairly disease resistant. Native to Japan. Zone 5.

M. halliana (flowering crabapple) is a shrubby form to about 15 feet. Rose red flowers and purple fruits. Native to Japan and China. Zone 6.

M. sargentii (sargent crabapple) This small, shrubby crabapple has been grown for years in oriental gardens. Its small size fits quite well in a small garden. Grows to about 8 feet with a spread of 12-15 feet. White flowers and small red fruit. Native to Japan. Zone 4.

PRUNUS PLUM, CHERRY *Rosaceae*

Prunus blossoms are called snow flowers in Japan because the plants often bloom early enough to accompany spring snows. Plum blossoms have long been associated with longevity and rebirth in oriental cultures and they are treasured because the flowers fall before withering. The cherry blossoms of Japan are known worldwide. This genus contains a wide variety of shapes and forms, from small and shrubby to tall and elegant. Most plums and cherries have colored bark, usually maroon, with obvious white lenticels. The single or double blossoms are often fragrant and vary from white to pink. Some plums and cherries have attractive gold-

en fall color; others lose their leaves while still green. Although oriental tradition precludes using double flowers because they are said to be vulgar and not in keeping with desired simplicity, the garden designer should decide whether to choose some of the striking double-flowering types available. The fruits vary with the species, from familiar edible plums and cherries to fruits that are merely ornamental to no fruit at all (sterile cultivars).

Most species of *Prunus* transplant very easily as balled-and-burlapped or container-grown specimens (a few will tolerate bare-root transplanting). They are tolerant of a wide range of soils, with one requirement—the soil must be well drained. They will even tolerate drought fairly well, but will wither in constantly wet soil. Prunus also perform best if planted in full sun. Pruning is dependent upon the species. If growing for fruit production as well as ornament, pruning can be an elaborate task, requiring a good reference on fruit production. Some of the shrubby types benefit from regular renewal pruning. Fertilization also depends upon the species, although all species should be regularly fertilized on poor soils to keep the plant vigorous enough to fend off the many insect and disease problems plums and cherries tend to have. Propagate by cold-stratified seed. Some species propagate well by cuttings; most fruit-producing types are grafted.

SELECTIONS ***P. armeniaca*** (apricot) is a small, round tree with a crown that flattens as the tree matures. Branches close to the ground; beautiful orange-red bark. Pale pink flowers and apricot-colored delicious fruits. Some cultivars have been devel-

Prunus serrulata 'Pendula'.

oped for spectacular blooms rather than fruit. Very susceptible to frost damage in cold climates. Native to China. Zone 5.

P. cerasifera (Myrobalan plum) is a small tree to 25 feet; white flowers, yellow to red small, sweet plums. One of the first plums to bloom. Used as rootstock for other plums. Several cultivars with purple leaves (of questionable worth because they are disease prone). Native to central Asia. Zones 3-8.

P. mume (Japanese apricot) is the most popular flowering plum in Japan and China. Grows to about 25 feet; flowers white to deep red; small yellow bitter fruits that are pickled and used for liqueur. Often used for bonsai. Native to China and southwestern Japan. Zone 6.

P. persica (peach) is grown especially for fruit production. Small pink to white flowers followed by juicy, large fruits. Choose cultivar carefully according to climate—often nipped by frost. Native to China. Zone 5.

P. serrulata (Japanese flowering cherry) Many cultivars available; grows 40-50 feet; white or pink flowers and black inedible fruits. Double or single varieties available. Attractive gold to red fall color. Native to Japan and Korea. Zone 5 or 6, depending on cultivar.

P. tomentosa (Nanking cherry, Manchu cherry) is a shrubby cherry to 6 feet; fuzzy leaves; white to pink flowers followed by bright scarlet edible fruits. Makes an attractive hedge, tolerates shearing, although at the expense of the flowers. Native to eastern Asia. Zone 3.

P. triloba (flowering almond) is shrubby and grows to around 10 feet; double flowers of pink or white; seldom has fruit. Overused in the landscape because it is beautiful in flower (but unfortunately, has little interest the rest of the year). Native to China. Zone 3.

P. x yedoensis (Yoshino cherry) bears single pink flowers that fade to white; most widely planted ornamental cherry in Japan. These are the cherries used in Washington, D.C. Can reach 40 feet; weeping form available. Naturally occurring hybrid in Japan. Zones 5-8.

SALIX WILLOW, OSIER *Salicaceae*

Some people complain about the willow's shortcomings: it needs copious water, is subject to insect and storm damage, and has weak wood that usually causes it to be short-lived. But a well-grown willow in its magnificent weeping form is an unquestionable asset to the landscape.

Willows need full sun and moist or even wet soils. They are traditionally grown at the edge of a body of water. They will grow in average soil if water can be supplied whenever the weather turns dry. The soil need not be of greater than average fertility. Transplant in fall or early spring. Willows are known for their greediness. Unless they are planted in wet soil, be prepared to water them in dry weather. An organic mulch helps keep average soil moist for willows. Trim off lower branches so they won't rest on the ground. Because willows "bleed" sap, they should be pruned only in winter or spring. It is easy to propagate willows from cuttings taken anytime. Willows have weak wood that is easily damaged by ice and wind. They are also prone to insect damage, particularly from caterpillars. Do not plant near septic tanks, drains, or in cultivated areas because they tend to seek water and become a nuisance.

SELECTIONS *S. alba* (white willow) has an excellent loose and open shape and delicate texture, growing to about 30 feet tall and is hardy in Zones 3-7. It has yellow wood and catkins. ***S. a.* 'Tristis'** (golden weeping willow) is readily available, hardy to Zone 2 and also has good yellow bark. ***S. a.* 'Argentea'** has stunning silver foliage. ***S. babylonica*** (Babylon weeping willow) is known for it shape; it is considered the best of the weepers. But it is hardy only in Zones 6-8 and is subject to canker, twig blight, and powdery mildew. ***S. b.* 'Crispa'** has interesting curled leaves.

SOPHORA JAPONICA PAGODA TREE *Fabaceae*
This large native of China and Korea grows 60-70 feet tall with a rounded, loose crown. Its shiny blue-green compound leaves remind one of honeylocust and mountain ash, although they are more substantial. The trees are grown most often for their beautiful flower display in late summer when panicles of cream to yellow fragrant flowers droop elegantly from the ends of the branches. The flowers are followed by pods that remain into the winter, adding a pleasing effect for winter enjoyment. Although the tree is large, it is still a splendid focal point and has the added benefit of providing filtered light and interesting patterns on the ground. Zones 4-8.

Transplant pagoda trees as young balled-and-burlapped plants. As with most other leguminous plants, they are quite tolerant of poorer soils. Ideally, they should be given loose, fertile soil, but they will do just fine in impoverished, dry soils. Water well to establish, and then irrigate only in times of extreme drought. Prune as necessary to maintain its shape and do not fertilize. Propagate by scarified seeds or softwood cuttings.

STEWARTIA PSEUDOCAMELLIA JAPANESE STEWARTIA *Theaceae*
This small-scale tree grows 25-40 feet tall and is a wonderful addition to the oriental garden as a focal point. Its gray, brown, and cinnamon mottled bark is one of its best features, yet is rivaled by its magnolialike flowers in summer and its orange-red fall color. This native of Japan is truly a plant with year-round interest. Zones 5-8.

Stewartias require moist, somewhat acid soil, and should be transplanted as very young balled-and-burlapped plants. Provide copious amounts of water for establishing the first year, and be ready to add supplemental water in subsequent years. A soil high in organic matter will help retain moisture as will mulching as soon as it is planted. Pruning is seldom necessary; fertilize annually after the first year. Propagate by warm- and cold-stratified seed or softwood cuttings (stewartia is not easy to propagate).

STYRAX JAPONICUS JAPANESE SNOWBELL *Styracaceae*
Japanese snowbell is native to Japan and China and grows to about 20 feet high. Its bark is mottled, somewhat like stewartia, but its primary focus is the flowers. The white flowers are borne in clusters that dangle on long, delicate pedicels, putting on a spectacular show in spring. As a focal point in the landscape, snowbells have few rivals, especially with the added reward of beautiful bark. Zone 5.

Transplant as a balled-and-burlapped plant very early in spring. Plant in rich, organic, somewhat acid soil that is moist but well drained. This plant must be supplied with plenty of water, especially when becoming established. Choose a site that is in full sun or partial shade with some protection form winter winds. The flowers are especially prone to frost damage. Prune only as necessary for shaping and fertilize annually after the first year. Propagate by softwood cuttings.

Salix babylonica.

SALIX INTEGRIFOLIA 'ALBA MACULATA' (HAKURO NISHIKI WILLOW)
Small tree to 15 feet tall. Average, moist soil. Full sun.
Zones 8-10.

SOPHORA JAPONICA (PAGODA TREE) 20-30 feet at 20 years, 60-70 feet at 50 years. Rounded, loose crown, shiny blue-green compound leaves, panicles of cream to yellow flower. Full sun, loose fertile soil is best. Zones 4-8.

STEWARTIA KOREANA (KOREAN STEWARTIA) To 50 feet tall. Zigzagging branches, toothed leaves turn red in fall, 3-inch white flowers with yellow centers. Moist, rich, acidic soil. Zones 6-9.

STYRAX JAPONICA (JAPANESE SNOWBELL) To 20 feet high. Mottled bark, clusters of dangling white flowers. Full sun or partial shade, rich, organic, somewhat acid soil. Zone 5.

DECIDUOUS SHRUBS

ABELIA X GRANDIFLORA GLOSSY ABELIA *Caprifoliaceae*

Abelias are flowering shrubs native to Asia and Mexico with shiny, semi-evergreen leaves and delicate, profuse white bell-shaped flowers tinged with pink from
mid-summer through fall.

Plant abelia into moist, somewhat acid soil in a site that is protected from winter winds in cold regions. Abelias may be damaged in very cold winters, and for
this reason, they perform best in Zone 6 even though they may survive in Zone 5.
They will usually have dieback in colder zones and will need to be pruned in
spring to remove dead branches. Abelias will tolerate full sun to half shade
although the flowering may be somewhat reduced in shade. They transplant well
as balled-and-burlapped or container-grown plants as long as they are given plenty of moisture throughout the season. Fertilize every two or three years.
Propagate by softwood cuttings or by sowing seeds immediately when ripe (no
stratification needed).

BERBERIS THUNBERGII BARBERRY *Berberidaceae*

Barberries are thorny shrubs which are traditionally grown for their brightly colored fruits, attractive yellow to red flowers, and bright fall color. Different cultivars come in shades of green and red; some grow to only 1 foot tall, others up to
6 feet tall. Flowering and fruit set also varies by cultivar. The species is native to
southern Europe and central China. Hardy Zones 4-8.

In springtime, flowering deciduous
trees add color to Japanese gardens.

Rich, well-drained soil will provide the best growth, although barberries grow well in almost all types of soil. They are extremely tolerant of drought and thus seldom need supplemental watering. Barberries are adaptable to bare-root planting, although they are most commonly available as container-grown plants. Provide full sun for most intense leaf color when using red-leafed varieties. Green types will tolerate some shade although their shape will be more loose and open. When purchasing barberries, check carefully for dying branches, an indicator of a wilt problem. Propagate by softwood cuttings taken from June through August. Seeds can be sown outdoors in fall or cold-stratified and planted in greenhouse benches.

SELECTIONS *B. t.* **'Crimson Pygmy'** has sparse flowering and fruit set, but its size and red foliage are quite useful in the oriental landscape. 'Crimson Pygmy' is a good substitution for boxwood because of its fine texture and naturally small size. It rarely needs any pruning since it maintains a tight mound shape naturally.

CALLICARPA JAPONICA JAPANESE BEAUTYBERRY *Verbenaceae*

Native to Japan, Taiwan, and China, Japanese beautyberries are grown for their striking, abundant clusters of small, pale lavender fruits that are revealed when the leaves drop in the fall. The shrubs grow to about 5 feet and have pink to rose tiny flowers. Although hardy in Zones 5-8, the stems usually die back to the ground each winter in more northern areas. They do, however, bloom and fruit on new wood each year. The cultivar 'Leucocarpa' has white fruits.

Provide well-drained soil of average or low fertility–beautyberries transplant easily, whether bare root or container grown. Plant in full sun or partial shade and fertilize only every few years. Prune the stems back to the ground in late fall or early spring to allow new growth to emerge unhampered. Fertilize infrequently and add supplemental water only if the season is exceptionally dry. Propagate by softwood cuttings in the summer or by seed. Seeds need no stratification or scarification for germination.

CHAENOMELES FLOWERING QUINCE *Rosaceae*

This genus contains only three species but many hybrids. The shrubs are adorned with attractive roselike flowers in various colors and fragrant quincelike fruits. The fruits make delicious jellies and preserves. The shrubs are easily identifiable by their leafy stipules, and often have thorny spurs. Flowering quinces make attractive natural hedges or shrub borders, as well as lovely specimens.

Provide flowering quince with a sunny site and well-drained soil for the best performance. It will grow in partial shade, at the expense of flowers. Flowering quinces are tolerant of varying soil and moisture conditions, and are unharmed by pollution. They transplant best when balled and burlapped, although container-grown plants do well if purchased when quite young. Smaller, compact plants will have a nicer appearance in the landscape than those that have been left to grow leggy and open. Generally, no supplemental irrigation is necessary unless the season is extremely dry. Renewal prune by removing larger stems at ground level each spring. Since the plant blooms on new wood, it can be pruned to about 6 inches from the ground each spring to keep it quite compact. Propagate by softwood cuttings in late summer or by seed that has been cold-stratified.

SELECTIONS *C. japonica* (Japanese flowering quince) grows 2-3 feet; flowers usually

ABELIA X GRANDIFLORA 'EDWARD GOUCHER' (GLOSSY ABELIA) 4-5 feet tall. Small leaves, tubular pink and white flowers. Moist, somewhat acid soil, full sun to half shade. Zones 6-9.

BERBERIS THUNBERGII 'CRIMSON PYGMY' (BARBERRY) To 1 foot tall. Fine-textured red foliage, compact mounding habit. Full sun for best color, rich well-drained soil. Zones 4-8.

CALLICARPA JAPONICA (JAPANESE BEAUTYBERRY) To 5 feet tall. Small pink flowers, clusters of small, pale lavender fruits. Well-drained, average soil, full sun or partial shade. Zones 5-8.

CHAENOMELES SPECIOSA 'GRENADA' (COMMON FLOWERING QUINCE) 6-10 feet tall. Red, pink, or white flowers, 2- to 3-inch yellow fruits. Zones 4-8.

salmon to orange to scarlet to dark red; greenish yellow fruits; native to Japan. Zones 5-8.

C. speciosa (common flowering quince) usually grows to 6 feet but can reach 10 feet; red, pink, or white flowers; 2- to 3-inch yellow fruits. Native to China. Zones 4-8.

CORYLOPSIS PAUCIFLORA BUTTERCUP WINTERHAZEL

Hamamelidaceae

Native to Japan, winterhazels are planted for their early fragrant hanging clusters of yellow flowers. The medium green leaves are pale green on the undersides. *Corylopsis pauciflora* grows to 4-6 feet and is wide-spreading, quite delicate in texture and stature. They are valued in the oriental landscape for their early fragrant flowers that appear in sun or partial shade. Winterhazel can be used for a specimen or as part of a natural shrub border. Zone 6.

Plant winterhazel in moist, well-drained soil rich with organic matter. The flower buds may be killed by early warming in colder climates, so plant in an exposed, colder location to keep the buds dormant as long as possible. Transplant balled-and-burlapped plants and amend the soil with organic matter if it is not already rich. Because they are slow-growing they seldom need pruning, but you can prune these early flowering shrubs to shape just after they finish blooming. Provide plenty of moisture throughout season and fertilize every one or two years. Propagate by softwood cuttings in summer, and do not move cuttings until they go through a full dormant period. Seed propagation is quite difficult since they require warm and cold stratification.

DEUTZIA CRENATA DEUTZIA *Saxifragaceae*

These small shrubs are native to Japan. They grow to 5 feet with erect branches and a delicate, soft texture. They have 3- to 5-inch panicles of white to cream flowers in early spring, making a spectacular flower display in early spring. They are well suited to the oriental garden as focal points, for shearing (at the expense of flowers), or for low hedging. Zone 6.

Plant in any well-drained soil in full sun or light shade. They are adaptable to a range of moisture, soil conditions, and pH. Deutzias are generally grown as container plants, although they will transplant readily in almost any form. Deutzias will almost always need pruning after a cold winter because many stem tips die, although it is best to wait until after they flower. Provide an average amount of water throughout the season. Propagate by softwood cuttings in summer.

ELAEAGNUS *Elaeagnaceae*

Native to southern Europe and Asia, this group's common feature is the striking leaf color. The leaves appear silvery due to small scales covering both sides. The fruits are drupelike and also covered with silvery scales. The flowers are inconspicuous but quite fragrant. These plants are desirable in the oriental landscape for their foliage color and fragrant flowers. Use with discretion, however, since they can be somewhat ungainly in shape.

Plant in full sun and light, well-drained soil for best performance. Elaeagnus are quite adaptable to pollution, salts, moist and dry soils, and a wide range of

CORYLOPSIS SINENSIS (CHINESE WINTERHAZEL) To 15 feet tall. Gray-green leaves, pale yellow flowers in 2-inch racemes. Moist, rich, well-drained soil. Full sun to partial shade. Zone 6.

DEUTZIA CRENATA 'NIKKO' (DEUTZIA) To 5 feet tall. Erect branches, 3- to 5-inch panicles of white to cream flowers. Full sun or light shade; wide range of soil types. Zone 6.

ELAEAGNUS PUNGENS 'FRUITLANDII'(THORNY ELAEAGNUS) To 15 feet tall. Dense shrub with spiny leaves, clusters of fragrant flowers. Full sun, light, well-drained soil. Zones 7-9.

ENKIANTHUS CAMPANULATUS (REDVEIN ENKIANTHUS) Upright shrub with pagodalike habit. Pure white flowers, brilliant red fall foliage. Full sun to partial shade, well-drained peaty soil. Zones 5-9.

Enkianthus campanulatus.

pH. They "fix" nitrogen, so are able to thrive on poor soils. They transplant easily in most forms, although because of their size, they are usually found as balled-and-burlapped plants. They need pruning regularly to remove dead branches and branch tips and to keep them vigorous. If allowed to go unpruned, they tend to become bedraggled and ugly. Their tolerance for drought precludes any additional water except in extreme cases. Propagate by cold-stratified seed; cuttings are unreliable.

SELECTIONS *E. commutata* (silverberry) grows 6-12 feet; upright habit; silver leaves and showy yellow flowers followed by silver fruits; native to northern North America. Zones 2-6.

E. multiflora (cherry elaeagnus) grows 6-10 feet with a wide spreading flat top; red edible fruits that are favored by birds. Native to Japan and China. Zones 5-7.

ENKIANTHUS PERULATUS WHITE ENKIANTHUS *Ericaceae*

These deciduous plants are related to the rhododendrons and are native to Japan. White enkianthus grows to 6 feet with a horizontal, pagodalike branching habit. Their simple leaves are clustered at the branch tips. The subtle, drooping flowers in late spring give the plants grace and softness, and the plants have exquisite fall colors of orange, yellow, and red. In the oriental garden where fall color is treasured, these plants function as attractive specimens. Zones 5-7.

Provide well-drained acid soil, much the same as for rhododendrons. They will grow well in full sun or partial shade. Since they are deciduous, they do not need to be sited for winter protection as other ericaceous plants do. Transplant as balled-and-burlapped or container-grown plants into soil that has been amended with organic matter (peat moss if your soil is naturally alkaline). Mulch immediately to keep soil cool and prevent cultivation near their shallow roots. Fertilize yearly after flowering. Propagates easily from untreated seed or softwood cuttings in summer.

EUONYMUS SPINDLE TREE *Celastraceae*

This genus contains every type of plant from deciduous to evergreen, and from tree to shrub to vine. Most species have angled stems that remain green at least during their first year, if not several years beyond. The flowers are inconspicuous, and the seeds are surrounded by orange or red fleshy arils which are in turn enclosed in a yellow, pink, or tan capsule. The capsule splits to reveal the arils, which makes a striking display on heavily fruiting plants. The fall color and fall fruiting aspects are desirable for the oriental garden, as are the angled stems that catch snow.

Most euonymus will tolerate average soil and sun or partial shade. They languish in extremely wet or very dry soils. One of their most attractive features is that most euonymus produce vivid fall color even in shade. They transplant well balled-and-burlapped plants although many nurseries now grow them in containers. Plant them into soil that has not been amended. Euonymus tolerate heavy pruning and can be sheared as hedges, although trying to prune a large plant into a small shape rarely works well. Provide an inch of water a week by rainfall or irrigation. Propagate by softwood or semi-hardwood cuttings, and maintain cuttings at cool temperatures (40° F) for three to four months.

FORSYTHIA X INTERMEDIA BORDER FORSYTHIA *Oleaceae*

These shrubs, native to eastern Asia, are grown for their masses of yellow, bell-like flowers in early spring. Border forsythia grows 8-10 feet with long arching branches, and its habit can be somewhat rangy. It has medium green foliage with some purple to it in fall. Much breeding work has been done to develop cultivars that have hardy flower buds in very cold climates, and there are many cultivars available commercially. On non-hardy species, the only flowers that often survive to bloom are those below the snow line where they are protected. In the oriental garden, forsythias make a beautiful spring display. Their large size fits well in an informal hedge or naturalistic planting. Zones 5-8.

Provide full sun and average garden soil. They will tolerate dry conditions. Most forsythias benefit from annual pruning either completely to the ground or by removing the oldest canes. Prune after the plant has finished flowering. Transplant balled-and-burlapped, bare-root, or container-grown plants. Forsythias generally need no supplemental irrigation since they tolerate drought. Propagate by softwood or hardwood cuttings. If propagating from seed, they need no stratification.

HYDRANGEA *Saxifragaceae or Hydrangeceae*

Few flowers are as consistently showy as those of the deciduous or evergreen shrubs in the genus *Hydrangea.* Dozens of small blooms are carried in large flat-topped or pyramid-shaped clusters in colors that range from pure white to intense pink and nearly pure blue. Many are native to Asia and are refined enough to work well in an informal oriental garden.

Grow hydrangeas in partial shade to full sun in a fertile, porous soil. Avoid overly dry or waterlogged soils. Soil pH should be slightly acid; soil over pH 7.5 will produce chlorotic (yellowed) flowers. The exact flower color depends on both the pH and the aluminum content of the soil. Plant in early spring or fall, keeping the rootball intact. Add organic matter sparingly—an excess will produce foliage at the expense of flowers. All varieties, however, will benefit from a surface mulch of organic matter. As their name implies, hydrangeas are water-loving; water well to keep them from wilting during dry spells. Supply a complete fertilizer in spring. Prune directly after flowering. Cut back all winter damage severely, but leave at least two or three sets of buds above ground level to obtain bloom the next season. Propagate from cuttings taken almost anytime during the growing season, or sow seed in pot

SELECTIONS *Hydrangea macrophylla*, bigleaf hydrangea, has an upright, rounded habit and flowers prolifically. It reaches 3-5 feet, depending on region and pruning. *H. paniculata* produces large white flower clusters in mid to late summer. Prune in late winter or early spring to restrict size and enhance flowering. **'Grandiflora'**, commonly known as PeeGee hydrangea, is widely planted, and justifiably so. Its mostly sterile flowers resemble huge, pyramidal snowballs.

JASMINUM JASMINE, JESSAMINE *Oleaceae*

This large genus contains trees, shrubs and vines that are native to the tropics and subtropics of eastern and southern Asia, the Malay Archipelago, Africa, and

Hydrangea aspera, an Asian native, grows 6 feet tall and bears flat-topped clusters of lilac flowers. It is hardy to Zone 7.

EUONYMUS ALATA (BURNING BUSH) 15-20 feet tall. Horizontally branched shrub with green leaves that turn bright pink or red in fall. Full sun or partial shade; average soil. Zones 3-8.

FORSYTHIA X INTERMEDIA (BORDER FORSYTHIA) 8-10 feet tall. Long, arching branches, masses of tiny yellow flowers. Full sun, average soil. Zones 5-8

HYDRANGEA MACROPHYLLA (BIGLEAF HYDRANGEA) 3-5 feet tall. upright, rounded habit, abundant, large clusters of flowers. Full sun to partial shade, fertile porous soil. Zones 5-8.

JASMINUM NITIDUM (STAR JASMINE) Climbing plant with long, pointed leaves and white flowers; very fragrant. Full sun, any soil, moist is best. Zones 8-10.

Australia. Many have fragrant flowers of yellow, white or pink. The vining types should be trained onto a trellis or arbor, where they will spread a sweet fragrance overhead.

Transplant container-grown plants in early spring into well-drained, moisture retentive soil. Jasmines are rampant growers and thrive in most soil or moisture conditions as long as they are given the warmth they need. Maximum flower display occurs in full sun, but the plants tolerate shade as well. Prune by thinning shoots after the plant blooms. Fertilize annually until the plant covers the trellis or arbor, and then hold back on fertilization to every few years to control growth. Propagate by semi-hardwood cuttings.

SELECTIONS *Jasminum officinale* (common white jasmine, poet's jasmine) climbs to 30 feet; compound leaves and white tubular flowers in clusters; beneficial to cut back entirely every few years. Native to Himalayas. Zones 7-10.

J. sambac (Arabian jasmine) evergreen climber with shiny whorled leaves; waxy white clustered flowers that turn pink with age–highly fragrant; oil used to flavor tea. Native to India. Zone 9.

KERRIA JAPONICA JAPANESE ROSE *Rosaceae*

This genus contains only one species which is native to China and Japan. It grows 3-6 feet tall, has many green stems with few side branches and showy golden yellow flowers. Cultivars have been bred to produce variegated leaves and double flowers. In oriental gardens, kerrias provide an interesting flower display in late spring and colorful stems through the winter months. Zones 4-9.

Kerrias grow well in full sun or partial shade although the flowers fade quickly in sunny spots. Provide well-drained soil to prevent winter injury. Transplant as balled-and-burlapped or container-grown plants. Provide average moisture as necessary to supplement rainfall. Kerrias will need pruning regularly because the twigs die out occasionally. Do not fertilize kerrias and provide only average soil to avoid the plants becoming weedy with reduced flowering. Propagate by softwood or semi-hardwood cuttings any time in summer or fall.

RHODODENDRON AZALEA, RHODODENDRON *Ericaceae* [SEE ALSO ENTRY UNDER DECIDUOUS SHRUBS]

The genus *Rhododendron* includes over 900 species and thousands of cultivars. This genus includes evergreen, semievergreen and deciduous plants. The distinctions between rhododendron and azalea are somewhat arbitrary, depending on which authority is consulted. Generally, azaleas are deciduous and have funnel-shaped flowers, where rhododendrons are evergreen or semi-evergreen and have more bell-shaped flowers. There are exceptions to both cases, however. In oriental gardens, tightly pruned azaleas are often used to represent stones, or are used as western gardeners use boxwood. In either case, they are severely pruned to keep their shape at the expense of blooms. In other instances, they are used as a focal plant because of their flowers. Most bloom in spring.

The one necessity to keep rhododendrons healthy is acid soil. Provide them

Stone pathways and a lantern are the defining features of this small garden–except in spring, when the azaleas are in bloom.

A row of 'Fedora' azaleas curves along a stone staircase at the Portland Japanese Garden.

with peat-based, rich soil with plenty of moisture and they will thrive. They perform best in a somewhat protected sunny spot, but will tolerate semi-shade. Using rhododendrons or azaleas in partial shade may mean reduction in the number of flowers. Rhododendrons are usually grown as container plants, and care must be taken to avoid damaging the root system when transplanting. Plant into well-amended soil and provide plenty of moisture. Apply mulch immediately to keep the soil moist. Depending on the species, propagate rhododendrons by softwood cuttings or seed.

SELECTIONS *Rhododendron* **Exbury hybrids** (Exbury azalea) yellow, orange, red fall color; pink, red, orange, white trusses of flowers. Zones 5-7.

R. molle (Chinese azalea) grows to 5-6 feet; leaves to 6 inches long; yellow flowers with green spots; native eastern to central China. Zone 7.

R. reticulatum grows to 25 feet; leaves 2½ inches long; red-purple to magenta flowers appear before the leaves; native to Japan. Zone 6.

R. simsii (Sim's azalea) semi-evergreen; grows to 5-9 feet; 2-inch-long leaves; rosy to dark red, spotted flowers; native to China and Taiwan. Zones 7-8.

SPIRAEA SPIREA *Rosaceae*

This large genus of shrubs contains species found throughout the northern hemisphere. Leaf shape and size vary as do the form and habit of the shrubs. The white, pink, or rose flowers are generally tiny, but are borne in clusters, providing an abundant display. Spring flowering types bloom before the leaves, and summer flowering species bloom heavily in spring and then sporadically throughout the summer. Spireas are widely used in oriental gardens, particularly for their spring flower display.

Spireas are tough plants that will survive almost any conditions except full shade and very wet soils. They appear to thrive in dry, impoverished soils. Most species benefit from annual pruning to remove old canes and rejuvenate the shrub. Pruning requirements depend on the species and when it flowers. Spireas are almost exclusively grown as container plants and transplant quite easily. Fertilize infrequently and provide average moisture while they are establishing a new root system. Propagate by softwood cuttings.

SELECTION *Spiraea x bumalda* (bumald spirea) grows 2-3 feet in rounded form; white to pink to deep rose flowers on new growth; many cultivars are available. Hybrid of *S. japonica* and *S. albiflora*. Prune in early spring Zones 3-8.

S. cantoniensis **'Lanceata'** (double reeves spirea) grows 4-6 feet with long, blue-green leaves; showy double white flowers. Species is native to China and Japan. Zones 6-9.

SYRINGA LILAC *Oleaceae*

There are about 30 species of these popular ornamental shrubs. Lilacs are famous for their showy, early spring flowers. Some of the shorter species are well-used in oriental gardens, not only for their fragrance, but also for their refined shape and lack of maintenance requirements. The small leaved varieties may be sheared.

Lilacs will tolerate many types of soil, but thrive in rich, moist conditions. They must have full sun in order to flower. Remove the flower stalks each

KERRIA JAPONICA (JAPANESE ROSE) 3-6 feet tall. Multiple green stems, few side branches, showy golden yellow flowers. full sun or partial shade; average soil. Zones 4-9.

RHODODENDRON MUCRONULATUM (KOREAN RHODODENDRON) 8 feet tall. Upright to rounded habit, rosy pink flowers. Partial shade, peat-based, rich, acid soil with plenty of moisture Zones 4-7.

RHODODENDRON 'BOW BELLS' (EXBURY AZALEA) 4-6 feet tall. White flowers edged in pink. Full sun or partial shade; peat-based, rich, acid soil with plenty of moisture. Zones 4-8.

RHODODENDRON 'ROSE POINT' (GLENN DALE AZALEA) 3-5 feet tall. Very large crimson flowers. Full sun or partial shade; peat-based, rich, acid soil with plenty of moisture. Zones 4-8.

In autumn, viburnums' bright berries provide color as well as food for birds.

spring to encourage heavy bloom the following year. Lilacs should be renewal pruned annually by removing older stalks at ground level. This keeps new, fresh growth coming forth. Older lilacs can be cut entirely to the ground to rejuvenate them, but it will take a few years to bloom again. Transplant balled-and-burlapped plants in spring or fall into loose soil. Provide average moisture. Propagate by softwood cuttings or cold-stratified seed.

SELECTIONS *Syringa meyeri* (Meyer lilac) grows 4-8 feet; small leaves and small panicles of slightly fragrant pale purple flowers give it a fine texture. Native to China. Zones 3-8.

S. microphylla (littleleaf lilac) grows to 6 feet; wide spreading; pale lilac flowers in 3-inch panicles. Native to China. Zones 4-8.

S. oblata (early lilac) grows 10-12 feet; only lilac with attractive fall color; large leaves and pale lilac flowers in 5-inch panicles; earliest blooming lilac; coarse texture. Native to China. Zones 3-8.

S. pekinensis (Pekin lilac) grows to 15-20 feet; flowers yellow-white in 6-inch panicles; beautiful cherrylike peeling bark. Native to China. Zones 3-7.

VIBURNUM *Caprifoliaceae*

This genus consists of over 200 species of deciduous and evergreen shrubs native to America, Europe and Asia. They all have clusters of showy white to pink flowers, followed by blue, black, purple, red or white berries. This group of shrubs is used extensively for landscape purposes because of their year-round interest. They perform beautifully as specimens, screen plants, for hedges and for naturalistic settings. Their fruits attract a wide range of birds and other wildlife. Oriental gardens make effective use of the species with fruits that remain in winter.

In addition to having beautiful flowers, fruits and leaves, they are tolerant of a wide range of conditions. They are best adapted to moist soils, but viburnums will thrive in sun or partial shade, and in moist (not permanently wet) or dry soils. They seldom need pruning and they transplant easily as balled-and-burlapped or container-grown plants. Very young plants can be transplanted bare root. Provide average moisture throughout the first season and fertilize infrequently. Propagate by softwood cuttings; seed germination is difficult because of double dormancy.

SELECTIONS *Viburnum dilatatum* (linden viburnum) grows 8-10 feet; upright habit; dark green leaves that turn russet in fall; red fruits remain in winter. Native to Japan. Zones 5-7.

V. farreri (fragrant viburnum) grows 8-12 feet; white to pale pink fragrant flowers and red fruits that turn to black; dark green foliage turning to red-purple in fall. Native to China. Zone 6.

V. macrocephalum (Chinese snowball viburnum) semi-evergreen; grows 6-10 feet; white showy balls of flowers that are sterile (no fruits are produced); needs some protection for full floral display. Native to China. Zones 6-9.

V. plicatum var. tomentosum (doublefile viburnum) grows 8-10 feet with widely horizontal branches; pure white flowers of lacecap variety–the cluster will have large sterile flowers ringing a cluster of small fertile flowers; fruits red turning to black; must have well-drained soil. Native to China and Japan. Zones 5-8.

SPIRAEA JAPONICA (JAPANESE SPIREA) To 6 feet tall. Erect shrub with pink flowers in large corymbs. Full sun or part shade, any soil except very wet. Zones 4-8.

SYRINGA VULGARIS (COMMON LILAC) To 20 feet tall. Tall, slender, erect shrub with white, purple, or lilac flowers. Full sun, average soil. Zones 4-8.

VIBURNUM PLICATUM (JAPANESE SNOWBALL) 8-10 feet tall. Horizontal branches, rounded clusters of pure white flowers; red fruits. Full sun or partial shade, well-drained soil. Zones 5-8.

VIBURNUM PLICATUM VAR. TOMENTOSUM (DOUBLEFILE VIBURNUM) 8-10 feet tall. Widely horizontal branches, pure white flowers; red fruits. Full sun or partial shade, well-drained soil. Zones 5-8.

VINES AND GROUNDCOVERS

ASARUM WILD GINGER *Aristolochiaceae*

These deciduous or evergreen herbaceous groundcovers are found natively throughout North America. They get their name from the strong scent of the leaves and flowers although they are not the source of culinary ginger. Their heart-shaped leaves are shiny or matte deep green and borne on long slender petioles that arise from underground rhizomes. The inconspicuous flowers vary from red to brown and are borne right at soil level underneath the leaves–the plant is obviously grown for its foliage which makes a beautiful groundcover in shade. Wild gingers are not a groundcover to be trodden upon, although *A. canadense* is extremely tough and recovers quickly.

Wild gingers naturally grow in deep woods, so the greatest success will be achieved with moist, rich soil that is slightly acid. Plant container-grown plants in full to dense shade in soil that has been well amended with organic matter. Water well while the plant becomes established and apply mulch to help retain moisture. Plant the evergreen gingers in sites that will be somewhat protected from the winter sun, especially when there is no snow cover. Plant in spring only. No pruning is necessary except to remove evergreen leaves damaged by winter. Fertilization is seldom needed. Propagate by dividing rhizomes in very early spring.

SELECTION *Asarum canadense* (Canada snakeroot, wild ginger) bears deciduous leaves 5-6 inches long and leathery, dark matte green. Grows about 6 inches high. Reddish purple flowers in April and May; the toughest and fastest spreading species of wild ginger. Zone 3.

A. europaeum (European ginger) has shiny dark evergreen leaves that come directly from nodes on the surface rhizomes. Grows about 6 inches high. Brown flowers. Zone 4.

A. shuttleworthii (mottled wild ginger) has semi-evergreen to evergreen leaves that are mottled with silver markings. Zone 6.

CLEMATIS VIRGIN'S BOWER *Ranunculaceae*

Clematis appear in herbaceous, woody types and shrubby or vining forms. They are native to the northern temperate zones, and are widely grown throughout the world for their beautiful blossoms and attractive fruits. The flowers occur as clusters of small flowers, urn or bell-shaped flowers, or large open flowers. The flowers have no petals, but have four showy sepals that appear as petals. The compound leaves are green to gray-green with twining petioles that enable the plants to climb. Clematis have clusters of small fruits, each with a feathery plume, making them quite showy summer through fall. There are thousands of hybrids, each chosen for specific flower or fruit character. Clematis are well used for screening, to adorn a light post, as a focal point and as a backdrop for a shrubby border. The small-flowered, subtle varieties are particularly appropriate for an oriental garden.

Clematis perform best when planted in a spot that provides full sun for the upper portion of the plant and shade to keep the roots cool. They will survive

Clematis requires specialized pruning. Although the species vary considerably in their blooming times and habits, the hybrids are classified into three groups according to their bloom times and pruning needs. Group I, the Florida group, blooms in summer on old wood and should be pruned only occasionally and very slightly after the plant has flowered. Group II, the Patens group, blooms in spring on old wood and should be pruned as the Florida group except in spring after blooming. Group III, the Jackman group, blooms in summer and fall on new wood. This habit makes these plants perform well when pruned to the ground each winter. Many of the small-flowered species can become rampant if not pruned regularly, so it is important to prune diligently if growing several types. *Clematis macropetala,* above, is in Group II.

partial shade, but flowering may be reduced in some of the large-flowered types. Planting them on a trellis with a groundcover at their bases is the best situation for healthy plants. Transplant them in spring as container-grown plants into well-drained soil that is rich in organic matter and immediately mulch their roots. Water well to establish and monitor moisture throughout the first season. Clematis are prone to rot if planted in constantly wet soil. Fertilize hybrids once a year; do not fertilize small-flowered varieties or they will become rampant. Propagate by cold-stratified seed or softwood cuttings.

SELECTION *Clematis armandii* (armand clematis) is an evergreen vine with long, shiny tapering leaflets and white to cream abundant flowers followed by plumy fruits. Fertilize early spring; provide ample water. Prune after flowering. Zone 7.

C. maximowicziana (sweet autumn clematis) is a rampant grower that produces clouds of small white, extremely fragrant flowers in fall. Prune to ground in early spring. Zone 5.

C. montana var. *rubens* bears rosy pink larger flowers with exquisite fragrance. Prune after flowering. Zone 5.

C. tangutica (golden clematis) bears delicate 2-inch bell flowers of yellow-gold through summer, followed by showy fruits. Prune to the ground in spring. Zone 5.

C. virginiana (virginsbower) produces panicles of creamy white flowers through summer; attractive bright green foliage. Zone 4.

PACHYSANDRA TERMINALIS JAPANESE SPURGE *Buxaceae*

Native to Japan, this evergreen groundcover is perhaps one of the most widely grown for all landscape situations. It grows to about 1 foot high, and its whorls of glossy, bright green leaves provide unique interest as well as an effective, sturdy groundcover. The plants spread readily by underground stems. Spurge flowers are borne in creamy white spikes that stand above the foliage in spring, and although they are not particularly showy, they are borne quite early and emit a sweet fra-

Left: Groundcovers pachysandra, buglewood (*Ajuga reptans*), and lily-turf (*Liriope muscari*) along with hydrangea

ASARUM EUROPAEUM (EUROPEAN GINGER) 6 inches high. Shiny dark evergreen leaves, tiny brown flowers. Partial to full shade, moist, rich, slightly acid soil. Zones 4-8.

CLEMATIS MAXIMOWICZIANA (SWEET AUTUMN CLEMATIS) Vigorous vining plant produces abundant tiny, fragrant white flowers. Well-drained, rich moist but not wet soil; shade for roots, sun for upper portion. Zones 5-9.

PARTHENOCISSUS QUINQIFOLIA (VIRGINIA CREEPER) Vigorous vine or groundcover. Compound leaves turn red in fall. Full sun to full shade, any soil. Zones 3-9.

WISTERIA FLORIBUNDA (JAPANESE WISTERIA) Twining woody vine to 35 feet. Compound leaves, grapelike clusters of violet, purple-red, white, or pink flowers. Rich, deep, well-drained soil. Zones 4-9.

grance that is welcome after a long winter. Pachysandra is a superb groundcover for full shade, particularly under large trees. It also performs well on a slope although it will take some time to become established. Zones 3-8.

Transplant as container-grown plants into a partially or fully shaded site. If grown in sun, Japanese spurge fades to yellow and fails to thrive. Also, plant in a site that is somewhat sheltered from winter sun and wind to avoid it being severely damaged in winter. Plant in well-drained rich, amended organic soil and provide copious amounts of water during its establishment. Pachysandra peforms best in slightly acid or neutral soil—alkaline soil prevents it from thriving and turns the leaves yellow. Fertilize once a year with an acidic fertilizer if on neutral soil. On acidic soil, fertilization is only necessary every few years once the planting is established. For the first two to three years as the planting is becoming established, pinch out the plant tips to encourage branching and faster coverage. After that, pruning is generally unnecessary except to remove leaves and stems damaged in winter. Propagate by divisions, softwood cuttings or rooting the stolons.

PARTHENOCISSUS WOODBINE *Vitaceae*

This genus contains several species of woody, climbing vines, only three of which are in frequent use in the landscape. The vines produce tendrils with sticky pads on the ends that adhere easily to masonry or wood (although they sometimes cling just as tenaciously to metal). The leaves are usually lobed or compound, glossy green and brilliantly colored in fall. The flowers and fruits are insignificant as ornamental features. These vines are commonly used for screening or to soften a wall, which they do rapidly. Another excellent use which may be overlooked is as a groundcover. They cover fairly quickly, but do lose their leaves in fall so will be a mass of bare vines through the winter. In areas without constant snow cover, this may create a somewhat unattractive area if visible in winter.

Transplant container-grown plants into average soil in full sun to full shade. Water to establish and then only as needed in extremely dry times. These vines are uncommonly tough and will withstand city pollutants, drought and almost any situation imaginable. Fertilization is unnecessary and pruning should be done only to keep the plant in bounds. Contrary to popular belief, the sticky substance on the tendril pads does not undermine masonry or wooden walls. The vines may hold moisture near a wall, causing some deterioration, although there exist many brick or stone buildings that have been covered for hundreds of years with no appreciable damage. Be warned, however, that the sticky pads are almost impossible to remove short of sandblasting, so be absolutely certain when choosing a site. Propagate by cold-stratified seed, hardwood or softwood cuttings or layering.

SELECTIONS *Parthenocissus quinquifolia* (Virginia creeper) native to the northeastern U.S. Palmately compound leaves; brilliant red-orange fall color. Blue fruits are somewhat showy after leaves fall in autumn. Performs well as climbing vine or as groundcover. Zones 3-9.

P. tricuspidata (Boston ivy) is the ivy known for covering old buildings; native to central China and Japan. Three-lobed shiny leaves that turn bright red in fall. Blue fruits. Covers more densely than *P. quinquifolia*. Zones 4-8.

Above: A carefully tended gourd-shaped bed of creeping thyme in the dry garden of Portland Japanese Garden.

THYMUS SERPYLLUM CREEPING THYME *Lamiaceae*

This species of thyme is native to northwestern Europe and is an excellent fine-textured groundcover that will tolerate some foot traffic. It is commonly used between paving stones in oriental gardens because it gives off a pleasant odor when trod upon. Creeping thyme has tiny gray-green leaves and stems that form a large mat that is rarely more than 3 inches high. The stems root readily at the nodes. The tiny reddish purple flowers are borne in clusters at the ends of the stems throughout the summer. When the plants are in full bloom, they have an attractive purple haze even though the flowers are small. Zone 4.

Plant container-grown plants or divide clumps from existing stands in spring or fall. Plant in full sun to partial shade in well-drained, impoverished soil. The plants perform best in hot, dry conditions and tolerate drought well. Plants grown in fertile, moist soil will be larger, more open and unattractive, so the secret for a beautiful groundcover is to not water, not fertilize and generally neglect—the perfect plant! If the plants do begin to stretch out and become too loose, prune them back substantially before they begin to flower. Propagate by division, seed or softwood or hardwood cuttings.

WISTERIA FLORIBUNDA JAPANESE WISTERIA *Fabaceae*

The familiar wisteria is native to Japan and the twining woody vines grow to 35 feet or more. The stems always twine in a clockwise direction, and many of the most widely known oriental gardens have hundred year-old wisterias carefully tended by professional gardeners. The compound leaves are green to gray-green and downy. Although the vines are beautiful in themselves, wisterias are usually grown for their intensely fragrant flowers. These flowers are great grapelike clusters in violet, purple-red, white, and pink. The clusters hang elegantly from the stems, and an arbor draped with a wisteria in bloom is enough to make you forget that any other place in the world exists. The flowers are followed by brown pods that remain into the fall. Hundreds of cultivars of Japanese wisteria exist, giving a wide array of flower color and intensity of fragrance. Zones 4-9.

Wisterias do not transplant readily, so transplant container-grown plants only. Provide rich, deep, well-drained soil, a site in full sun and ample water to establish strong roots. Japanese wisterias need to be pruned to keep them in top blooming condition, and the gardener intending to grow wisteria would be wise to consult a pruning manual, especially if an established plant is not flowering well. Pruning involves cutting back shoots to only a few buds and doing some root pruning. Fertilize annually with a low nitrogen fertilizer such as superphosphate. Too much nitrogen causes heavy leaf growth and sparse flowering. Propagate by seed, division, layering, cuttings, root cuttings, grafting.

Left: Spring color at the Portland Japanese Garden is provided by azaleas and *Wisteria sinensis.*

MOSSES

Moss gardens have been used in traditional oriental gardens for many years, especially in gardens that are almost completely shaded. Moss is used to replicate or remind the visitor of nature, with its soft green to enhance rocks, trees and shrubs. Practically, it can decorate areas where nothing else will grow such as deep shade, constantly moist soil, acid soil, and over tree roots that compete with plants for nutrients and moisture.

The most common way to start a moss garden is to purchase moss sod, although a moss garden can also be started from spores. The soil should be amended to retain moisture by adding organic matter. A soil test will determine the soil's pH; neutral to alkaline soil should have sulfur added before planting moss. Once the moss is planted, it is essential to keep it moist while it becomes established, and the gardener must keep it well weeded. Once it is established, the moss does a fairly good job of choking out weeds, and the only requirement to keeping the garden looking good is constant moisture. If planting a moss garden in a sunny area, it is usually necessary to add a sprinkler system set at regular intervals to keep the moss moist.

Always purchase moss sod from a reputable nursery (there are several specializing in this). Collecting from the wild can easily destroy the balance in nature and

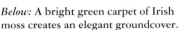

Below: **A bright green carpet of Irish moss creates an elegant groundcover.**

Left: Mosses cover the rocks and shaded areas in this Japanese garden.

eventually endanger the plants.

True mosses are small, non-flowering, rootless, non-vascular plants. The mosses that are used in gardens are usually club mosses. Culture is similar for all of them. Transplant container-grown plants into very well-drained, sandy soil in full sun or partial shade in early spring. Plant where not exposed to extreme winter winds and sun. If snow cover is not constant through the winter, mulch with a lightweight mulch such as straw or pine boughs, removing it in early spring. Water well to establish, and if planting in full sun, provide supplemental irrigation in dry times. The plant has shallow roots, so cannot use water reserves deep in the soil. If the planting becomes too bumpy and undulating, indicating crowding, alleviate by digging clumps from the planting and allowing it to fill in again. Fertilize annually with low-nitrogen fertilizer. Propagate by seeds or division.

ARENARIA (moss sandwort) is a low-growing perennial that resembles moss; it is hardy to Zone 5.

LYCOPODIUM (club moss) is often used in baskets. It is not frost-tolerant.

POLYTRICHUM COMMUNE (haircap moss) is very bright green, low-growing, and dense.

SAGINA SUBULATA (Irish moss, Corsican pearlwort), forms 4-inch-tall evergreen mats of tiny, bright green foliage with flowering stalks. They make effective groundcovers as well as an attractive addition to the rock garden or as filler between paving stones since they will tolerate some foot traffic As the mats spread, they give a soft, undulating appearance to the landscape. Zone 2.

SELAGINELLA (little club moss, spike moss, kurama moss) is easy to grow and ornamental. Different species vary in color from bright green to tawny brown. They need moist, shady sites.

SOLEIROLIA SOLEIROLII (baby's tears) is a mosslike mint that is very resistant to heat and forms a dense, bright green mat.

ANNUALS, PERENNIALS, BULBS

ANEMONE X HYBRIDA JAPANESE ANEMONE *Ranunculaceae*

Japanese anemone grows to around 5 feet, with the flowers borne on graceful slender stalks high above the dark green compound leaves. This perennial is commonly planted for autumn color in the landscape where it makes a lovely statement because of its height. The flowers are white or pink and absolutely glow when used against a background of evergreens or dark deciduous foliage. Zone 5.

Transplant into the garden in fall or spring into moist, well-drained loamy soil. Anemones are versatile enough to thrive in partial shade or full sun as long as they are somewhat protected from dry, windy sites. Mulch immediately upon planting and water abundantly while the plant becomes established. Cut back flower stalks after blooming. Anemones seldom need dividing and are best propagated by root cuttings or seed sown in the fall.

ASTER X FRIKARTII FRIKART'S ASTER *Asteraceae*

Asters are indigenous to all parts of the world, and commonly grace not only home and commercial gardens, but also fields and meadows in all climates. Frikart's aster grows to 2½ feet with many branches arising from the soil, and pale blue-purple daisylike flowers with yellow centers. The midsummer to fall flowers can be up to 3 inches across and are pleasantly fragrant. The leaves are dusty green and slightly fuzzy. Asters are most commonly used for their blooms in summer and fall. Often this aster will still be blooming as the first snow falls. Frikart's aster makes a beautiful addition to a sunny spot, and can be effectively used with most other flower colors. Zone 5.

Plant asters in fall or spring into very well-drained soil of average fertility and full sun. Wet soil is almost always detrimental, particularly in winter. Asters need perioidic division to keep them healthy and floriferous. The center of the clump dying out indicates a need for division–divide the clump in early spring. This is an excellent way to propagate, although cuttings also work effectively. Frikart's aster will need staking if the desired look is for an upright, tidy plant. A network of twiggy branches put in place early in spring will eventually be covered by foliage, and will hold the aster upright. The aster does, however, look especially nice when allowed to drift among other plants as part of a tapestry. Mulch heavily in fall after the ground has frozen.

ASTILBE FALSE SPIREA *Saxifragaceae*

Astilbes are well-used landscape plants in cultivated gardens of all types. Their divided graceful leaves and feathery plumes of flowers are a perfect accent or edging to a shady perennial border. Sizes range from dwarf types that only grow 6-8 inches tall to large-leaved varieties of 4 feet or more. Most often they form a mound of foliage with flower spikes in white, pink or red extending well above the leaves. The flower plumes bloom in midspring, and the showy stalks remain on the plant throughout the summer, sometimes appearing to bloom the entire

ANEMONE X HYBRIDA 'HONORINE JOBERT' (JAPANESE ANEMONE) 3-5 feet tall. Pure white flowers, large leaves. Full sun to partial shade. Blooms in late summer to early fall. Zones 6-10.

ASTER X FRIKARTII 'MÖNCH' (FRIKART'S ASTER) 2-3 feet tall. Sturdy upright stems, lavender flowers. Full sun. Blooms in late summer to fall, Zones 5-10.

ASTILBE X ROSEA 'PEACH BLOSSOM' (FALSE SPIREA) 3 feet tall. Pale pink flowers, ferny compound leaves. Full sun to partial shade. Blooms in early summer. Zones 4-8.

ASTILBE CHINENSIS VAR. TAQUETII 'SUPERBA' (FALSE SPIREA) 3-4 feet tall. Narrow plumes of strong magenta flowers, strong erect stems. Full sun to partial shade. Blooms in late summer. Zones 4-8.

White chrysanthemums and asters have a magical affinity like that of the intimate converse between a man and a woman. When the effect would be appealing, prepare a special place that suits them and plant them there to good advantage. Or, plant them on opposite sides of a formal wooden fence, so that they appear to be peeking at one another through the fence.

FROM *SECRET TEACHINGS IN THE ART OF JAPANESE GARDENS,* DAVID A. SLAWSON

season. Astilbe's love of moisture makes it an excellent plant for use along a stream bank or beside a pond. The white flowering types offer a glowing spot when tucked into a shady garden.

Transplant astilbe in spring into well-amended, organic soil. Water heavily to establish and then provide ample moisture throughout the season. Astilbes will grow in full sun as long as there is plenty of supplemental moisture, although they perform with less effort in partially shaded areas. Fertilize annually and prune only if the flower stalks become unsightly. Plants perform best if divided every four or five years. Propagate by dividing in very early spring.

SELECTIONS *Astilbe x arendsii,* the most commonly available astilbe, grows 2-3 feet depending on cultivar. Flower colors range from white to pale pink to dark pink to lavender to deep red. Zone 4.

A. chinensis (Chinese astilbe) bears soft purple-pink flowers about 12 inches high; most tolerant of dry soil; stoloniferous habit makes good groundcover. Native to China. Zone 4.

CHRYSANTHEMUM X MORIFOLIUM CHRYSANTHEMUM *Asteraceae*

Considered one of the three friends of winter by the Chinese (pine, bamboo, mum), chrysanthemums are often used for fall color in oriental gardens. They are usually trained into shapes, with the cascade being the most popular, or they may be cut for vases. Chrysanthemums range from 1-3 feet high in mounded or upright forms. Flowers have varying petal and flower head shapes, varying from spoon shaped, to tiny pompoms to single petals appearing as a daisy to the long, airy petals of spider mums. Although listed as hardy to Zone 5, these flowers are often treated as annuals in cold climates since they are difficult to overwinter and do not bloom until late fall. A 16-petalled chrysanthemum has appeared in the official crest of the Japanese Imperial family since the Meiji period.

Transplant into very well-drained, rich soil in full sun. Wet soil in winter is the most common reason for their demise. Fertilize annually and pinch out the growing tips three times in summer to force the plant to be compact and full. To provide fewer but much larger flowers, cut out all stems except the four or five strongest. Pinch out all flower buds except the one at the growing tip. This gives a few beautiful large blossoms at the expense of a plant covered with smaller blooms. Provide plenty of water, and mulch immediately when planting. Taller varieties may need staking, especially if they have large flowers. Apply winter mulch after ground freezes, but only on very well-drained soil. Propagate by division or cuttings. Most commercial producers propagate by cuttings.

HELLEBORUS NIGER CHRISTMAS ROSE *Ranunculaceae*

Hellebores, native to Europe, have been grown in oriental gardens for years. These attractive plants have the added bonus of blooming in February, March and April in colder climates. During unusual winter thaws, the plants may begin to bloom even in December and January. The mound of glossy serrated evergreen leaves supports 1-foot stems on which are borne showy white flowers with distinct yellow stamens. This plant definitely deserves a spot where the flowers can be

observed closely, such as the edge of a shrub border or near a path. Zone 4.

Hellebores perform best in partial to full shade where the white flowers appear as if they have an inner light. Provide rich, moist, somewhat acid soil and protection from winter winds and sun which may scorch the leaves. Mulch immediately upon planting and water well throughout the season, never allowing the soil to dry out. Do not fertilize. Propagate by seed or division in very early spring. Division is not needed for the health of the plant, and the plants respond very slowly to being divided or transplanted.

HEMEROCALLIS DAYLILY *Liliaceae*

Almost every perennial garden in the world has a daylily of one sort or another, a testament to their ease of care and their long-lived beauty. There are about 15

MUMS IN THE EAST AND WEST

Although the Greeks named the Chrysanthemum "Golden Flower," the earliest recorded reference to the flower comes from Confucius, who in *Li-Ki* (Ninth Moon) extolled "the chrysanthemum with its golden glory." These small, mostly single, usually yellow wildflowers were a far cry from the ebullient blooms that characterize current mums. In the ninth century, the Japanese embraced the mum as a garden plant, and the new forms they developed were jealously guarded and long confined to Japan. In the mid nineteenth century, Robert Fortune was able to carry a few plants to Britain, resulting in a major breakthrough in Western mum culture when British and French botanists further improved the Japanese cultivars. America's first experience with mums was in 1798, with the introduction of a variety called 'Dark Purple' by John Stevens of Hoboken, New Jersey, but it was not until the 1920 'Fortune' that more varieties were available. In 1932, Alex Cumming of Bristol, Connecticut crossed existing garden varieties with the Korean mum (*Dendranthem zawadskii*), creating vigorous, handsome plants that eventually became available in a wide variety of colors and forms. Practically all hardy mums have ancestries stemming back to the Korean hybrids.

Above left: Chrysanthemums in many colors, shapes, and forms.

HELLEBORUS ORIENTALIS (LENTEN ROSE) 2 feet tall. Small clusters of cup-shaped, nodding pink, deep purple, pale green, or white flowers. Partial to full shade. Blooms in late winter to early spring. Zones 3-10.

HEMEROCALLIS FULVA (TAWNY DAYLILY) 3-6 feet tall. Cultivars available in many colors and sizes. Full sun or partial shade. Blooms in midsummer. Zones 4-8.

HOSTA VENTRICOSA (FUNKIA, PLANTAIN LILY) 12-18 inches tall. Edging hosta; large bluish leaves; tall lavender flowers. Shade to 1/4 sun. Blooms mid to late summer. Zones 4-8.

HOSTA SIEBOLDIANA 'ELEGANS' (FUNKIA, PLANTAIN LILY) 18-24 inches tall. Background hosta; large bluish leaves; white flowers with light fragrance. Shade to 1/4 sun. Blooms mid to late summer. Zones 4-8.

species of daylilies and thousands of cultivars available with every possible combination of flower shape, color and plant size. The long, grasslike, medium green to gray-green foliage sets off flowers with six long petals that may be cup-shaped or open and reflexed. Flowers range from white to yellow to orange to red to violet, and many are scented. Each flower only lasts a day, but the plants produce many buds so the display is fairly long-lived. Daylily flowers are edible as are the thickened roots. Daylilies perform well as a groundcover or as a bank planting, and make a beautiful focal point when viewed from the opposite side of a pond. After the flowers finish blooming, the foliage is lovely for the rest of the season. Zone 4.

Daylilies are tolerant of almost any conditions, but perform best in full sun to partial shade and well-drained soil of average to poor fertility. Provide average amounts of water to establish, but subsequently they will need little supplemental irrigation since they are quite drought tolerant. Do not fertilize and prune only to remove spent flower stalks. Fertilization will tend to produce lush foliage and few flowers. Propagate by division in spring or late summer.

SELECTIONS *Hemerocallis fulva* (tawny daylily) is perhaps the most common daylily; a stalwart performer with flower stalks up to 6 feet. Orange to reddish flowers with maroon stripes; no fragrance. Cultivars available in all colors and double flowers. Native to Europe and Asia.

H. middendorfii grows to 1 foot tall; clusters of small orange blossoms that are pleasantly fragrant. Native to eastern Siberia, Japan, Korea.

HOSTA PLANTAIN LILY, FUNKIA *Liliaceae*

Hostas are perhaps the perfect plant for partial to deeply shaded areas. They are most often grown for their tropical-looking foliage, but the flowers on many species are beautiful as well. The leaves vary from being slender and grassy, giving a delicate soft texture to a large, bold, almost rounded shape that is large enough to hold its own with any shrub. Foliage color varies from lime green to deep green to blue, with many types of yellow and white variegation available as well. Some leaves are puckered like seersucker. The flower stalks emerge in mid to late summer and extend high above the foliage. The flowers are bell-shaped and borne along the upper half of the flower stalk. Flowers are either blue-violet or white and some are delightfully fragrant, reminiscent of jasmine. Hostas make excellent edge plants with their tidy appearance, and they also make a superb groundcover under shade trees.

Plant into well-enriched soil in spring or fall. Once established, hostas need little care, but water well throughout the first season and in times of drought thereafter. Do not fertilize and prune only to remove the spent flower stalks. Hostas seldom need division although they will form large, tightly bound clumps. Propagate by division—part of the clump can be separated from the parent plant or the entire plant can be dug and divided into many smaller plants. Hostas recover very quickly when divided or transplanted.

SELECTIONS *Hosta lancifolia* (narrow-leaved plantain lily) bears slender medium green 6-inch leaves and stalks with many flowers of pale lilac. Native to Japan. Zone 4.

Hostas combine well with grasses and other foliage and flowering plants; they are natural choices for the shade garden.

CLASSIFICATIONS OF HOSTAS

• Small hostas are up to 8 inches in height. They are best suited to shaded rock gardens or between the roots of trees where the soil is poor and shallow. 'Sea Sprite' and 'Chartreuse Wiggles' are examples.

• Edging types are 8-12 inches tall. These are especially useful for edging shaded beds or borders, woodland paths and walkways. Here their rapid growth and vigor inhibits weeds and eliminates the tedious task of edging. 'Ginkgo Craig' (below) is a good cultivar.

• Ground covers range from 12-15 inches tall. These, such as 'Janet' and *H. tokudama* "Flavocircinalis' (above left and above right), can be planted singly or massed at close spacing.

• Background types may reach 24 inches. They are usually planted as feature plants or a centerpiece around which the rest of the shade garden is designed. Good examples are and *H. sieboldiana* 'Elegans' and *H. s.* 'Mira' (right).

• The largest hostas are called specimens. These are 2-4 feet tall, usually slow growing and excellent as accent plants. *H. tokudama* 'Aureo-Nebulosa' (above, far right) and 'Wide Brim' fall into this category.

H. plantaginea (fragrant plantain lily) yellow-green foliage up to 8 inches; large, fragrant white flowers. Native to China and Japan. Zone 4.

H. sieboldiana (seersucker plantain lily) 10- to 15-inch-long matte blue-green leaves with distinct veins and rippled surface; lilac flowers. Native to Japan. Zone 4.

H. ventricosa (blue plantain lily) bears dark green leaves to 9 inches; 2-inch deep violet flowers. Native to eastern Asia. Zone 4.

IRIS IRIS, FLAG *Iridaceae*

Irises are native to northern temperate regions all over the world. They are easily recognized by their wide-bladed grassy leaves and distinct flowers consisting of three inner petals called "standards" and three outer petals called "falls". Iris flowers vary widely in shape and color and the plants vary in size from the tiny crested iris to the large German iris. Irises have been used traditionally in oriental gardening for hundreds of years for their ethereal flowers and attractive foliage. They make quite a focal point when used in a mass, and are particularly attractive at the edge of a pond. Some irises tolerate wet soils quite well, thriving on riverbanks.

Iris culture varies according to the species grown. Most will perform well in full sun or partial shade, although flowering will be reduced in shade. Unless the species is one of the swamp irises, provide well-drained average soil. Most irises benefit from a summer mulch and a winter mulch applied after the ground freezes in cold climates. Propagation and division needs depend on whether the iris is a rhizome or bulb-producing plant. The usual method for propagation is by division. Some irises are quite prone to iris borers which can destroy the plants.

SELECTIONS *Iris cristata* (crested iris) grows to about 6 inches; small dark lilac flowers are borne very early in spring. Spread by rhizomes and can make a dense ground cover in shady areas. Provide well-drained soil and do not fertilize. Plant in full sun only if plenty of moisture is available. Division is seldom needed. Cultivars are available with deep blue or white flowers. Zone 4.

I. ensata [Iris kaempferi] (sword-leaved iris, Japanese iris) produces very large flowers in blue to purple to lavender; the flowers are somewhat flattened. Grows 3-4 feet high; medium green leaves. Performs best in very moist to wet soil that is somewhat acid and has plenty of organic matter. Plant in full sun to light shade. Zone 5.

I. laevigata grows 2-4 feet tall; the species has blue-violet flowers but cultivars are available with white, pink and yellow flowers. This plant is often used for its lovely variegated foliage. Grow in wet areas such as on shelf in a pond; divide in fall. Native to eastern Asia. Zones 5-9.

I. siberica (Siberian iris) grows 2-4 feet tall; small flowers in all shades of blue, purple, and white. Tolerant of poor, dry soil but best growth achieved in moist, somewhat acid soil. Division rarely needed; forms large clump. Zone 2.

Above: Iris cristata.
Below: Iris pseudacorus growing along a stream in Denver Botanic Gardens' Japanese Garden.

LILLIUM *Amaryllidaceae*

No one has ever accused lilies of blending into a landscape; indeed, some people consider them a bit too showy for an oriental garden. But if you're looking for a graceful splash of color, any of the hundreds of varieties available are worth considering. Lilies are grown from bulbs and come in vast array of sizes, shapes, and colors. They bloom at different times of the year and a succession of bloom from mid spring to early fall can be had with a little planning.

Almost all lilies need full sun and good drainage; wet feet will kill these otherwise hardy plants. Most hardy lilies are best planted out in early to mid fall; the exceptions are madonna and nankeen lilies, which can be planted at the end of summer. (Lilies can, however, be planted at any time and bulbs should not be stored for any length of time). Plant the bulbs about 8 inches deep—work the soil deeper—and space them according to size. Adding bone meal to the planting hole is beneficial. Taller varieties may need staking. Lilies need little maintenance if they are planted in a suitable site; deadhead as necessary but don't remove stalks or the lily will not flourish the following year. Lilies will reappear year after year, producing 8-10 blooms on each. Propagate by seed, by planting the outer curved covering of the bulb (bulb scales) or by separating and planting bulbils.

SELECTIONS *Lilium aurantum* (gold-banded lily) is native to Japan; it bears up to 20 large, fragrant flowers and grows up to 10 feet tall.

L. canadense, native to North America, produces bell-shaped yellow flowers.

L. candidum (madonna lily) bears 15 or more fragrant white flowers; to 4 feet.

Oriental lilies are hybrids of *L. aurantium* and *L. speciosum.* They generally flower late and bear large flowers. The 'Elegance' cultivars are among the best.

Asiatic lilies are generally 3-4 feet tall and flower in late spring to early summer. 'Enchantment', deep red and 3 feet tall, is a popular cultivar.

MECONOPSIS ASIATIC POPPY *Papaveraceae*

Found mainly in the high elevations of the Himalayas, Asiatic poppies–particularly the blue poppy–have flocks of devoted admirers. Unfortunately, the plants are extremely fussy in their requirement and are easily grown in North America only in the Pacific Northwest. These requirements include cool, moist summers and mild winters. Rich, acid, moist but perfectly drained soil is also necessary. Most species are perennials, but reseed themselves in the proper site, sometimes to the point of invasiveness.

SELECTIONS *Meconopsis betonicifolia* (blue poppy) is a short-lived perennial with nodding, intense clear blue flowers. Though demanding, they are also rewarding. Zones 7-9.

M. cambrica (Welsh poppy) produces yellow flowers and will tolerate conditions in most gardens. Grow in full to partial shade. Zones 6-9.

NELUMBO NUCIFERA SACRED LOTUS *Nymphaeaceae*

The sacred lotus is the primary symbol for Buddhism, and has been used for centuries in oriental gardens for its beauty and its edible roots, seeds, and leaf stalks. It is native to eastern North America, western Asia and Australia. This water

Overleaf: Lotus at Ganna Walska Lotusland, Santa Barbara.

The Himalayas are the source of many plants that thrive in the Pacific Northwestern region of North America, including several species of meconopsis (below).

IRIS ENSATA [I. KAEMPFERI] (SWORD-LEAVED IRIS, JAPANESE IRIS)
3-4 feet tall. Medium green leaves, very large flowers in many patterns and shades of blue, purple, and gold. Full sun to light shade; rich moist or wet soil. Zones 5-9.

LILIUM AURATUM 'PLATYPHYLLUM' (GOLDEN RAY MOUNTAIN LILY)
4-6 feet tall. 10- to 12-inch waxy white flowers with yellow markings and orange anthers, slightly acid, well-drained soil. Zones 5-9.

LILIUM 'ENDEAVOUR' (HYBRID ASIATIC LILY) 3-4 feet tall. Medium green leaves, 6- to 8-inch gold flowers, orange at center. Full sun to light shade; rich moist or wet soil. Zones 3-10.

MECONOPSIS BETONICIFOLIA (BLUE POPPY) 3-5 feet tall. Intense, clear blue flowers. Full sun to partial shade, moist, rich well-drained soil. Zones 7-9.

plant has large leaves of matte green up to 2 feet wide, with some emerging above the water line and some floating. The plant can reach 8 feet in height in warm climates. It is prized for its giant cup-shaped waxy pink, white or yellow flowers that stand high above the leaves. The flowers are many-petalled and quite fragrant. In the center of the flower is a fleshy receptacle that turns brown to black and is used frequently in dried arrangements. Lotus are essential to give the finishing touch to a pond, providing it is of a size to handle these large plants. When seen from a distance, they take one's breath away. Zone 9.

Although only listed as hardy to Zone 9, lotus are easily used in colder climates as long as the plants are lifted and stored for the winter in a frost-free area. Plant in a tub or basket with heavy garden soil amended with manure. In spring after danger of frost, anchor the tub in at least 24 inches of water and remove foliage and flowers as they fade. In fall, gradually reduce the water level (by moving the lotus up the side of the pond bank or onto shallow shelves). Before the first frost, either lift the tub and move it into a greenhouse or heated storage area and keep moist through the winter. An alternative is to dig a deep hole, place the tub into it, and then mulch very heavily to keep the plant from freezing. This method is always somewhat of a risk. There are some cultivars that are hardier than the species. Propagate by division or seed–plants do not like to be disturbed once planted in the tub.

NYMPHAEA WATER LILY *Nymphaeaceae*

Water lilies are staples of still pools, and even a small tub pool can support at least one beautiful plant. There is an endless variety of cultivars available. Hardy water lilies survive outdoors all winter unless their roots freeze; tropical water lilies are hardy only in Zone 10, but are easily overwintered indoors. Tropical water lilies can be night-blooming or day-blooming. Many water lilies are fragrant, and flowers come in all colors from pink to white to yellow to red, as well as purple to blue for tropicals. Water lilies are a beautiful addition to the garden.

Water lilies vary in their requirements according to the species or hybrid. They all must have their roots well below the water line. They are usually grown in containers sunk in manmade ponds.

PAEONIA PEONY *Paeoniaceae*

Peonies are perhaps the most traditional flower used in oriental gardens. Although there about 20 species, native to Eurasia and North America, only two are widely used as garden plants. Peonies have dissected leaves on sturdy stems and many-petalled large showy blossoms in all shades of red, yellow, pink and white. Some peonies have visible yellow stamens, while others have the center structures completely engulfed in ruffly petals. Their dark, glossy foliage remain beautiful long after the flowers have faded in early summer. Herbaceous peonies make a beautiful blooming hedge, and tree peonies are inspiring focal points. There are an infinite number of cultivars available.

Peonies are tolerant of most soils, although a rich, well-drained loam will produce the best results. Although plants are often available in nurseries in the

PEONY CATEGORIES

The American Peony Society recognizes four different forms of peony flower:

1. **Singles** have five or more petals surrounding a central mass of fertile pollen-bearing anthers.

2. **Doubles** have five or more guard petals surrounding a mass of anthers and carpels modified to appear as a mass of petals. There is no trace of typical stamens in the double form.

3. **Semidoubles** have five or more guard petals surrounding a center intermixed with petallike carpels and distinct pollen-bearing stamens.

4. **Japanese** types have flowers with five or more guard petals and a center consisting of a larger mass of staminodes (modified stamens with aborted non-pollen-bearing anthers).

Anemone types are classified with the Japanese types by the American Peony Society.

Below: Japanese peony.

NELUMBO 'MOMO BATAN' (EAST INDIAN LOTUS) 3 feet tall. Very large flowers and leaves. Full sun; plant in container submerged in water. Zones 9-10 (can be overwintered indoors in cooler climates.

NYMPHAEA 'JAMES BRYDON' (HARDY WATER LILY) Spreads 4-6 feet across. Cup-shaped red flowers, green foliage. Full sun (accepts part shade); plant in container submerged in water. Zones 5-9.

NYMPHAEA CAERULEA (SACRED EGYPTIAN LOTUS, TROPICAL WATER LILY) Spreads 5-7 feet across. White flowers with pointed petals edged in lavender blue. Full sun; plant in container submerged in water. Zones 9-10.

PAEONIA LACTIFLORA (CHINESE PEONY) Shrubby plant 3-4 feet tall. Dark green foliage, large double flowers. Full sun to partial shade (full sun for best flowering); moist rich soil is best. Zones 5-8.

Opposite: Nymphaea alba at Sun Yat-Sen Classical Chinese Garden, Vancouver, British Columbia.

spring, planting in August or September is recommended–find a garden center that offers the plants in fall. Plant in full sun to partial shade although flowering may be somewhat reduced in shade. In southern gardens, partial shade will keep the flowers from fading quickly. Water abundantly the first season and thereafter in dry times. Mulch will help conserve moisture. Peonies seldom need dividing and don't tolerate transplanting well. To propagate, divide in fall, making sure to have three to four "eyes" or growing tips per clump. Seed-produced plants seldom come true and will take four to five years to bloom. When planting peonies, the eyes must be exactly 1 inch below the soil line to produce flowers.

SELECTIONS *Paeonia lactiflora* (Chinese peony) grows 3-4 feet; blooms early spring, foliage dies to ground in winter. Native to China, Mongolia and Siberia. Zone 4. *P. suffruticosa* (tree peony) grows 3-5 feet on upright woody stems. Native to China. Zones 5-8.

PAPAVER ORIENTALE ORIENTAL POPPY *Papaveraceae*

Oriental poppies, native to southwest Asia, are outstanding in the landscape with their tall, papery blossoms gracefully waving well above the foliage. The leaves are fuzzy, gray-green and deeply serrated. The foliage dies away around mid-summer, so are best planted with another perennial to fill in the hole from summer into

Below: Chinese peony, *Paeonia lactiflora* 'Bev'.

fall. The foliage will begin to resprout in late August, but does not fill in as heavily as in spring. The flowers range from red to orange to pink to white, usually with a black to dark brown large center. Poppies should be used as a focal point and are beautifully effective when planted in large masses to be seen at a distance.

Plant poppies in fall in very well-drained soil. Wet soil, particularly over winter is usually fatal. Plant in full sun or partial shade. Mulch to conserve moisture only if the soil is well-drained. Poppies are tolerant of drought so seldom need supplemental irrigation. Poppies do not transplant well, so choose a permanent spot for planting. To propagate, take root cuttings in late summer. Remove foliage as it yellows. Do not fertilize–excessive fertility will force many leaves and few flowers.

PLATYCODON GRANDIFLORUS BALLOON FLOWER *Campanulaceae*

The common name of this Asian native refers to the flower buds, which are shaped like hot-air balloons. Long-lived and easy to grow, this perennial is tolerant of a wide range of sites and conditions. The compact form *P. g.* var. *mariesii* is offered by most nurseries and lends itself to flowerbeds, borders, and even rock gardens. Taller cultivars, such as 'Shell Pink' and the 'Fuji' series from Japan, also have their place and make excellent cut flowers; sear the base of the stem to prevent "bleeding." Plant balloon flowers in well-drained soil in

Below: A field of oriental poppies.

PAPAVER ORIENTALE (ORIENTAL POPPY) 2- to 3-foot-tall stems. papery blossoms, Gray-green serrated foliage. Full sun or partial shade. Average, well-drained soil. Zones 5-8.

PLATYCODON GRANDIFLORUS (BALLOON FLOWER) 1½-2½ feet tall. Erect toothed stems, oval gray-green leaves and balloon-shaped purplish blue flowers. Full sun to partial shade. Zones 3-10.

PRIMULA PULVERULENTA (CANDELABRA PRIMROSE) To 3 feet tall. 1½-inch-wide red, pink, or yellow flowers in clusters. Full sun, moist soil. Zones 7-9.

RODGERSIA AESCULIFOLIA (RODGER'S FLOWER) To 6 feet tall. Glossy green lobed leaves, panicles of creamy white flowers. Partial shade to full sun, moist, rich soil. Zones 4-8.

full sun in the North, but shade lightly in hot climates. Each spring apply a dressing of fertilizer to maintain fertility; water during dry weather. The deep, fragile roots resent disturbance, but careful division is possible after growth begins in late spring. Pot-grown plants are preferred, since root disturbance is minimal; either spring or fall planting is appropriate. Spring-sown seed germinates readily in pots. To prolong blooming routinely remove spent flowers. Pests and diseases are seldom a problem.

Platycodon grandiflora 'Alba'.

PRIMULA PRIMROSE *Primulaceae*

Only a few species of this large genus are widely grown, so many of them being too fussy for all but the specialists. Mostly native to temperate regions of the Northern Hemisphere, primroses do best where summers are relatively cool. Most primroses prefer a richly organic soil that remains moist. If the soil conditions are met, they will do well even in full sun, but also thrive in dappled shade.

Both spring and fall are good planting times. Divide established plants after flowering or sow fresh seed as soon as it is ripe. Young seedlings are best overwintered in a cold frame, prior to spring planting. Primroses are subject to winter-heaving in cold climates; protect with evergreen boughs. Slugs can be devastating in damp shady places; in sunnier spots be alert for aphid and red spider mite infestations.

SELECTIONS *Primula* x *polyantha* (polyantha primrose) is most widely cultivated. Countless millions are raised annually and sold as early spring pot plants. As soon as the ground warms up, these can be planted outside and will usually continue to bloom for several seasons. The 'Pacific Giant' strain is widespread; it has flowers of yellow, blue, red, pink, and white, mostly with yellow throats.

P. japonica (Japanese primroses) if allowed to self-seed naturally, will form large colonies in rich, moist to wet soil where they are partly shaded. If the roots can be kept moist, Japanese primroses will thrive in sunny places, too, and adapt well to border conditions. They are especially attractive in bog gardens, or alongside streams or ponds; best where the water is not stagnant.

P. sieboldii (Japanese star primrose) is summer deciduous.

Candelabra primroses are Asian hybrids which do best in the Pacific Northwest.

RODGERSIA AESCULIFOLIA RODGER'S FLOWER *Saxifragaceae*

Native to China, this species of Rodger's flower grows to 6 feet and has distinct palmately lobed leaves, closely resembling those of the horsechestnut. The leaves are glossy green and add a tropical air to the garden. The panicles of creamy flowers in summer make a beautiful complement to the bold, striking plant. Rodger's flower is well used as an accent in a woodland garden or along a pond bank. Zone 4.

Plant in partial shade or full sun if plenty of moisture is available. The most common reason for these plants to die is lack of adequate moisture. Plant into well-amended rich soil and mulch immediately to retain moisture. Fertilize only every couple of years. Propagate by division in early spring.

WATER GARDENS

Gardening in water has been done for centuries and has now reached new popularity because new materials, such as flexible pool liners and preformed pools, have made it easier than ever. There is a vast range of plants that can be planted in containers submerged in water. Members of the family Nymphaceae, including water lilies and lotus (see pages 138-143) are perhaps the most spectacular. Many foliage plants, such as sweet flag, papyrus, rushes, and reeds will also thrive in these conditions. Plants used with water lilies in water gardens are often called marginals; some sources refer to them as bog plants or emergents (if their leaves emerge from the water). Many other plants, including irises, are well-suited to the marshy ground around the edges of a pond or stream.

For information on creating a pond, see pages 204-205.

FOLIAGE PLANTS

ACORUS GRAMINEUS GRASSY-LEAVED SWEET FLAG *Iridaceae*

Native to China, southeast Asia and Japan, this perennial grows to about 18 inches tall with slender, delicate leaves. The flowers are green and not particularly noticeable; it is grown for its attractive foliage. It generally maintains a clump form, but will spread somewhat by fleshy rhizomes. It is a favorite for wet areas and grows particularly well on the edge of a pond. There are cultivars available with variegated leaves. Zone 6.

Provide full sun to partial shade and constantly moist soil. These plants grow well in boggy areas, indicating the need for moisture. Water well when planting; make certain to plant at the same level at which it was planted in its pot. Do not fertilize; trimming or pruning is unnecessary. Propagate by division.

CYPERUS HASPEN DWARF PAPYRUS *Cyperaceae*

Dwarf papyrus is native to Africa and grows in marshy, wet areas. It is an annual plant that is often used in water gardens because of its unusual habit. It has 1- to 2-foot stalks that hold an umbrellalike structure with spiky bracts throughout the summer. Dwarf papyrus is most effectively used in a small pond or water garden although it is becoming popular as a container plant. Zone 7.

Dwarf papyrus is often used as an annual aquatic plant in colder climates. Plant in full sun or partial shade in marshy soil or standing water. Keep constantly moist or the plant will die. Pruning and fertilization are unnecessary. Propagate by seed or division..

IMPERATA CYLINDRICA VAR. RUBRA JAPANESE BLOOD GRASS
Poaceae

Japanese blood grass is a relatively new addition to the spectrum of ornamental grasses that can be found in most nurseries. It is listed most often in the nursery trade as *Imperata cylindrica* 'Red Baron', which is synonomous with *I.c.* var. *rubra*. It is a slow growing species that is unusual in that it is grown for its upright colorful foliage rather than for its flowers, which rarely appear. In the spring, its leaves emerge as medium green, but as the season progresses, the green foliage turns increasing red; by fall it is the "blood red" color of its common name. In late fall, the foliage ripens to a coppery tan, adding winter interest to the garden.

Japanese blood grass prefers full sun, but will tolerate and even benefit from partial shade in the warmer sections of its range; shade will produce inferior color. Plant in soil that is well-drained but remains evenly moist and rich in organic matter. As with many other warm-season grasses, Japanese blood grass responds well to division in the spring rather than the fall. Cull out any plants that stay green rather than turn red in the fall for they are not only less attractive, but will also be invasive. **NOTE:** Some forms of this species are so invasive that they have been illegalized.

ACORUS CALAMUS 'VARIEGATUS' (VARIEGATED SWEET FLAG)
Upright; 2- to 4-foot green lance-shaped leaves striped in creamy white, tiny greenish flowers, citrusy fragrance. Full sun. Zones 4-10.

CYPERUS HASPEN (DWARF PAPYRUS) 1-2-feet tall. Umbrellalike plant spiky bracts. Full sun, moist, rich soil. Zones 7-10.

IMPERATA CYLINDIRICA VAR. RUBRA (JAPANESE BLOOD GRASS) 18-24 inches tall. Narrow grass emerges green, turns deep red. Full sun for best color, partial shade tolerated; rich, evenly moist, well-drained soil. Zones 5-9.

LIRIOPE 'MUNSON WHITE' (LILYTURF) Grassy plants to 12 inches tall with spiky white flowers. Shade is best, full sun is tolerated; any well-drained soil. Zones 5-10.

MISCANTHUS SINENSIS 'ZEBRINUS' (ZEBRA GRASS) 6-8 feet tall. Loose-growing clump with horizontal yellow bands on green leaves, pale pink 8- to 10-inch-long flowers. Full sun, any well-drained soil. Zones 5-9.

MUSA ACUMINATA 'DWARF CAVENDISH' (EDIBLE BANANA) 6-8 feet tall. Treelike plant with very large paddle-shaped leaves and clusters of edible fruits. Partial shade, moist, rich soil, humid conditions. Zones 9-10, Zone 8 with protection.

OPHIOPOGON JAPONICUS (MONDO GRASS, LILYTURF) 15 inches tall. Glossy dark green grass, lilac or white flower spikes. Sun or shade, any well-drained soil. Zones 7-10.

PENNISETUM ALOPECUROIDES (CHINESE PENNISETUM) 3½ feet tall. Clump-forming grass with 6-inch-long bottlebrushlike flowers; green foliage turns golden in fall. Full sun to light shade, any well-drained soil. Zones 5-9.

LIRIOPE LILYTURF *Liliaceae*

Native to Japan, China, and Vietnam, these lily relatives are valued as impenetrable ground covers massed in sun or shade, as well as for edgings at the front of beds and borders, foundation plantings, and along woodland paths. Under urban conditions, their tolerance of pollution and heat is unbeatable.

While lilyturf tolerates full sun, most are at their best where they are shaded during the heat of the day. Almost any type of soil is satisfactory as long as the drainage is adequate; even during droughts additional water is unnecessary. Plant in spring or fall. As growth commences in spring, cut back the overwintered foliage and fertilize lightly. Propagate by dividing the plants anytime from spring till fall.

SELECTIONS *L. muscari* (big blue lilyturf) is the species grown most widely, and many cultivars are on the market. 'Majestic' is popular, as is 'Big Blue', taller than some at 15 inches. 'Variegata' has yellow margins to its strappy leaves and is especially effective during northern winters when there is little interest. *L. spicata* (creeping lilyturf) is a better choice where temperatures dip below -10° F., in spite of its invasive tendencies.

MISCANTHUS SINENSIS EULALIA GRASS *Poaceae*

Ornamental grasses are coming into more frequent use and are perfect complements to oriental style gardening. Eulalia grass, native to eastern Asia, grows to about 10 feet in thick, sturdy clumps. The long gray-green leaf blades arch elegantly and spikes of frothy flowers stand high above the leaves. The flower heads are silvery pink and may remain into winter. If left standing through the winter, the leaves turn tawny and rustle quietly, providing the element of sound even in the winter garden. Because of its size, eulalia grass needs a place of prominence, as a focal point to be viewed from a distance. It also adds an interesting element when planted to drape gracefully over water. Many cultivars are available with variegated leaves or in smaller sizes. Zone 5.

Eulalia grass will grow in most types of soil as long as they are well drained. Plant in spring in a sunny spot and water in well. Keep somewhat moist through the first season. Irrigation is needed only in extremely dry times. Do not fertilize and prune to ground in very early spring, before the new shoots begin to emerge. Plants will need to be divided when they begin to die out in the middle and form a doughnut-shape. Propagation is easiest by division.

MUSA BANANA *Musaceae*

These plants are used in oriental gardens for their dramatic foliage and the sensory delight of the sound of wind and rain on their large leaves. The spirally-arranged leaves are oblong with parallel veins and red midribs. Some species have attractive flowers in large clusters followed by long fruits that are actually berries. They are also grown in pots in northern climates and brought indoors for the winter. There are over 40 species, native to tropical Africa, India and southeastern Asia.

Plant in partial shade in rich, organic soil with plenty of moisture. The soil should be neutral to slightly acid and very well-drained. Protect from wind to

Above: Bananas and bamboo.

prevent tattering of leaves and protect from cold temperatures - the minimum temperature most species can tolerate before damage is 50 degrees. Fertilize annually and prune off suckers that form at the base. Water well during growing season and hold back in the winter, particularly if the plant is being grown for fruits.

SELECTION *M. basjoo* (ornamental banana) stems grow to about 8 feet; bright green wide leaves reach 4 feet. Yellow-green to yellow flowers; there is a cultivar with variegated leaves. Native to Ryukyu Island. Zone 8.

M. x paradisiaca (edible banana) grows to 25 feet in warm climates; over 300 cultivars available, some with striped or red leaves. Medium green leaves; yellow seedless fruit with white pulp. Native to the tropics. Zone 9.

OPHIOPOGON JAPONICUS MONDO GRASS, LILYTURF *Liliaceae*

Native to Japan and Korea, mondo grass is an excellent attractive groundcover or edging for a path. It grows to about 15 inches high with glossy dark green grass-like leaves. The plants flower in summer with loose spikes of pale lilac or white flowers, followed by blue fruits. The plants spread by underground rhizomes and once established, make a dense ground cover that weeds cannot penetrate. Zone 7.

Plant in sun or shade in almost any type of soil providing it is well-drained. Water well to establish and keep weeded during the first year. Fertilize sparingly every few years. In cooler climates, mondo grass can be grown in a pot and lifted and stored cool and dry over the winter. Propagate by seed or division.

PENNISETUM FOUNTAIN GRASS *Poaceae*

This genus contains annual and perennial grasses, most of which are graceful and airy with narrow leaf blades and feathery arching flower plumes. The leaves and flower stalks arch at differing angles, giving a true image of a water fountain. Fountain grasses grow in clumps, and the annual species often reseed themselves readily and can be a nuisance, particularly in warm climates.

Plant fountain grass in spring into very well-drained soil and full sun. Water well when establishing, but supplemental irrigation should only be necessary in times of extreme drought. Do not fertilize and prune to ground in very early spring, before the new shoots begin to emerge. Plants will need to be divided when they begin to die out in the middle and form a doughnut-shape. Propagation is easiest by division.

SELECTIONS *P. alopecuroides* (Chinese pennisetum) grows to 3½ feet, in discrete mounds that beautifully edge a walk or stream bank. Bright green leaves turning tawny golden in fall and winter. White to cream seedheads long seedheads that appear in mid-fall and remain partially into the winter. Native to Asia. Zone 5.

P. setaceum (fountain grass) grows to about 3 feet high; gray-green leaves turn golden in fall. Perennial to Zone 8; grown an annual in other zones. Pink or purple flower plumes that arch among the arching leaves. Native to Africa.

P. setaceum* var. *rubrum (red fountain grass) is similar to the species but has red leaves and flowers.

FERNS
ADIANTUM PEDATUM MAIDENHAIR FERN *Adiantaceae*
The delicate maidenhair fern is native to the northwestern United States, and is found in cool, moist woodlands. The finger-like fronds are lacy and medium green with a dark petiole. Maidenhair ferns look most appropriate when used in their natural setting, as a groundcover or accent under shade trees. Plant maidenhair ferns in partial to full shade. Mulch when planted and keep moist throughout the season. Zone 2.

ATHYRIUM FILIX-FEMINA LADY FERN *Aspleniaceae*
The delicate lady fern is native to the temperate northern hemisphere and is always found in moist, damp woods. The bright green arching fronds with tiny leaflets grow to 3 feet, forming a vase. Lady ferns are effective as a ground cover under shade trees or shrubs or when massed along the banks of a shady stream or pond. Although lady ferns are tolerant of a wide range of soils, their best performance will occur in rich, moisture retentive soil. They will tolerate full sun if given plenty of moisture; otherwise, plant in partial shade. Prune only to remove tattered fronds. Zone 2.

CYRTOMIUM FALCATUM JAPANESE HOLLY FERN *Polypodiaceae*
Native to South Africa, Asia and Polynesia, this fern has stiff arching dark green fronds with points on the pinnae (hence its common name). The stems are hairy and reddish-brown. Holly fern makes an attractive focal point or ground cover in a partially or fully shaded woodland where the glossy fronds are striking. Holly ferns perform best if planted in a situation similar to their native habitats of cool, damp woods. Plant in partial to full shade. Mulch when planted and keep moist throughout the season. Zone 9.

DRYOPTERIS ERYTHROSORA JAPANESE SHIELD FERN *Aspleniaceae*
Native to China and Japan, the Japanese shield fern occupies partially or deeply shaded moist woods. Its compound leaves grow to $1\frac{1}{2}$ feet long and have a reddish cast when unfurling in spring changing to very dark glossy green in summer. Because of this spring color and the red sori, this fern is also called Japanese red shield fern. Shield fern makes a beautiful ground cover or accent plant in moist woodland gardens. Plant in partial to full shade. Mulch when planted and keep moist throughout the season. Zone 5

POLYSTICHUM ACROSTICHOIDES CHRISTMAS FERN *Aspleniaceae*
One of the most wonderful characteristics of this native of eastern North America is that it is evergreen. The rich green shining leaves to 2 feet long hover above the snow in cold climates. It naturally grows in moist woods although it can also tolerate some sun. In the oriental garden, it is a welcome sight when the snow melts, particularly as a companion to snowdrops in very early spring. Use it as a groundcover, as an accent along water, or as an edging for a path. Plant Christmas fern in very well-drained organic soil that remains somewhat moist. Plant in full shade to partial shade. Water well during the first season and apply mulch immediately upon planting to keep the soil moist. or dividing the crowns in spring. Zone 2.

Ferns are wonderful accent plants for oriental gardens, adding a lacy touch in shady areas. Most have similar requirements, needing moist rich soil. They should be divided only for propagation; most can also be propagated from spores.

Bamboos. *From top to bottom: Chusquea coronalis* (weeping bamboo); *Sasa veitchii* (kuma bamboo grass); *Phyllos-tachys aureosuicata* (yellowgrass bamboo).

Opposite: Phyllostachys nigra (black bamboo).

BAMBOOS *Poaceae*

Bamboos have long been associated with oriental gardens because of their graceful, grassy appearance. Sizes range from giant to the small pygmy bamboo that is under one foot. Bamboo is symbolically associated with strength and resilience because of its size, with the family because of its habit of growing in clumps, and with modesty because of its lack of flowers. Depending on the species, bamboo is used for groves, hedges, screening, accent and in containers. Bamboo can be clump-forming or running, and can become rampant if not controlled carefully. The rhizome bamboos are excellent for holding a bank in place. Whatever the reason for including bamboo in the oriental garden, the gardener will find a sturdy plant with few care requirements. See page 177 for bamboo fence-making.

Bamboos perform best in warm, moist soil. They will tolerate poor soil but not poor drainage. Most thrive in partial shade although some species will do well in full shade. Water well while establishing (which can take two to three years). Bamboos are somewhat invasive by nature, so fertilization is generally unnecessary. Prune by removing the largest culms or stems to let in more light and appreciate more fully the grace of mature plants. Shorter varieties should be cut back to the ground in early spring, much the same as ornamental grasses, to allow fresh new growth to emerge. In order to confine running species, sink a non-degradable barrier at least 20 inches deep. Propagation is usually by division since most species take many years to produce a flower.

SELECTIONS *Arundinaria gigantea,* native to the United States, has a ½-inch culm and grows 10-12 feet. A clumper, it produces a dense screen. Zone 6. *A. pygmaea* (pygmy bamboo) has bright green leaves to about 1 foot high. It spreads by rhizomes and makes an excellent groundcover. Native to Japan. Zone 8. *A. simonii* (Simon bamboo) grows to 25 feet; leaves bright green with some variegation; fully variegated cultivar available. Native to Japan. Zone 8.

Bambusa arundinacea (giant thorny bamboo) grows to 100 feet in clumps with stems to 5-inch diameter; medium shiny green leaves. Native to India; Zone 8. *B. glaucescens* (hedge bamboo) is sometimes called bamboo of filial piety since the new shoots arise from the center and are thus protected. Grows to 10 feet; leaves medium green changing to yellow. Native to China. Zone 9. *B. vulgaris* (common bamboo) grows to 60 feet with stems to 5-inch diameter; stems may be yellow, green, or striped; leaves bright green and arching. Cultivated throughout the world. Zone 5.

Phyllostachys aureosulcata (yellowgroove bamboo) grows to 30 feet high; yellow and green striped stems. Native to China. Zone 7. *P. bambusoides* (Japanese timber bamboo) grows to 75 feet with 5-inch stems; dark green glossy leaves. Native to China. Zone 8. *P. nigra* (black bamboo) grows to 25 feet; green stems turning purple and then black. Native to China. Zone 8 (can be grown in Zone 6, but die back in winter). *P. pubescens* (moso bamboo) grows to 75 feet with 5-inch diameter stems; pale green stems. Native to Japan. Zone 8.

Pleioblastus pygmaeus grows to 1 foot and has small blue-green leaves. It is useful as a groundcover and its invasive tendencies are controllable. Zone 5.

Sasa veitchii (kuma bamboo grass) grows 2-3 feet tall; medium green leaves turn tawny in winter. Good groundcover. Native to Japan. Zone 6.

Shibataea kumasaca (bamboo) grows to 6 feet; dark green leaves. Native to Japan. Zone 6.

Sinarundinaria nitida has arching culms that reach 13 feet. This clump-former may be used as a speciment or hedge. Plant in semi-shade. Zone 6.

Oriental gardens—whether they are authenic in every aspect or simply seek to capture the spirit on which they are based—are different from Western gardens in many ways. As discussed in Chapter 1, the goal of an oriental garden is more than the artful display of plants; it is the creation of an atmosphere of peace and serenity that will promote meditation and enlightenment. To achieve that goal, the garden designer manipulates every element of his or her space. Plants are only one of the many facets that are combined to form the oriental garden; others include rocks, water, sculpture, walkways and pathways, as well as the surrounding landscape. The rules that can be learned about creating an oriental garden are less important than the attitude under which they are followed.

Perhaps the most important element in the success of any garden design is the establishment of the long term goal you hope to attain by building it. Think about the garden's intent. Ask yourself the following questions: what do I want my garden to be, how do I intend to use it and what does it need to blend with? Creating a sense of harmony between the land and the existing structures will give the garden a sense of belonging by creating the illusion that it has always been there. If, after an honest evaluation of your garden wishes, you have a strong interest in developing an oriental garden, your primary aim should be to create a

In each of these gardens, natural elements have been carefully manipulated; the results emulate nature without being totally natural.
Above: In this Chinese garden, land has been molded to form gentle contours, leading the eye to water features.
Right: The Japanese Garden at Ganna Walska Lotusland unfolds slowly, revealing new features at every turn. The surrounding landscape is drawn into the scene as it is reflected in the pond and glimpsed through breaks in background trees.
Opposite: An authentic Japanese moon bridge at The Portland Japanese Garden leads viewers through carefully arranged displays of plants and stones.

garden design

In a dry garden, rocks, gravel, or pebbles symbolize water. Raked patterns, created with a special tool, add texture. The raking procedure instills peace and reflection. *Above:* **The dry garden at The Portland Japanese Garden.**

peaceful space that emulates nature. This objective can be achieved by providing a place for reflection, meditation, and inspiration. Therefore, it is not only helpful but essential to have a clear vision of the garden you want, before you begin implementation.

Designing an oriental garden is a process. Be sure that your garden is well matched to the site and the native surroundings. Adapt the garden to the site by demonstrating sensitivity to slope, soil, water, and plant selections. At the same time, remember that an oriental garden is not completely naturalistic, even though its aim is to emulate nature. Stone arrangements are a primary consideration for enhancing the garden's sculpture and focus and proper placement are key to ensuring the attainment of your long term goal. As you select special features, remember the oriental appreciation for seeing beauty in simplicity.

In most oriental garden designs, the creation and placement of varying elevations and water features is inspired by the natural landscape. Thus, the plantings are encouraged to grow in informal shapes, with trunks that are irregular and, thereby, mimic the growth typically found on mountain tops. Individual plant selections are extremely important and the random addition or removal of plants will take away from the design. As in a great oriental flower design, each piece fits together to make the whole and each needs the other to complete the creation.

CHOOSING A GARDEN TYPE If your house is not oriental in design, it is advisable that you place your oriental garden at the side or back of the house. Tucked into a corner, along a wall, or as a viewing expanse, your oriental garden can be an oasis—a magical place for contemplation and relaxation. If the land is sloped, you can create the feeling of mountains by incorporating a dry stream or a rocky outcropping. The use of smooth curves and a conscientious effort to keep the garden simple and uncluttered are important. Also, installing an enclosure that is in keeping with the oriental design will greatly enhance your garden.

How have you determined you wish to use your garden: for viewing from a window or balcony, for entertaining, as an outdoor living space, or as an architectural accent, a courtyard or an entrance garden? Begin on a small scale until you are comfortable with the care involved. Remember, a small garden can be designed to appear much larger.

Begin formulating your plan by considering the use of certain physical elements such as gravel, water, stone, and bonsai. If you are considering a gravel or raked sand garden, keep in mind that they tend to be high maintenance. The leaves must be blown or raked because a weed problem inevitably develops as they decay and as seeds germinate. Instead of gravel or raked sand, use a ground cover or grass to lower the need for maintenance.

Planning on Paper Once you have a vision for your garden, study your survey plan of the property that includes the location of all buildings and property lines. Put in the main walkways and consider how the outdoor space will be divided to create garden rooms and give the necessary enclosure. Be sure to block any unattractive views by planting tall evergreens.

Let's assume that you are working with a rectangular lot and you have decided to place the oriental garden in the rear area. Create a bed line that varies from 4-

Above: Acer palmatum 'Dissectum'
with caladium and hardy begonias.
Right: Azaleas add bright color to this
garden; when they fade, the contrasts
in texture between the maple in the
background and the stones will be the
main features of the garden.

10 feet from the property line. The amount of variation depends on the size and scale of the property. Do not make the shapes on both sides as mirror images. One corner should have more depth than the other, although both corners should have a wide planting bed. Adding a peninsula on one side can make an interesting focal point and provide a planting space for light-loving and low-growing plants. Select the spaces where rocks will be placed. Consider what type of water you want and place it appropriately; thus, thinking in terms of size and the most advantageous viewing and listening points.

For a garden along the side of a house that connects the front and rear areas of the property, straight lines and formal shaped walkways can be considered. Since this space is primarily for access, its design can be done in a number of ways. The use of irregular flagstone as a walkway and planting trees and moss will result in a woodsy feeling.

Choosing Plants Select plants in order to achieve year-round interest. Plan on 60-70 percent of them being evergreens. Your choices do not need to be Asian plants. In many cases, the American counterparts will be fine. One exception is the Japanese maple which has such a distinctive shape, color, and texture that it usually deserves inclusion somewhere. Many of the different native species of pines can be used as needled evergreens. The remaining 30-40 percent of the plants chosen should be selected for their textural qualities.

Primary plantings will be the tall screen plants chosen for their height. The most commonly selected evergreen for this purpose is the Leyland Cypress (*Cupressocyparis leylandii*). This particular cypress is not the best choice for many

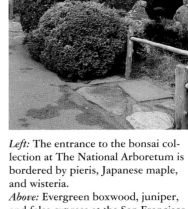

Left: The entrance to the bonsai collection at The National Arboretum is bordered by pieris, Japanese maple, and wisteria.
Above: Evergreen boxwood, juniper, and false cypress at the San Francisco Tea Garden.

situations because it grows so quickly that its roots are not well established and it may fall over. Some better choices would be *Cryptomeria japonica* (Japanese red-cedar), *Cunninghamia lanceolata* (China fir), *Sciadopitys verticillata* (Japanese umbrella pine), *Magnolia grandiflora*, or species of *Tsuga* (hemlock), *Cedrus* (cedar), *Abies* (fir), or *Picea* (spruce).

Next, choose plants that are a bit lower in height such as *Chamaecyparis pisifera*, *Chamaecyparis obtusa*, *Pinus* sp., *Taxus* sp., *Juniperus* sp., *Thuja* sp., and bamboo. As you arrange them try not to make them too busy. For example, a pattern of 2-1-2-1 would be too congested. Try thinking of rhythm and use patterns like 3-5-2-7-1 with only occasional small numbers. Vary the textures of selected plants as you combine them. For example, use a rounded, shiny leaf, like *Magnolia grandiflora*, next to a needle-leaf, such as *Cryptomeria japonica*. Thus, the plants will stand out in the landscape rather than disappear.

Contrasts in texture. *Above:* Stone, *Hedera helix* 'Glacier', *Acer palmatum* 'Dissectum Viride'. *Top:* Lilyturf, bugleweed, pachysandra, azalea, impatiens, and hardy begonias.
Right: Spring color provided by azaleas will be followed by irises.

Color, texture, shape, size Successfully designing with plants means taking into account the color, texture, shape, and size of the plants. When you have a strong color, do not use too much of it. For example, blue can be an interesting color if used against a green background. Too much blue would be a distraction from the overall effect of the garden. The same is true with the red-leaved Japanese maples; they make a wonderful accent when used sparingly. Choose certain spaces for plants with strong color and strong texture. As in designing with flowers, you do not want too much competition between your flowers.

Narrow, grasslike leaves contrast beautifully with bold leaves. For example, using sedge or lilyturf in front with the bold leaves of hosta behind it and then a dwarf needled evergreen behind the hosta, would gives a superb contrast of three interesting textures. Combining the gray leaves of *Stachys byzantinus* with green lilyturf will make the green stand out against the silver. Try the rounded leaves of azalea next to the shiny, pointed leaves of leucothoe.

Bamboo, with its fine leaves and vertical lines looks wonderful against a redbud, maple, or amelanchier. Placing a horizontally branched plant in front of a vertical plant is elegant. Think about the layers you create as you arrange for contrasts in rich colors, textures and shapes.

PLANNING FOR THREE OR FOUR SEASONS

Spring In spring we feel the warmth of new life coming to the garden. We observe the new leaves coming out and notice the interesting colors of the emerging growth as it develops. The new foliage of the deciduous plants brings its screening benefits as well. There are plenty of early spring blooming plants to enjoy for color. Ideally, a spring garden combines a blend of new evergreen growth, the furry, bright green of many conifers, and the shiny fresh green of most broadleaved evergreens along with the refreshing burst of spring flowers and the fragile

Oriental gardens change dramatically from season to season. *Above and above left:* In spring, dogwood, wisteria, and azaleas burst into bloom. *Left:* In summer, shades of green predominate, presenting a lush, healthy effect; a ginkgo tree is underplanted with pachysandra.

new shoots of perennials. In a shady garden there is a host of wildflowers, both annuals and perennials, that will provide early color.

One of the most beautiful groups of trees for dramatic emerging leaf color is the red-leaf Japanese maple. Its rich red, young leaves contrast effectively with the flowers of early spring blooming trees like the redbud (*Cercis canadensis*) and the yoshino cherry (*Prunus yedoensis*). Some of the choice spring blooming shrubs include Japanese pieris (*Pieris japonica*) or the mountain pieris (*Pieris floribunda*)

Top: Crape myrtle's exquisite bark is attractive all year. *Above:* The feathery foliage of Japanese maple turns vivid red in autumn, in sharp contrast to the gravel below it. *Opposite top:* In autumn dark green evergreens stand out against brilliant maple foliage. *Opposite bottom:* Winter.

with their lovely weeping flowers which are reminiscent of the lily-of-the-valley. Flowers of deciduous azaleas are especially lovely as they appear to be floating in the air. Camellias and their extraordinary flowers also enliven the spring garden.

A host of reliable perennials will add interest to the oriental garden in spring. Siberian iris (*Iris siberica*), for example, combines lovely foliage with distinctive flowers. In the shade, try blending astilbes with hosta. The native pachysandra (*Pachysandra procumbens*) makes a fine groundcover. Solomon's seal (*Polygonatum odoratum* var. *thunbergii*) adds an architectural element to the back of a border with its arching habit and pendulous flowers.

Summer In summer we rely more on shapes, forms, texture, light, patterns, and shade. To enjoy color in summer, plants need to be carefully selected. In most oriental gardens, you would not see much in the way of color in summer. Since most Americans want to have color, which is best provided by annuals, you can use impatiens or New Guinea impatiens for this purpose. Perennials such as daylilies, peonies, balloon flowers, and Japanese iris also provide a subtle splash of color to a typically monochrome scene.

One of the best trees for summer color is the crape myrtle (*Lagerstroemia indica*) which has a stunning bark that adds year-round interest. Flower colors vary but white is highly recommended for an oriental garden. Larger trees should be planted to create shade in selected places during summer time. For example, near the terrace or deck, place a tree such as redbud, Japanese maple, zelkova, or sophora and allow it to grow over the deck forming a natural umbrella.

Some grasses provide a rich texture for summer effect. Two examples of appropriate grasses are sedges and lilyturf. Sedge has a finer texture than lilyturf whose leaf is more rounded. These two grasses are particularly valuable as edging plants.

Most likely your garden will need some watering during the dry parts of summer. If you miss a critical period for water application, the garden will have difficulty recovering from the damage. Keep a close watch on dryness during any hot, dry spells.

Fall Oriental gardens are known for their brilliance in the autumn. In part this is because of the changing colors of the Japanese maples with their rich and varied hues. Redvein enkianthus (*Enkianthus campanulatus*) is famous for its fall color. It makes a wonderful specimen plant and combines well with rhododendrons around a patio. Katsura tree (*Cercidiphyllum japonicum*) has a rich yellow color with a touch of apricot in the autumn and its leaves smell like cotton candy. The dwarf winged euonymus (*Euonymus alatus* 'Compactus') provides an intense red color and can be used as a hedge or a specimen. Bush clover (*Lespedeza bicolor*), one of the seven flowers of autumn, brings rosy purple blooms to the garden late in the year.

A myriad of chrysanthemums are known to be featured in the oriental garden in autumn. The Nippon chrysanthemum (*Chrysanthemum nipponicum*) is a great perennial chrysanthmum for your oriental garden.

Winter Winter is also a beautiful time in the oriental garden. If well-designed, winter is the time to appreciate the bones of the garden. Often there are flowers on the autumn higan cherry (*Prunus subhirtella* var. *autumnalis*). The Japanese plum (*Prunus mume*) comes into bloom, even in the middle of a snow storm, with its fra-

grant cherrylike blossoms and is, appropriately, a symbol of endurance. The fragrant wintersweet (*Chimonanthus praecox*) with yellow flowers can be smelled for a long distance throughout the garden. Japanese winter hazel (*Hamamelis* species) will bloom sweetly in the waning days of winter.

Trunks and barks are an important consideration for the winter garden. The exfoliating bark of the paperbark maple (*Acer griseum*) glistens in the winter sunlight. The snakelike bark of the Asian quince (*Cydonia sinensis*) peels and exposes a multitude of colors—forming an interesting pattern of green, gray, white, and tan. *Acer palmatum* 'Ozakazuki' has stunning red twigs to color the winter landscape.

Evergreens are the nucleus of the winter garden. Perhaps the conifer most often seen in oriental gardens is the Japanese black pine (*Pinus thunbergiana*). It is considered a high maintenance plant because it requires pruning every year in order to be properly shaped. Proper pruning often achieves wonderfully sinuous branching patterns which are worth the effort. Japanese red pine (*Pinus densiflora*) requires less pruning and is a great specimen because of its decorative orange-red bark. The peeling bark of the lacebark pine (*Pinus bungeana*) makes it a striking plant and should be placed so that its trunk can be viewed easily.

Bamboo adds interest to the garden in winter, and creates a wonderful, musical sound when it blows in the wind. For fragrance combined with evergreen foliage, the sweetbox (*Sarcococca hookerana*) makes an excellent low plant. The sacred lily-of-China (*Rohdea japonica*) is attractive in every season. In winter, its strap-shaped leaves are a dark green and it has an interesting red fruit nestled in the center, resembling eggs in a bird's nest.

Moss is an important feature for interest in winter as well as in all seasons. Moss provides a low maintenance groundcover—requiring no mowing. Only try to create a moss garden where you find moss wants to grow—usually this is a place with wet soil that is shady. Initially, it seems labor intensive to keep it weeded, but once stabilized, a moss garden will provide rich textures and lovely year-round shades of velvety green.

Special Features

Features do not make a successful oriental garden—good garden design makes it great. Features can enhance the design but they must be incorporated with sensitivity to the space.

WATER The placement of a water feature is a key decision. If you are creating a waterfall or pond, be sure to install it near an area of activity so that you can appreciate its beauty and sounds. If the water feature or pond is further away from the house, then consider making a pavillion and terrace so that it can be used for entertaining. Within the water feature, a bridge makes a delightful addition, particularly if it goes over a stream or creek.

The inclusion of water and the sounds of water will give your garden vibrancy. Depending on your site and budget, water can be in the form of a pond, creek, waterfall, or simple garden pool. If you want to have fish, then the water will be dirty and you will need a biological filter and aquatic plants to keep it clean. Carefully placed rocks within a garden with moving water will produce pleasant gurgles, babbles, and gushes. To enjoy the sounds of water, place the water fea-

Planting around water features. *Below:* Mosses and evergreens. *Opposite top left: Ilex glabra, Liriope muscari,* and irises. *Opposite top right:* Pines and maples overhanging. *Opposite bottom left: Acer palmatum* 'Dissectum Atropurpureum', *Liriope muscari,* azaleas, impatiens, false cypress, and *Lamium maculatum. Opposite bottom right: Liriope muscari,* Christmas ferns, hostas, and heuchera.

ture close to the house so you can enjoy the water music.

Another feature always worth considering is a stone water basin. These basins are easy to install and require little space, but are significant in their representation of the water or ocean. As master Sen No Rikkyo said "When you hear the splashing sounds of the water drops that fall into the stone bowl, you will feel that all the dust of your mind is washed away."

CONSTRUCTING A WATERFALL The simplest sort of water feature to install is a boulder or group of boulders over which water can gently trickle into the pond. Choose boulders that have natural crevices to serve as water channels, and if you're using more than one, make sure that they fit together snugly to avoid backwash. Angle the boulders properly, again to avoid backwash; if you're using a flexible liner, let the boulders sit atop the liner, pulling it gently so that it surrounds the bottom, back, and sides of the rocks. The pump's tubing should be hidden behind the boulders.

Features like bridges and waterfalls add immensely to the garden, but they must be used carefully and can't be allowed to substitute for good garden design.

You can also buy a preformed fiberglass waterfall unit. These units are easy to install, but unless nature has provided you with a grade, you'll have to construct one yourself. Excavate the soil so that it fits the waterfall unit, making sure that the base is level; for a natural look (and to protect the unit against the deteriorating effects of sunlight), cover it with rocks of some sort. Both boulder and preformed waterfalls should be softened with plantings.

BRIDGES A well-placed bridge will add a wonderful sense of connection in your oriental garden. Anything that allows you to get from one side of the water to the other is a bridge, whether a series of sawn logs or stepping stones, or wooden decking or planking. In a woodland setting, consider a rustic log bridge. Bridges may be flat or slightly arched. Even if the bridge is not serving a utilitarian purpose it should always look as if it is there for a reason. It should invite visitors to

walk to the other side. In a more naturalistic setting, you might well have groundcovers softening the edges of the pond, and unless you need one for access, you probably won't want a bridge; in a formal garden the pool will most likely have a paved or constructed edge, and here a bridge will look right at home. Stepping stones will also provide a sense of connection and they, too, invite visitors to explore the garden further.

LANTERNS AND OTHER SCULPTURE A lantern provides an important focal point. Often a lantern is incorporated for the sole purpose of highlighting a specific feature of the garden. They are most at home near a waterfall or other water feature but can also be skillfully placed along a walkway. Real stone lanterns can offer a peaceful quality to an oriental garden as well as help to pull your eye to a particular place of beauty.

Pagodas or pavilions are most effective when viewed from afar. They need space and should never be jammed into a small area. They offer a quiet place for rest and reading where one can retreat from the hectic world into serene surroundings.

Lanterns, pagodas, and other sculpture often enhance a garden's design, but no one feature should be relied on to make it work. Their incorporation adds perspective to the landscape and helps to draw the eye to its different elements. Several types of lanterns exist. The Japanese Garden includes four. *Yukimi doro,* the "snow-viewing" lantern, has graceful lines that are enhanced by a covering of snow. The *kotoji doro,* or "harp tuner" lantern stands on two legs, resembling a tuning fork; this lantern is always placed with one leg on land and the other in

Above: Chinese lion. *Below and opposite page: Tachi-gati,* or pedestal lanterns. *Far right:* Stone tower. *Opposite top right:* Brightly-colored foliage in the southern Chinese style. *Opposite top left*: Raised bird feeder.

water, reflecting the interdependence of land and water. The *nure sagi* lantern, with its rather stooped and tapered shape, is said to resemble a heron standing in the rain. *Yu ki mi,* the peace lantern, was given to the City of Portland by the Mayor of Yokohama in 1945; its inscription reads, "Casting the light of everlasting peace" and its curved legs represent cat claws. The garden also boasts a beautiful 18-foot, five-story pagoda (*goju-no-to*) presented to the Garden by Portland's sister city, Sapporo, Japan.

STONE Stone is an essential ingredient in an oriental garden. Large rocks add drama to the garden. Take care to change the shape of the ground when setting a stone so that it looks natural. In other words, a rock should never simply be laid on top of the ground as this would cause it to appear "placed" rather than having occurred there naturally. Therefore, you need to exercise great patience in placing the large stones. Remember, once placed, they are almost impossible to move. Arrangements should be artistic. The creation of a pleasing rock arrangement is so important in an oriental garden that it is highly recommended you hire someone whose work you have admired to place the stones. The use of slender, droop-

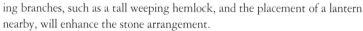

ing branches, such as a tall weeping hemlock, and the placement of a lantern nearby, will enhance the stone arrangement.

If the site is flat and you are unable to change the elevation, it is possible to place the stones to produce an illusion of elevation changes. If you dig out soil for a pool, you can take the excavated soil and use it to build up a slope for a wet or dry stream bed. Stepping stones should be used to visually connect you with the water, as well as provide acess.

In his book, *Secret Teachings in the Art of Japanese Gardens*, landscape designer David A. Slawson discusses the primacy of stone work in classical gardens. Slawson translates the carefully controlled rules devised by early masters for arranging stones. Among the 94 points are the following; material taken directly from *Secret Teachings* is noted by quotation marks.

Left: Ornate doors separate rooms at The Sun Yat Sen Classical Chinese Garden. *Below:* Natural and manmade borders and fences delineate sections in a Japanese garden.

Opposite: Raked stones represent mountains at Kennin-ji, a classical Japanese Garden near Kyoto.

• When structuring a garden, trees and stones should be regarded as structural elements; "you must consider full the relationships of Mutual Destruction and Mutual Production in respect to the Five Colors of rocks." (The five colors–blue-green, red, yellow, white, and black–are connected to the Five Elements of Chinese cosmology, and also involve the connection of directional orientation to human nature: earth=yellow=North; wood=blue-green (green dragon)=East; fire=red=South; metal=white (white tiger)=West; water=black=North). To do so, you must harmonize the client's nature with the cosmic, geological, and climatological nature of the site, and the aesthetic qualities of the material.

• When setting rocks, bear three forces in mind: horizontal, diagonal, and vertical, equivalent to the triad Heaven, Earth, and Man. "Once you have set the

triad—Heaven, Earth, and Man—and then planted an upright tree to complement it, the result is a flawless gem fit for a king."

• In places where water flows turbulently, set rocks at eccentric angles.

• Don't change the position of a rock from what it was in the mountains; "reversing" the rock, or placing it so that the part that was underneath in the mountains is now on top, is considered bad luck.

• Don't use rocks (or trees) that are exotic or showy near windows of family members.

• Rocks should work well together; do not use disharmonious rocks.

• "In setting the rocks, first of all, when you are about to set the Happiness & Prosperity Rock for the master, select with consideration for its place in the overall balance a nameless rock, so that people will not know which is which. Then, after the hole is dug, the proper mantra is invoked. Have ready about 1 *sh o* of rice (depending on the size of the garden), and when you set the named rock with the rice still in the measuring box, put it into the hole. Here again, so that people will not know it is the named rock, after you have had the hole dug for the nameless rock, put the rice while still in the measuring box into it, too, then remove the measure and put a little rice into each hole. This is done so that people will not be able to distinguish between the named rock and the nameless rock."

• Smallish rocks set in beds of white sand so that they barely protrude are called subordinate rocks. They can be set in patterns like crescents, or scattered randomly to create a quality like gently rustling leaves.

• Torii stones are set in ponds, toward the East shore, close to the Water-dividing rock. They are used in groups of three, set in horizontal triad configuration, and are flat-topped. The Water-dividing rock has diagonally sloping sides and stands in the middle of the current where the water flows into the pool.

CLASSICAL ORIENTAL DESIGN IN YOUR GARDEN The Japanese garden design principles above are part of a long tradition, passed down from master to master. A lifetime of study is necessary to master this art. Slawson lists the stages of study: viewing the work of past masters, learning from nature, apprenticeship, oral transmissions, and secrets. But the study of the work and canon of past masters cannot substitute for creativity and true understanding of nature. As garden master Matsuo Basho wrote, "Go to the pine if you want to learn about the pine, or to the bamboo if you want to learn about the bamboo. And in doing so, you must leave your subjective preoccupation with yourself. Otherwise you impose yourself on the object and do not learn."

Learning the rules and the names and shapes of rocks used by past gardeners can connect a Western gardener to a venerable tradition and culture. But It is the spirit of these masters—their willingness to meditate upon nature and themselves—that should be copied, not their work. As Slawson writes, ". . . without human purpose and deep feelings born of experience to guide their use, these design tools are worthless and may even be a curse." Placing stones or lanterns in a garden is not what connects them to the oriental traditions; the use of specific plants and other materials is not necessary. What is necessary is studying nature and whatever materials you use until you come to your own understanding of them. This is much more difficult—and much more rewarding.

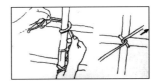

Separations are an important element of oriental gardens, both conceptually and aesthetically. Separation can be achieved with borders of plants, such as the border of cherry laurel or the backdrop of evergreens on the opposite page or with gates or fences. One popular material for fencing is bamboo. Bamboo fencing can be created from dried bamboo stalks. If you need long poles, insert one stalk into a slightly wider one. Vertical poles are inserted into the ground and horizontals are woven or tied with twine, as above.

Below: The five basic stone shapes used in oriental gardens (clockwise from top left): Low vertical, tall vertical, reclining, flat, and arching. Stones are given names according to their scenic effect (Hovering mist rock, Falling Water Rock); sensory effect (Rock of Perfect Beauty); cultural values (Master Rock and Attendant Rock; Happiness & Prosperity Rock); or use (torch-cleaning Stone). The most common composition is the triad, an archetype which appears throughout oriental philosophy and design, corresponding to the triad of Earth, Heaven, and Man. Paving stones, as in the photograph opposite, can be used to represent flowing water.

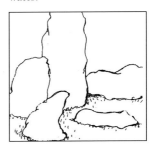

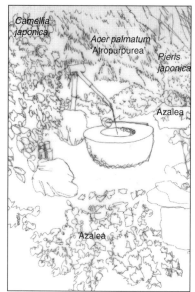

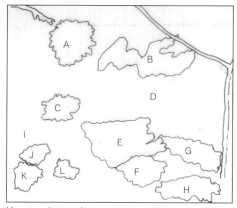

The photos on these pages show oriental garden design adapted to North American home gardens. At left, a stone basin surrounded by azaleas, camellias, pieris, and a Japanese maple creates a vivid picture in spring; in summer and fall the colors will be more muted. Above, foliage plants are carefully combined with stones in a multi-layered garden; summer color is provided by impatiens. Each garden fits nicely into a medium-sized backyard.

Key to photo above
A=*Cryptomeria* 'Bandai Suji'
B=*Acer palmatum* 'Osaka zuki'
C=*Stachys byzantina*
D=*Hedera helix* 'Glacier'
E=*Microbiota decursata*
F=*Asarum canadense*
G=*Ophiopogon japonica*
H=*Mentha pulegium*
I=*Abies* sp. (dwarf)
J=impatiens
K=*Vinca major* 'Variegata'
L=*Sedum* 'Dragon's Blood'

Plants are only one element in the oriental garden, but they are cared for meticulously. With experience, most gardeners develop their own techniques for tending their gardens; trial and error eliminates the procedures that are overcomplicated or unnecessary for a particular site and confirms those that work well. Personal style will also dictate the way a gardener works, choosing labor-intensive or time-saving methods according to his or her personal needs. But there are some basic techniques that all gardeners need to know, practices that will help assure dependable success.

ANALYZING THE SITE The first step in choosing a site for an oriental garden or border is carefully examining the entire existing plot. Is there shade, and if so what kind and how much? Is the site sunny, and if so how much sun is there and at what time of day? Does the area drain well, and if not, how wet is it and what can be done about it? Is the area flat or sloping, and if sloping to what degree? Is the soil deep or shallow, poor or rich, sandy or clayey? All these factors should be considered before you decide which elements–plants and non-plants–to include. Existing plants on the site should be accounted for by incorporating them into the plan where they are (building the garden around them), or planning for their removal. A stately oak tree may be incorporated into your new plan, but a row of scraggly shrubbery may have to be eliminated. Unwanted trees and shrubs can be relocated or removed entirely, but doing so can be time and energy consuming as well as costly.

If you are fortunate enough to have a natural feature such as water or rock outcroppings, you will probably want to plan your garden around it; these features can become interesting and integral parts of the garden. Sites that are flat to slightly sloping are easiest to work with, but a sloping area can be used to great effect, particularly if you can build steps or artificial hills into or of them. You may want your garden to unfold, winding around a complex area. A great part of oriental garden design involves using your site to its best advantage even before placing a single plant in it.

SHADE OR SUN Shade or sun is a basic consideration. Many species, particularly flowering plants, need full sun, but if well done, a shaded garden can be lovely and satisfying. Shade gardens are subtle and delicate, cool, green, quiet, and inviting. In the shaded garden, the harmonious nuances of foliage and flower color are quietly blended into a symphonic whole that appeals strongly to the senses, which are so often jaded by too much exposure to the overpowering brilliance of the full-sun garden. Because it often utilizes a natural location, the shaded garden is easier and less expensive to install than the sun garden; trees, shrubs, water, and rock are assets rather than liabilities. Maintenance is lower, for weeds do not flourish in the shade, and less watering is required.

Shade can be categorized into three types: deep shade, partial shade, and light shade. Deep shade is the condition when plants receive no direct sunlight, and the light intensity is low. This type of shade results from having a heavy canopy of trees that allows no sun to reach the ground. Year-round shade, such as that from evergreens, will further reduce the selection of plants that can be used in this type of garden. Such conifers as pine, spruce, and fir will also provide a shallow root system that will compete with perennials and further reduce plant selection. All-year shade from a wall or fence can also prohibit sun from reaching the surface of the ground, but the light intensity may be strong enough to create a greater selection of plants.

Partial shade is the condition that occurs when the plants receive direct sun for part of the day. It is important to note that the time of day, season, and area of the country will influence this type of shade. Morning or late day sun will be weaker and less intense than sun during the midday to early afternoon hours, for even sun-loving roses can perform well in only five to six hours of direct sun provided it comes during these times. The sun in the spring or fall is less intense than during the summer months, and in many northern areas plants will be able to tolerate more direct sun at the same time of day (because of decreased intensity) than sections of the South and West. In the South many perennials that are typically known as sun plants will benefit from shade during the midday in summer.

Light shade—or dappled sunlight, as it is sometimes referred to—is the condition that arises when plants receive no direct sunlight, but the light intensity is high or is the result of sun filtering through a light canopy of branches from deciduous trees. This allows a dappling of sunlight to reach the foliage of the plants, yet the sunlight moves as the branches sway in the breeze or as the sun moves in the sky. Although sun will reach the foliage, it will not be intense enough or stay in one place long enough to harm even the most shade-loving plants. This is by far the most desirable type of shade, for it allows the greatest number of species to be successful.

Sun gardens are best described as those gardens that receive at least five to six hours of direct sun during the times when sun intensity is strongest; the types of plants that can be grown under these conditions prosper because of these conditions.

SOIL Just as shade or sun can be a limiting factor in the selection of plants, soil and drainage are factors in determining which plants can be grown. Before building the garden, dig a few widely spaced 18-inch-deep test holes. These will give you a soil profile, showing the depth of the topsoil, its makeup, and the makeup of the subsoil.

For most perennials and grasses, the topsoil should be 8-10 inches deep and well drained, but for trees and shrubs, 12-24 inches of well-drained soil are not unreasonable and will actually be preferred. The condition of the soil will have to be remedied before planting if the topsoil is not at least 8-10 inches deep, or if the drainage is poor because of a hardpan layer of subsoil.

The preferred method of amending and preparing soil to be planted is by "double-digging," which consists of digging down to a depth of two spades while incorporating organic material, sometimes coarse sand. This is

To determine whether your drainage is adequate, dig a hole large enough to hold a gallon pot. Fill the hole with water, and see how long it takes to drain.

BUYING PLANTS

Signs to look for when when purchasing plants:
• Plants with the most flowers will probably continue to flower well.
• Plants should be established beyond the seedling stage and have developed into good, sturdy individuals–a minimum pot size of 3 inches is recommended.
• If the plant is a rooted cutting, it should have been pinched when young, which creates bushy and full growth, with more than a single stem.
• Foliage should be turgid (full, slightly swollen) and solid green.
• Leaves should be upright and undamaged.
• No infestation or damage by insects or disease should be evident. Pick the plant up for a close inspection.
• A potted plant should have a sturdy root system. Some buyers knock the plant out of the pot to be sure a healthy root system has been established. Often the top growth is an indicator of a healthy root system.
• Many yellow leaves at the base of a plant or roots growing out of the bottom of the pot are often an indication that the plant is pot-bound. A few roots is no problem, but many roots out the bottom is not a good sign.

a backbreaking and time-consuming task, and if possible it should be accomplished using a back-hoe–unless, of course, you need the exercise and have the time.

An extremely attractive alternative to double-digging is single-digging, which sounds like–and is–half the work. Single-digging will provide enough soil preparation except for those gardens where there is a shallow hardpan or a drainage problem. It can be accomplished by digging to the depth of one spade or by rototilling to a depth of 8-10 inches and incorporating organic material into the soil. Never add more than 2 inches of organic material to the soil at one time, for larger quantities are hard to mix into the soil–the soil and organic material will have a layer-cake look and will not mix well. If necessary or desired, more organic material can be added in subsequent diggings or rototillings.

It is important to use organic material to improve all types of soils, for it will add drainage to heavy soils and fluff up sandy or poor soils and help them retain moisture. Cow, steer, or horse manure, leaf mold, well-decomposed sawdust, peat moss, or any type of compost will give good results.

Whenever possible, after preparing the soil for planting and especially before putting in a new bed or garden, let the soil settle or age for a few months before planting. A new garden prepared in the fall should, if possible, be planted in the spring, and a garden prepared in the summer should be planted in the fall.

FERTILIZER Another important consideration in soil preparation is soil fertility. Before fertilizer is applied to the soil a soil test should be taken to determine the fertility of the soil and the pH. Most plants perform best in soils that are slightly acid to slightly alkaline, although some benefit from an acid or alkaline soil. The most common example is rhododendron, which needs an acid soil. The pH is measured on a scale of 0-14, with 7 being neutral, 0-6.9 being acid, and 7.1-14 being alkaline. A soil test will give you instructions on how to raise the pH if your soil is too acid or how to lower your pH if the soil is too alkaline. The soil test will also give recommendations as to how much of a specific fertilizer should be added per square foot to bring the fertility of the soil up to balance.

Most fertilizers have varying proportions of the three major elements needed by plants: nitrogen, phosphorus, and potash or potassium. Complete fertilizers, such as 5-10-5 or 10-6-4, contain a percentage of all three of these elements, while fertilizers such as superphosphate (0-46-0) are incomplete because they do not contain a percentage of all three elements. Overfertilization can lead to spindly plants that produce masses of foliage and few flowers.

PLANTING

Once your soil is prepared and your plan is decided upon, it's time to begin planting. As noted in Chapters 2 and 3, choose plants that will do well in the conditions you are providing them. The most common reason for a plant's failure is that it was placed in the wrong site.

1. Carefully remove existing plants.

2. Place plants on burlap or other material so that they can be moved easily, and remove to a protected spot.

If the soil in your garden does not meet your requirements, it can be amended or replaced. A soil test, which can be done at your local nursery or county extension office, will indicate what your soil needs. Amending or replacing poor soil is most easily done before starting a garden, but it can also be accomplished in existing gardens. Though time-consuming and labor-intensive, this process will contribute greatly to the health and success of your garden.

3. Remove the old soil, one or two spades deep.

4. Amend the removed soil with fertilizer, compost, or other necessary amendments, and mix well.

5. Replace plants and water generously but carefully.

PLANTING TREES AND SHRUBS When buying shrubs and trees, you can usually choose between bare-root, containerized, and balled-and-burlapped specimens. Bare-root plants should be planted only during their dormant seasons. Containerized and balled-and-burlapped specimens can be planted at any time when conditions are not harsh–the newly planted tree or shrub should not have to deal with midwinter cold or midsummer sun, especially in extreme climates. Buy plants from reputable nurseries, and make sure that they have healthy root systems before you put them in the ground. If you cannot plant your new trees immediately, store them in a cool place and water them regularly. If possible, dig a trench, lay each tree into it, and cover it with soil up to the lowest branches. Planting is a gardener's most rewarding task and also one of the most crucial. Without the right start, even the most carefully tended trees will languish. Whether the tree is bought bare-root, containerized, or balled-and-burlapped, the roots need to be kept moist before planting. The maxim is simple, but apt: if they dry, they die. When digging the planting hole, make sure it's large enough to fit the roots without crowding. Prune any crushed or damaged roots back to sound wood. Finally, be sure to plant at the proper depth; too deep is just as wrong as too shallow. The hole should be at least as wide as it is deep, and the sides should be roughed up so that the soil around the roots does not become solid. Rule-of-thumb is that the hole should be two to three times as wide as the rootball. Do not dig deeper than the bottom of the ball or the container or the tree will sink. Never dig when soil is very wet or very dry, as this will damage the soil structure.

Recent research indicates that amending soil before planting a shrub or tree is not beneficial. If the soil in and around the planting hole is richer than the surrounding soil, the roots will not leave the hole. A "potbound" effect will be created. Amend the soil only lightly.

To plant a bare-root tree or shrub: Because very little soil is packed with bare-root trees, they must be kept moist. Remove packing material, clods of earth, and broken or dead roots. Prune off dead or broken branches, and soak the plant for at least one, and not more than four hours. Mound soil in the bottom of the hole so that the center of the plant can be placed on the mound with the roots resting around it. Fill in half the soil; pack the soil firmly enough to avoid large air pockets, but not so firmly as to compact it. Water thoroughly; fill with soil; water again.

To plant a containerized tree or shrub: Containerized trees are started above ground in special plastic pots; they do not need to be dug up, and their roots are not damaged by transplanting. Remove the container (even if the manufacturer suggests leaving it on). It is important to break the rootball only if it has become potbound. Using a sharp knife or pruning shears, make cuts into the roots on all four sides of the rootball. Fluff out the roots with your fingers. Place the plant into the hole, and fill in soil.

To plant a balled-and-burlapped tree or shrub: The burlap needs to be removed halfway down the ball (entirely if it is synthetic), and all string, twine, and other packing material should be taken off. Place the plant in the hole and make sure it is at its proper depth by placing a rod across the hole; if

1. Dig a shallow hole, wider than deep.

2. Scatter fertilizer or other amendments if necessary. Recent research has shown than amending the hole causes the tree to become "potbound" within its hole.

3. Place the tree. Find the root flare, the place where the trunk of the tree hits the roots. Nurseries sometimes cover this up and you may have to remove burlap or soil. Place root flare at a point ⅓ of rootball higher than existing grade in heavy soils, level in light soils.

4. Fill in the hole.

5. Firm up the soil before you water. If you water first, you will compact the soil.

6. Create a 3- to 6-inch mound, called a berm, around the outer edge of the roots to hold water that can soak in deeply.

1. Add soil amendments as necessary–compost, leaf mold, peat moss, etc. Shovel necessary amendments on top of bed to be prepared.

2. Turn over soil, one shovel deep, incorporating amendments and breaking up any clods of soil. If you can, do this two or even three times. Soil should become loose and friable.

3. Using a steel rake, smooth and level surface of bed. Remove any stones, debris, or clods of earth.

4. Walk down the bed, firming up the earth; this prevents the soil from settling unevenly.

5. Rake smooth again, checking one more time for rocks. Smooth and grade the surface.

6. Dig the hole. Hole should be deep enough so that top of crown is even with surface of soil.

1. Carefully remove plant from container. If roots are pot-bound, tease them out a bit.

2. If necessary, add fertilizer, such as super phosphate, while preparing soil.

3. Place plant in hole. The crown should be level with the surface of the soil. A plant that is placed too deeply may develop crown rot; a plant that is not covered may become stressed from exposure.

4. With your feet, firm up soil under plant, pushing in earth that was removed.

5. With your hands, smooth out the area under the plant, removing hand- and footprints.

6. Water gently, but fully. Check plant daily several days after planting and make sure soil remains moist.

the top of the rootball is not level with the rod, put in more soil, or dig deeper. Make sure the hole is not dug too deep; if soil has been dug below the rootball it is likely to settle. Fill in remaining soil, and firm.

At some nurseries, a metal cage is placed around the rootball; in that case, make sure to cut the metal cage in many places so that the rootball is not restricted. Bend back the top of the wire cage but don't attempt to lift the tree out of the cage or to cut the cage before the tree is in the hole, as the rootball is likely to fall apart.

It is a good idea to create a 3- to 6-inch mound, called a berm, around the outer edge of the roots to hold water that can soak in deeply. When the plant is in place, water well. During the first few months (and up to two years) after establishment, check frequently to make sure that the plant is kept moist. Inserting your finger into the root zone 1-2 inches will let you know if you need to water.

PLANTING PERENNIALS Three main factors influence when to plant perennials. First and foremost are the plant's cultural requirements. For example, some perennials like irises are best when planted one to two months after they flower, for this is the time when they produce new roots. Second, and almost as important, is the region in which you live, for the gardener's spring (planting time, not calendar spring) comes earlier in the South than in the North. In the coldest areas of the North it is better to plant in the spring, for fall plantings might not have time to establish themselves if winter comes early. On the other hand, it may be preferable to plant perennials in the fall in the South, for spring planting might be stressed by the onset on an early, hot dry summer. The third factor is simply the availability of plants, for many nurseries may have only certain plants in the spring or will ship only bare-rooted perennials, such as peonies, in the fall.

Most perennials can be easily planted in the spring or early fall from either containers or bare-rooted stock. It is preferable to plant bare-rooted stock in the spring while they are dormant, just starting growth, or in the early fall, for although the foliage may be going dormant the root system will still be active well into the fall to early winter in some areas. Container-grown material can be planted with excellent success in the spring, early fall, or even in the heat of summer, but those planted in summer will require more care and may establish slower than if planted in spring or early fall.

Tough perennials like ferns or lilyturf can be successfully planted in the spring, summer, or fall. These bare-rooted perennials can even be planted when they are in flower and with a little aftercare will recover almost immediately. Knowing the conditions for the specific plant will increase the gardener's success rate.

When planting container perennials it is important to keep them at the same depth as they were in the container, but bare-rooted plants do not have the same guidelines. They should be planted to the depth where the old stems and the crown of the plant meet. Peonies and bearded iris are two of the exceptions to this rule; specific requirements for these and other plants that do not follow the general rule can be found in Chapter 2 of this book.

If the soil that has been prepared for the perennials was recently roto-tilled or dug and has not had a season to settle, it is best to "walk it down" before planting. This does not mean stomping, and it should never be done when the soil is wet (which ruins the texture of the soil by removing air spaces): simply walk over the area in your normal stride until you have covered the whole area, then rake to get it somewhat level and to remove debris, such as large stones, roots, or any other material that does not belong in the soil. Don't worry: if the soil isn't wet, and if it has been prepared with enough organic material, walking it down will not compact it.

Make the hole for the plant larger than the root area of the plant; this will give the roots room to expand. And spread the roots outward and downward; this enables the plant to establish itself quickly without choking or girdling itself by wrapping its roots around one another. Since water moves through soil in an up and down movement, spread-out roots—since they cover more area—will be able to acquire more water and nutrients. If you find that the roots of a container-grown plant have become pot-bound, tease the roots out before planting. Otherwise, they might not be able to break free of this girdling.

When you have placed the plant at the proper depth and spread out the roots, fill the hole with soil. Be sure to firm the soil around the roots to remove any large air pockets in the soil and to give the roots good contact with the soil.

The final step is to water the plant well, remembering that you cannot overwater a plant with just one watering and that a shallow watering will leave many air pockets.

MAINTENANCE

MULCHING Mulching involves covering the surface of the soil with either organic or inorganic materials. Mulching is done for several reasons. It discourages weeds, keeps the soil evenly moist, conserves water, gradually adds some nutrients to the soil (if organic mulches are used) keeps the foliage of the plants free from soil, and gives the garden a pleasing appearance (many mulches are decorative) while reducing the labor involved in weeding or frequent watering. Mulches can be organic or inorganic, but most plants perform better with organic mulches. Organic mulches decay and add nutrients to the soil, while inorganic mulches do not decay and thus do not add nutrients to the soil. Inorganic mulches like stones, gravel, pea gravel, or pebbles can be used with good effect in oriental gardens. The aesthetic effect of the mulch must be weighed against the cultural advantages.

DEADHEADING The process of removing spent flowers is called deadheading, and is important for several reasons. Many plants will rebloom if deadheaded. Deadheading also removes seed-bearing structures, eliminating unwanted

---

VIEWPOINT
MULCHING IN ORIENTAL GARDENS

We mulch with leaf mulch because it has a deep, dark color. Since plants are not typically mulched in oriental gardens, we try to keep our mulched area as small as possible.
BENJAMIN CHU,
MISSOURI BOTANICAL GARDEN

We limit our mulching because it detracts from the aesthetics of the garden; we prefer using groundcovers. In areas where mulch is beneficial, we use a hardwood bark mulch.
JIM HENRICH,
DENVER BOTANIC GARDENS

We use fine-textured wood chips, but much of the mulched area also has groundcover over it.
NANCY ROSE, MINNESOTA
LANDSCAPE ARBORETUM

We mulch to conserve moisture and reduce soil temperature in summer and extreme cold in winter. We use wood chips from the city's forestry section. If the chips are aged (or, better yet, composed), they add to the aesthetics of the garden by providing a woodland look.
HENRY PAINTER,
FORT WORTH BOTANIC GARDEN

Under large shrubs–like rhododendrons and camellias–we mulch with compost and partially composted live oak leaves. The fine texture and dark color blend fairly well and the mulch is not too noticeable.
VIRGINIA HAYES,
GANNA WALSKA LOTUSLAND,
SANTA BARBARA

Controlled irrigation saves water and protects plants.

Weeding is critical to a garden's success; it prevents unwanted plants from competing with the ones you wish to thrive.

seedlings. Seed production can stress plants, resulting in fewer blooms the following year or weaker plants. Plants will put their strength into producing stronger root systems or next year's flowers if not allowed to set seed.

Last, but certainly not least: Most plants are aesthetically more pleasing when not in seed; plants that have gone to seed can give the garden a tired appearance. Vigilant deadheading maintains a neat, healthy, fresh look.

WEEDING Although weeding is not much fun, it is important to the health of your garden. Weeds compete with other plants for nutrients, water, and sunshine; they need to be removed continually. Hand-weeding–going through the beds regularly and pulling any weeds you see–is the best approach. Try to get to the weeds before they flower and go to seed and multiply ten- or a hundred-fold. In a short time, you'll be able to recognize weed seedlings by just their first pair of leaves. If you are working with a very large area, you can hoe weeds, although with a hoe, you run the risk of damaging the fine roots of adjacent plants. The best time to hoe weeds is on a hot, sunny day; the hoed weeds will wilt and die quickly. If you hoe on a cool, damp day, a lot of the hoed weeds will reroot themselves and keep on growing.

IRRIGATING Some plants require a little extra water. You can irrigate by hand with a hose, which is very time-consuming, or you can set up various sprayers or sprinklers to cover an entire area. The advantage to overhead irrigation systems is that they cover a large amount of space quickly; the disadvantage is that they waste a lot of water. Overhead irrigation should be done on sunny days, and completed early in the day so that the plants can dry before nightfall, reducing the risk of disease caused by wet foliage. Soaker and drip irrigation use less water, but are more expensive to install and make it necessary to exercise extreme care when digging in the garden to divide or move plants. Don't irrigate so the water just penetrates the first inch of soil; irrigate so the soil is moist to a depth of perhaps 6 inches. Plants send their roots down as deeply as water is available, so deep watering will produce better-anchored plants that are less susceptible to wilting when the soil dries out (which it does from the surface first).

PROPAGATION

At some point in their lives, most plants should be propagated. There are three main reasons for propagation: To keep the plants young and vigorous; to keep overly vigorous plants in bounds; and to increase the number of plants without buying more. All methods of propagation can be grouped into two categories: sexual (or seed) production, and asexual (or vegetative). Sexual reproduction results in the production of new plants from seed while asexual reproduction is defined as reproduction using part of the parent plant–stems, roots, buds, etc.

SEXUAL (SEED) REPRODUCTION Many plants can be grown from seed. When sowing seeds indoors or outdoors, the rule of thumb is to cover the seeds with about the same amount of soil or planting medium as the seeds are thick. Extra-fine or small seeds should not be covered at all. After sowing, water the

1. Collect seeds after they have completely ripened.

2. Store them in a clean envelope; mark the envelope with the identification of the seeds and the date on which they were collected.

3. Place seeds in soil or other planting medium. Place an identification marker in the pot.

4. Cover seeds with soil or planting medium; depth of covering should be the same thickness as size of seeds. Very fine seeds can be left uncovered.

5. Water thoroughly but gently.

6. Most seeds will germinate in a few weeks at a temperature of about 60-75° F.

1. Cuttings are usually 4-6 inches long and have several sets of leaves.

2. To prevent the spread of disease, clean and disinfect all surfaces before you start.

3. Propagation supplies: rooting hormone, soil mix, cuttings.

4. After stripping off leaves, dip cutting in rooting hormone.

5. Insert the cutting into rooting medium to a depth of ⅓-½ of its length.

6. After misting, place the entire cutting-filled container into a plastic bag and seal.

seed containers or ground in which seeds have been sown gently, so as not to
wash away the seeds. If the seeds are in containers, this can be accomplished
by placing the seed container in a tray of water that is slightly shallower than
the container and letting the water percolate up from the bottom. Outdoors,
it is preferable to use a fine watering hose or water breaker, that, when
attached to a watering can or hose, gently disburses the flow of water. It is
also important to keep the seed containers out of the direct sun and to cover
them with clear plastic or glass to help keep the soil evenly moist until germination takes place. Most seeds will germinate in a few weeks at a temperature
of about 60-75° F. Some plants do not like to be disturbed and are hard to
transplant; these should always be sown in individual pots or outside in the
area in which they are to be grown. When the seedlings germinate, move the
pots into the sun or under growth lights. Light from most windows will not
be sufficient and will lead to weak, leggy seedlings. When the seedlings show
their first set of true leaves, move them from community pots into individual
pots. In a few weeks these transplanted seedlings can be transferred into a
cold frame or other protected area for the summer. In the early fall, they can
either be left in the cold frame or transplanted into their position in the garden. It is important to protect these young plants for at least the first winter.

ASEXUAL (VEGETATIVE) REPRODUCTION In most cases, it is preferable to propagate
plants by vegetative means rather than by seed. Seed-produced plants are
more or less genetically different from their parents, and although many
species do not show these differences, seedlings of hybrids or cultivated forms
will in most cases result in offspring that are not identical to the parent.
Plants that are propagated by vegetative means will, except in a very few
cases, result in offspring identical to the parent.

Vegetative propagation can be accomplished in many ways; cuttings and
division are the two most frequently used and generally the most successful
methods.

Cuttings Reproducing plants by using pieces of plants is probably the easiest
and most popular means of propagation. Chrysanthemums, sedums, and
many other bush, low-growing perennials and shrubs can be increased effi-
ciently and easily through cuttings.

Tip cuttings are 3- to 4-inch sections of leafy stems taken from nonflower-
ing side shoots that are healthy, semi-firm, and have three or four nodes.
These sections should be cut just below the bottom leaf node with a sharp
knife, razor blade, or shears. The cut section should be dipped in water, then
in a rooting hormone before being inserted into the rooting medium. A rooting hormone specific to the type of plant being propagated can be purchased
in most nurseries. Success can often be achieved without use of the hormone
with many types of vigorous plants.

Rooting mediums can be quite varied; gardeners have used washed
builder's sand, soil, vermiculite, perlite, peat, sphagnum moss, combinations
of these materials, and plain water. Many of these materials, including soil and
water, hamper root development and aftercare and should not be used. Equal

parts of peat moss and sand or perlite can be easily mixed and will be more than adequate for most cuttings; for succulent types such as sedums, which hold a good deal of moisture, a higher percentage of sand should be used to ensure proper drainage.

The medium should be moist and packed firmly before the cuttings are inserted, which will give the cuttings a firm foothold. Make a small hole in the medium with the eraser end of a pencil, a small piece of plant stake, or your finger, then press the medium firmly toward the base of the cutting. It is very important to have good contact between the base of the cutting and the medium or the cutting will dry out and die.

After the cuttings are inserted, they should be watered well, and the container they are in should be placed in an area that can provide humidity. A plastic bag with a few airholes or an empty fish tank can provide an excellent rooting chamber. After several weeks, check the cuttings to see if they are rooted sufficiently to be transplanted into individual pots. This can be accomplished by gently tugging on the cuttings; or lift one cutting out of the medium; if it does not have sufficient roots, it can be replaced in the medium and watered.

Some plants can be reproduced by root cuttings, which consist of 2- to 3-inch pieces of their fleshy roots. Take the cuttings when they are not in active growth, and place them in equal parts of peat, sand, and perlite. In a few weeks, the cuttings will have a few new sets of leaves and can be transplanted into individual containers and then into the garden or cold frame.

Hardwood cuttings Propagating deciduous trees and evergreen genera such as *Taxus, Chamaecyparis, Juniperus,* and *Ilex* from hardwood cuttings is a useful method for home gardeners since the cuttings are relatively nonperishable, easy to prepare, and require no special equipment or facilities for rooting. Unlike leafy softwood cuttings, which are prepared in spring or early summer when plants are actively growing, hardwood cuttings are made in late autumn, after defoliation but before severe winter weather has arrived.

Cutting wood is collected in the form of long, healthy, vigorous stems of the past-season's growth. These will vary in length depending on the species, and diameters will range from ¼-1 inch. In most cases, each stem will be sufficiently long to yield more than one cutting. To prepare the cuttings first remove and discard the thin terminal portion of the stem. The balance of the stem is then cut into 4- to 12-inch uniform lengths so that each cutting has at least two sets of buds. Where possible, make top cuts just above a bud and ½ inch below a bud at the base. Dust the lower inch of the cuttings with a rooting-hormone/fungicide mixture formulated for hardwood cuttings and secure with elastic bands in conveniently sized bundles. If you are making a lot of cuttings, make the bottom cut on a slant so you can easily tell top from bottom.

Pack the base of the cuttings with damp sphagnum moss and place them in a plastic bag. Seal the bag with a twist-tie and attach a label that indicates the date, name of plant, and required treatment. Store the bag at temperatures of 55-65° F for 14-21 days to promote callusing, and then place it in cold storage (the refrigerator will do) at 35-40° F until spring.

1. This large clump of daylilies is ready to be divided.

2. The entire clump can be lifted out with a spade or digging fork.

3. After lifting, insert a spading fork into the clump.

4. Insert a second fork, with its prongs between each other and using the handles as levers, pry apart.

5. Divide the roots by gently shaking and twisting the fans.

6. After reducing foliage, replant each division at the proper spacing; photo above shows peonies being replanted. Peonies, and other tuberous-rooted perennials resent being redug, and should not be divided often.

When dividing peonies and other tuberous-rooted perennials, keep in mind that three to five buds or "eyes" are needed for a flowering-size plant.

Spring planting should be done as soon as the ground is workable. Select a particularly well drained area of the garden and plant the cuttings deeply so that only one or two buds are above the soil. The location and spacing of the cuttings must be adequate to allow the plants to grow undisturbed for a year.

In mild areas, the period of cold storage may be dispensed with and the cuttings planted out directly in the autumn. For colder regions, however, this is not advisable as repeated freeze and thaw cycles during the winter and early spring will heave the cuttings from the ground.

Not all deciduous trees will root from hardwood cuttings, but for those that will–including willow and dogwood–this method provides a simple, low-cost form of propagation.

Division For most gardeners, division is both the easiest and quickest way to propagate. In the broadest of definitions, division is the splitting of one plant into two or more plants with each part having roots and stems or roots and a portion of a crown that contains buds that will become stems.

Some plants have the tendency to be overly vigorous need to be divided on a regular basis to keep them in good health and to keep them from overwhelming other weaker or less invasive plants; plants such as peonies may not need to be divided for many years. Shrubs should be divided if they begin to outgrow their bounds.

Although most plants can be successfully divided in the spring or early fall, a very loose general rule states that plants that flower in the early spring be divided in the fall and plants that flower in the fall are divided in the spring. Although both spring and fall are both acceptable times for dividing, there are people who prefer the early fall. In spring, gardeners have more tasks to complete than they do in the fall, and, more important, it is easier and less damaging to most plants to be divided in the fall. In the spring, division should take place as the plant emerges into leaf; lifting and damaging the foliage can set the plant back slightly, for it has to replace the foliage while making roots. Unexpected hot weather can also stress a plant. In the early fall, the foliage of most perennials will have started to go dormant and the plant will spend its energy to produce roots rather than foliage.

In the colder northern areas, it is preferable to divide plants in the spring or very early fall in order to give them time to establish root systems before winter. These plants should also be protected for at least the first winter.

Some plants have a more specific timetable for division. Peonies should be divided only in the fall. Daylilies can be divided in the spring, fall, or even in the summer while they are in flower. Most shrubs can be divided in spring or fall.

PRUNING

There are three basic reasons to prune a tree: to keep the plant healthy, to promote flowering and fruiting, and to shape and maintain the tree's size. Pruning for health entails the removal of dead, diseased, and weak wood; pruning for flowering and fruiting encompasses thinning, deadheading, and the removal of old wood; pruning for shape and size is essentially the selective removal of both old

To candle pines, grasp firmly and pull off the top 1/3 of the needles. This makes the plant healthier and bushier.

and new growth.

Extensive pruning of mature trees is serious business. Trees can be severely damaged by incompetent pruning, and, unfortunately it happens often. Aside from damage to the tree, pruning–particularly if done with a chainsaw, high in the tree, or anywhere near power lines–endangers the pruner's limbs and even life. We strongly recommend that arborists certified by the International Society of Arboriculture be hired for all except the most simple pruning tasks such as removing a low limb, removing dead wood, shaping young trees, and cutting off the tips of low, damaged branches. Make sure the person pruning your tree (and not just the contractor/owner) is licensed and check references.

To prune effectively and safely, you will need a few basic pieces of equipment: scissor-type (not anvil-type) hand shears (which perform a clean cut that doesn't promote a way for disease to enter plant), hedge shears (electric or manual), lopping shears (wooden-handled or steel with ratchet), a hand saw (sheathed or folding), gloves, and eye protection. Store all tools out of the reach of children, and maintain them regularly, keeping them sharp and free of dirt and moisture.

Whatever your reason for pruning, a few general caveats apply. When removing branches, cut as close to the branch collar of the main stem as possible, but do not cut into the branch collar. Leave only ⅛-¼ inch on smaller plants. Do not paint over the pruning wounds; this once-popular practice only promotes rot by providing a moist, sheltered environment for fungal organisms. Blooming trees should be pruned within two to four weeks after flowering, since next-season's flower buds will be formed on the new wood. Structural pruning can be done in winter, when the branching habit is clearly evident.

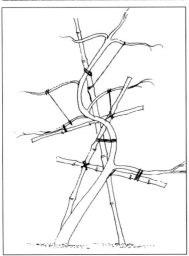

Training of conifers for oriental gardens is a specialized task but can be accomplished by a home gardener with patience. See text at right for description.

To maintain a tree's optimum health, prune regularly to remove dead, diseased, and weak wood and crossing branches. An experienced pruner will also remove branches that are growing toward the inside of the tree or the ground and weak crotches.

Two techniques encourage heavy bloom. Deadheading, the removal of spent flowers shortly after the blossoms fade, conserves the energy that would normally be spent on fruit production; it is commonly practiced on trees with profuse floral displays and nonornamental fruit, including rhododendrons, magnolias, and lilacs. Selective removal of old stems coupled with shortening and thinning of the remaining growth in early spring not only helps to maintain flowering trees, but is the key to better yield in fruiting trees.

Pruning to shape need not be daunting, especially if it is practiced regularly. To prune an ornamental tree, begin directly after planting by cutting out all dead, diseased, and weak wood. Then evaluate the branching structure and consider removing branches that overlap and rub, and those that form V-crotches that are likely to split apart; branches that have a crotch angle of less than 45° should usually be removed. Retain branch collars and keep branch stubs short (no more than ½-inch on younger trees); there should never be a stub.

Shape formal hedges twice a year, informal hedges just once; in the North, July 4 is generally considered the cut-off date for shearing. Remove one-third to two-thirds of the new growth at each pruning until the hedge nears mature size, then prune more severely. Hedges should be narrower at the top than at the base, so that adequate sunlight can reach the lower leaves. Though personal aesthetics and garden style will dictate the shape of a hedge, avoid flat-topped trees to minimize snow- and ice-load damage.

To reduce a tree's size without shearing, reach into the canopy and selectively prune branches back to a major limb, standing back from time to time to assess your progress. This method not only hides the cuts behind the remaining foliage, but gives the tree a more open and natural appearance.

Training Trees, particularly pine trees, in oriental gardens are sometimes trained to encouraged a desired form; the process is similar to training a child's teeth with braces. Untrained limbs tend to go up; training causes them to bend in curves or other shapes, or to hang over a pond.

Trees are usually trained with bamboo stakes and twine. For good results, choose young, pliant saplings and plant them in the ground at a slight diagonal angle. Prune off unwanted branches (see above). Bend the trunk to the desired curve and tie it to a bamboo pole that is driven into the ground near the tree. Next, secure horizontal poles, tying them to the pole and to horizontal branches of the tree. To avoid damaging the branches, place cloth or rubber padding between the twine and the bark. Pull some branches in front of the pole. It will take a few years before the tree is able to hold its shape on its own. During that time, candle the needles as described on the previous page and remove any unwanted branches. Once the tree is able to hold its shape, the poles may be removed, or they may be left indefinitely.

PESTS AND DISEASES

The use of the term pests and diseases can be misleading, for although we may think of pests as those members of the animal or plant kingdom that cause damage to plants we do not normally include most of the microorganisms in this definition. We normally consider pests as creatures–ranging from ants and beetles to deer and woodchucks–but weeds can also be put into this definition, as well as diseases such as bacteria, fungi, and viruses. In any case, we can categorize anything or anyone that causes damage to plants as pests and diseases. It is safe to assume that there is no way to rid the garden of all pests and diseases, but it is possible to prevent or control the level of pests and to keep them at an acceptable level.

The first step in insect control is always prevention, and prevention starts with good sanitation. Many pests such as slugs thrive in gardens that are unkempt for they hide and lay their eggs under flowerpots, weeds, wood, and wherever there is trash. Keeping the garden clean and free from weeds and trash effectively reduces the number of pests by reducing breeding and hiding spots. Removing dead or diseased foliage in the fall will have the same effect and will also reduce the number of pests for some of these pests lay eggs that overwinter on the food source–your plants.

Other insects such as whitefly are usually considered greenhouse pests but can and will prosper in the garden relatively quickly if allowed. In most cases, whitefly will be brought into the garden from infected plants, but by carefully inspecting plants that are purchased and buying pest-free plants they can be kept out of the garden.

Soft-bodied insects such as aphids, caterpillars, and slugs can be kept controlled with the use of diatomaceous earth, which is made from the ground skeletons of small fossilized animals. When spread around the plants, it forms a sharp barrier that will cut the bodies of the insects and cause them to die from dehydration. Diatomaceous earth can be expensive, but is easily available from nurseries or from swimming pool suppliers (it is used in swimming pool filters as well).

You can reduce some pests and diseases by selecting resistant species or cultivars, particularly if you know a problem is rampant in your area. Planting mildew-susceptible plants in areas that have excellent air circulation and thinning out some of the stems from crowded mature plants (which will increase air circulation) will also reduce the amount of disease.

In smaller gardens, it is possible to control certain insects by hand-picking or crushing them while wearing cotton gloves so as not to damage the plant. Slugs are easy to pick off, on a damp summer night, and aphids can be easily crushed by hand. Shallow trays of stale beer will attract and kill slugs. Aphids can be sliced off plants with a heavy stream of water that can be controlled by placing your thumb over the end of a hose, and a light, frequent syringing will also help control red spider mites, which do not like water.

YUKI ZURI (SNOW HANGING)

Yuki zuri is a technique designed by the Japanese centuries ago to protect their pine trees and other evergreen and specimen trees from heavy snows and ice during the winter months. A stout pole, one-third longer than the height of the tree, is sunk into the ground, with each length tied to a branch for support. The finished treatment looks like a maypole, with streamers haning down from the top, each one tied to a different branch. It has been said that to make a tree beautiful using this technique, at least 16 ropes must be used, coming from a central knot at the top, which may be adorned with decoration at the discretion of the garden designer.

In Japan, rice-straw twine is used; at the Portland Japanese Garden, nylon ropes are used and then stored for the next year. In parts of Japan where heavy, wet snow falls, *yuki zuri* is a necessity, but in Portland and other warmer areas, this technique is used only to symbolize a winter snow scene.

1, 2, 3. Once you've chosen a site, you'll need to mark out your pool's projected shape (unless you're installing a pre-formed liner). If you're constructing a geometric pool, use string and stakes as a guide. For irregular or naturalistic shapes, a garden hose or length of clothesline works best. When you're satisfied with the shape you've outlined, begin digging. Then remove about 2 inches of soil all around to make a permanent outline; you can remove the hose, clothesline, or string and stakes at this point.

CREATING A WATER FEATURE

Water is an important element in an oriental garden. If you are not lucky enough to have a natural water feature in your garden, you can construct one. Until recently, that meant pouring concrete, which was quite expensive. Now, plastic liners and preformed pools are available; using them, you can build a nice-sized pool for several hundred dollars in about a weekend.

CHOOSING YOUR POOL MATERIAL If you do decide to go with concrete, it's best to leave the work to a professional unless you have some experience with it. If you opt for a liner, you have two basic choices: preformed pools (generally constructed of rigid fiberglass) or flexible liners (the two basic types being laminated PVC and butyl rubber). Preformed pools are inexpensive and easy to install, and are available with built-in shelves for marginal aquatics. Unfortunately, they're limited as to depth and shape, and aren't nearly as long-lived as their flexible counterparts. Flexible liners, though just slightly more work to install, last far longer (ten to fifteen years for PVC and perhaps 40 or more for rubber) and are easier to repair. PVC costs about half what you'd pay for butyl rubber, but it will probably need to be replaced in under two decades.

STAKING OUT THE SHAPE Once you've chosen a site you'll need to mark out your pool's projected shape (unless you're installing a preformed liner). If you're constructing a geometric pool, use string and stakes as a guide. For irregular or naturalistic shapes, a garden hose or length of clothesline works best. Generally, in terms of design and ease of installation, the simpler the shape the better.

EXCAVATING THE SITE First, decide how you're going to dispose of the earth you dig up—it can be quite considerable, even from a small pond. Then remove about 2 inches of soil all around to make a permanent outline; you can remove the hose, clothesline, or string and stakes at this point. Continue digging, allowing the sides to slope at a gentle 20° angle. If you plan on building in any edges for marginals, excavate for them as well; you can place a 9-inch-deep edge 9 inches below the rim and, if you like, another one 9 inches below that. To make sure that the perimeter is level, place a carpenter's level atop a long, straight board laid across the length of the pool. When you've finished digging your hole, remove sharp objects and line the bottom with an inch or so of damp sand; sloping edges can be lined with old carpeting, geo-textile fabric, or even thicknesses of newspaper.

INSTALLING A FLEXIBLE LINER Lay the liner out loosely over the hole, weighting the sides down with bricks or heavy stones. If possible, let the sun warm it for a few hours before proceeding, so the material is more malleable. Don't bother trying to press the liner down into the hole; the water will do that. Fill the shell slowly, in 4- to 5-inch increments, backfilling with soil around the edges and tamping them firmly. Don't stop filling until water has reached the rim of the shell.

EDGING Whatever the style and form of your pool, you'll want to provide some sort of edging. If you use a preformed or flexible liner, the edging will disguise the exposed lining material, and protect it from damaging sunlight. In a more formal pool, where the edging is likely to be paved and geometric, you'll need to lay down a foundation. A naturalistic pool is easier to edge. You can simply place your edging material, whether it be rocks or other material, in an informal, random-looking pattern so that it disguises the pool edge. Make sure, however, that the material you use has no sharp edges and the edging is sturdy, wedging it into the soil slightly if possible. You may also want to bring your garden right up to the water, in the form of flowers, groundcovers, or even grass.

CONSTRUCTING A POOL WITH A FLEXIBLE LINER

4. Continue digging, allowing the sides to slope at a gentle 20° angle. If you plan on building in any edges for poolside plants, excavate for them as well; you can place a 9-inch-deep edge 9 inches below the rim and, if you like, another one 9 inches below that.

5. To make sure that the perimeter is level, place a carpenter's level atop a long, straight board laid across the length of the pool. Remove any sharp objects that could possibly puncture the liner.

6. Sloping edges can be lined with old carpeting, geo-textile fabric, or even thicknesses of newspaper.

7. Line the bottom with an inch or so of damp sand.

8. Lay the liner out loosely over the hole, weighting the sides down with bricks or heavy stones. Don't bother trying to press the liner down into the hole; the water will do that.

9. Fill the shell slowly, in 4- to 5-inch increments, backfilling with soil around the edges and tamping them firmly. Don't stop filling until the water has reached the rim of the shell. You're now ready to add your edging.

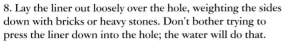

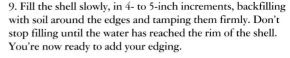

Above: **Flowering azalea.**
Top: **White pine.**

BONSAI

The ancient art of bonsai comes to us from many centuries of Japanese and Chinese tradition. In the usual form, a single tree or group of trees is grown in a decorative shallow pot and trained as a miniature version of a naturally occuring plant or landscape. Training a plant to achieve this look allows the gardener to have a part of the mountains or seashore or a spectacular old plant to contemplate and appreciate in a very small area such as a tea or courtyard garden.

Bonsai are designed according to time-proven principles, and the art has evolved five classic styles: formal upright, informal upright, slanting, semi-cascading, and cascading. The plant is trained with traditional design according to the attributes of the individual plant.

Bonsai involves elaborate and time-consuming pruning and training, beginning when a plant is very young. Although there are very old bonsai in homes and museums that are maintained by bonsai specialists and masters, an attractive bonsai specimen can be developed in only a few years. The goal is to produce a plant with the illusion of being very old, specifically by developing a rugged and gnarled trunk as the focal point.

Although the trunk is the main focus of a bonsai specimen, the size, shape, and placement of branches as well as the size of the leaves and the configuration of the surface roots are also important. These features are developed by extensive clipping, pruning, root pruning, and branch wiring.

Bonsai are produced from deciduous or evergreen plants from tropical or temperate climates. Those from temperate climates, such as junipers, must be wintered outdoors to give the plant the conditions it requires. Tropical bonsai such as serissa, on the other hand, can be kept indoors year-round or summered outdoors.

When creating a bonsai specimen, select a plant that has a sturdy interesting trunk and some roots of good size. Many bonsai aficionados haunt nurseries and garden centers, and bargain for junipers, arborvitae or other plants that have been damaged and are no longer salable as landscape plants. The plant's branches are initally pruned and shaped, and then the roots are pruned to compensate for the extensive loss of foliage and branches. The plant's root ball is then wired into its shallow pot which is filled with soil. Moss is planted on the soil to resemble a natural landscape.

The branches are shaped by wrapping them in annealed copper wire which is quite malleable and hardens once in place. The wires are left in place for several months, at which time the branch should remain in place after the wires are removed.

A bonsai must be groomed weekly to keep it healthy and attaractive. When grooming, remove dead or discolored leaves or flowers, slip off suckers or shoots arising from the main trunk, and remove any oversized leaves. New growth should be pruned by about half. Use this time to inspect carefully for insect or disease problems, and rotate the plant at one-quarter turn to keep it full on all sides. Because a bonsai has only the small amount of soil in the container from which to obtain water and nutrients, the gardener must provide them regularly. In spring and summer, plants may need to be watered three or four times a day if they are in small containers and rain is scarce. The gardener must pay careful attention to the plant's needs and water when it is needed rather than on a static schedule. Watering will vary depending on soil mix, type of plant, weather and size of container. Incorrect watering is a common cause of bonsai death.

Fertilization is usually done with every watering in spring through summer with a solution that is one-quarter to one-eighth the strength recommended on the fertilizer label. A complete fertilzer such as 10-10-10 is adequate unless the plant is specifically being grown for flowers or fruit. In this case, choose a fertilizer that is high in phosphorus such as 5-10-5. It is critical that a bonsai not be over-fertilized since the roots are extremly susceptible to burning if too high a concentration of fertilizer is used.

Most bonsai, whether tropical or temperate, benefit from a summer outdoors. In oriental gardens, specimens are placed by themselves on a table or pedestal to allow contemplation and enhance proper viewing from all sides. They should be placed where air can circulate freely all around the plant and its container. Bonsai are occasionally brought indoors in summer for viewing, but should only remain indoors for a few days. Temperate plants such as juniper and pine will not survive more than a few days.

Outdoors, most types of bonsai thrive in full sun, but tropical bonsai should be carefully acclimated before being taken outdoors. In winter, tropical bonsai must be brought indoors and given a place with high light and good air circulation. In cold climates, temperate bonsai should be allowed to go naturally dormant through the fall and then put into storage before cold weather hits. Plants are most easily stored in a cold frame with mulch under and around the plant. Plants should be kept at 25-32° F and checked periodically during the winter for water needs.

In spring, bring the plant out of storage gradually by moving it into an unheated garage or storage area. Water well and check often–plants coming out of domancy may need water twice a day. This is also the time to do a spring pruning if necessary.

When purchasing a trained bonsai plant, be certain of its identity so that you can provide the conditions it requires. Bonsai are becoming increasingly available in garden centers and florists; the gardener should take into consideration the amount of time and care necessary in order to maintain a healthy plant.

Above and below: **Bonsai at The National Arboretum.**

SOME SOURCES
American Horticultural
Therapy Association
 362A Christopher Avenue,
Gaithersburg, Maryland 20879
800-634-1603

Canadian Horticultural Therapy
Association
c/o Royal Botanical Garden
PO Box 399, Hamilton,
Ontario, Canada, L8N 3H8
416-529-7618

ENABLING GARDENS

Being forced to stop gardening is one of the worst fates that can befall a gardener, but the inability to get down on one's hands and knees owing to arthritis, a bad back, a heart problem, the need to use a wheelchair–or the normal aches, pains, and fatigues of advancing age–is no reason to stop gardening. By using a few different gardening techniques, modifying tools, following new criteria in plant selection, and tapping into the many resources for information and help, no one ever has to stop gardening.

Begin by thoroughly and frankly assessing your situation.
•How much time can you devote to gardening?
•Do you need crutches, a cane, or wheelchair to get around?
•Can you get up and down from the ground without assistance?
•How much sun or heat is wise for you?
•Can you bend at the waist easily?
•Is your coordination impaired? balance? vision? ability to hold tools?

Consult your doctor, occupational or physical therapist, and most importantly speak to a horticultural therapist.

Horticultural therapists are specially trained in applying horticulture in therapeutic programs for people with disabilities and older adults. They have developed specialized gardening tools and techniques that make gardening easier for every situation.

Once you've decided how much you can and want to do, the garden can be planned. For example, people with relatively severe mobility impairments should have firm, level surfaces an easy distance from the house and should use containers or raised beds to bring soil up to a comfortable working height–usually somewhere around 2 feet high with a maximum width of 30 inches if worked from one side and 60 inches if both sides of the container or bed are accessible. People with more mobility can work with easily worked, light soils mounded to 8-10 inches above grade and should use lightweight, long-handled tools. Smaller containers can be hung within easy reach on poles or fences, and an overhead structure can be used to support hanging baskets on ropes and pulleys so the baskets can be lowered for care and then replaced to an out-of-reach position.

Important considerations when planning the garden layout include:
•Start small: keep it manageable
•Use or create light, easily worked soils so less force is required to work them either by hand or with tools
•Keep all equipment and tools in accessible places
•Arrange for a nearby water source.

ORGANIC GARDENING

Few gardeners today are unaware of the devastating effect pesticides and other chemicals used in the past have had on our environment. Rachel Carson's searing exploration of the subject, *Silent Spring* (1962), exposed the "needless havoc" wrought by products designed to promote healthy plants. Not only were the chemicals poisoning our environment, they were also killing the natural predators of the pests we were seeking to destroy, making it impossible for nature to come to its own defense.

In the past few decades a vast and successful effort has been made to find new ways to garden without using harmful chemicals. The approach is directed at the soil and at the measures taken to control pests.

The soil is built up through the addition of organic materials, especially compost. The addition of compost, homemade or store-bought, and other organic material such as peat moss, green cover crops, and bone meal makes the soil so fertile and productive that petrochemicals are not needed.

Pest problems are handled through a practice called Integrated Pest Management (IPM), developed by the Council on Environmental Quality. IPM is defined as "maximum use of naturally occurring pest controls, including weather, disease agents, predators, and parasitoids. In addition, IPM utilizes various biological, physical, chemical controls and habitat modification techniques. Artificial controls are imposed only as required to keep a pest from surpassing tolerable population as determined from accurate assessments of the pest damage potential and the ecological, sociological, and economic costs of the control measures." In other words, gardeners must make reasonable assessments of how much damage a particular pest will do. If the pest is just munching on foliage, let it be. If controls must be taken, nonharmful ones should be tried first. Only in extreme cases is chemical warfare waged–and then in the most nonharmful ways possible.

The weapons in the IPM arsenal include:

•Careful monitoring to identify problems before they become widespread.

•Beneficial insects, such as ladybugs, praying mantises, and some nematodes, which feed on garden pests. Some of these reside naturally in your garden; others can be bought and placed there.

•Bacteria such as Bt (*Bacillus thuringiensis*) that attack garden pests. These bacteria can be bought by the pound and dusted on the plants; strains have been discovered that breed and attack many common pests.

•Insecticides such as rotenone, pyrethrum, and sabadilla and insecticidal soaps.

•Pest-repellent plants such as marigolds, which repel bean beetles and nematodes, and garlic, which repels whitefly.

•Hand-picking pests off foliage wherever they are seen in small numbers.

See Techniques, Chapter 4 for more information on pest control.

Oriental greens, like mizuna mustard greens (top) and 'Tatsoi' (above) are attractive and tasty, raw or cooked. They are cool-season crops; provide plenty of water and fertilizer.

GROWING ASIAN VEGETABLES

Since Asian vegetables are often expensive and difficult to find in most markets, those who appreciate their distinctive taste are amply rewarded by growing their own. North American gardeners find that growing Asian produce is relatively simple, with cultivation similar to that of more familiar Western varieties. The chief difference may be that the plants look more exotic–in fact, most make handsome ornamentals. Seed can be obtained through specialty catalogs (see page 219).

Brassica (cabbage) family. Among the best-known of these are Chinese (or Napa) cabbage, michihli, or chihli (green Chinese cabbage) and celery cabbage (or bok choy). Generally, these are short-day growers–summer days cause them to go to seed too quickly—so they're best grown in spring and fall. But the faster they are grown, the better their taste and appearance: enrich the soil beforehand with a high-nitrogen organic fertilizer, like well-rotted manure. Sow seed directly (about 1/2-inch deep, and 3-4 inches apart) in early spring (after danger of frost) or late summer. Keep seeds and plants amply watered. Thin young plants to 10 inches apart (18 for the Napa) and use the thinnings in salads. Side-dress with more manure after four weeks, adding a liquid fertilizer every two weeks. The chief pest is the cabbageworm: surround the patch with onion, garlic or tansy. Michihli doesn't store well, but the Napa and bok choy can last for weeks if harvested roots and all, buried in straw, and kept in a cool, dark place.

Chinese cucumber Prolific like its Western relative, but notably longer (6-36 inches), the Chinese cucumber should be planted early in the spring as soon as the soil warms up; it can bear until frost. Sow directly (1-inch deep) in humusy loam, preferably with a pH below 6.5 (add limestone or phosphorous if the soil is too acid). Thin to 1 foot apart. Unless a curly shape is desired, grow along a fence, trellis, or chicken wire on a frame: train the vines up, and gravity will pull the fruit straight. Chinese cucumber is highly resistant to disease, but requires lots of water to avoid a slight bitterness in taste. Otherwise, the cukes get sweeter as they grow larger.

Japanese eggplant (Nasu). This small, delicate eggplant needs full sun, plenty of water, and good drainage; the Japanese grow them on hills separated by trenches, which keep the sensitive roots from being trampled. Since the plants take three months to produce, and need hot days and warm nights, start seed indoors in peat pots in March, harden in a cold frame in April, and plant (15-18 inches apart) against a sunny wall after the last frost. Early growth will seem slow; pick off the first few flowers to strengthen the plant. Apply a potassium-rich fertilizer (use fish fertilizer in late summer) and a light mulch. Harvest the fruit when 6 inches long, before the shiny skin dulls.

Melons The distinctive bitter melon is grown like other melons: in warm, nitrogen-rich soil, with copious amounts of water and fertilizer–plus a long season. Train the vine on a fence or trellis. The fruit is least bitter when harvested before it reaches six inches long; if it loses its green color, it is too bitter to eat. The winter melon is cultivated in a similar way, except that, since its fruit can weigh 25 pounds, dry mulch should be piled to raise the fruit off the ground. Ripeness (after about 150 days) is denoted by a waxy white coating. It can be stored almost six months in cool, dry place.

Shungiku (Garland Chrysanthemum) This tasty green finds its way into many popular Japanese dishes, and is easy to grow as a cool-weather vegetable, like spinach. Seed in a cold frame in February or outdoors (1/4 inch deep) later in ordinary soil. It tolerates partial shade–even prefers light shade in summer. Thin to 4 inches apart, weed and water. After six weeks, when the leaves are 5 inches long, harvest either the whole plant or just the tender side leaves. Nip flower buds to retain tenderness and mild taste. Sow every few weeks for a continuous supply, and let some go to seed for next year.

Snow pea The chief difference from the garden pea is the lack of a parchment lining to its pod, which makes it edible. Cultivation is similar: it prefers cool weather and a moist, well-composted, slightly acidic soil. Soak seed overnight and mix with a legume innoculant to speed growth. Sow (March-May, and after mid-August) 1-2 inches deep along a trellis; thin to make the patch thick but not crowded. Weed constantly. After 60 days, expect the first of two harvests. For tastiest results, pick pods in early morning or cool evenings.

Vegetable soybean One of the most sacred foods in Chinese civilization, the soybean comes in many varieties and colors, from the sweet black type used in desserts to the more common green type. Most prefer a climate suitable for corn: hot and dry. Cool, wet weather is its chief problem, fostering bacterial blight and mildew. Start seed in late spring, in a light, loamy soil (rich soil is better than adding fertilizer later, which can slow maturity). The typical growing season is 100 days, although newer varieties deliver in 85-90.

Other beans The most commonly used beans for sprouts are adzuki beans and mung beans. The adzuki is grown like the typical green bean. Although it requires 120 days to full maturity (dried in the pod), it can be eaten immature like a green bean. The mung is exceptionally prolific, matures in 90-120 days, and can be used when young like a snow pea. To grow bean sprouts, fill a wide-mouthed jar about one-quarter full with the dried beans. Cover with a screen or cloth. Fill with clear, tepid water and drain immediately; repeat rinse two or three times a day. Keep in a dark place. The sprouts will be ready in three to six days.

Oriental vegetables that have become popular in the United States include cabbages, eggplants, beans, and bitter melons.

Above: Balsam, prepared for use.
Right: The University of California Berkeley Botanical Garden Chinese medicinal herb garden.

GROWING ORIENTAL HERBS

Many of the herbs used in oriental cooking are easy to grow and common in herb gardens. Mints, Chinese parsley (also called coriander), hot peppers, ginseng, Japanese parsley (mitsuba), many forms of garlic and chives, mustard, fennel, and basil are among the most popular herbs for cooking and all perform well in temperate regions. An herb that is somewhat new in the North American market–though it's been used in salads in Japan for a long time–is perilla, also called shiso or beefsteak plant. Perilla–particularly the purple-leaved forms–is also grown as an ornamental plant. Japanese horseradish (wasabia) needs to be grown near gently flowing spring water. One good source for oriental herb and vegetable seeds is Sunrise Enterprises, Box 1960, Chesterfield, Virginia 23838 (Telephone: 804-796-5796; Fax: 804-796-6735).

Chinese Medicinal herbs is another specialty, borrowing on centuries-old traditions; traditional Chinese medicine is one of the world's oldest systems of medical care. Chinese medical philosophy is based on the Taoist principle of yin and yang, the interdependence of qualities of change and relationship in the universe. Yang qualities are light, warm, active, external; yin are darkness, cold, rest, internal. When a person is sick, these qualities are out of balance; balance must be restored in order for the person to be cured. There are five pathogenic factors in Chinese medicine: cold, wind, damp, heat, and summer heat (sunstroke). These effects occur on 12 meridians (e.g., yin, yang, kidney, liver, lung, small intestine), the points used in acupuncture.

Health conditions are determined by the qualities of Chi, both internal (breath) and external (spirit). Chi moves along the meridians in the body, and when it is blocked, sickness occurs. Treatment can restore health by strengthening these weak and blocked areas. Typically, a Chinese doctor will prescribe nine to fifteen herbs, that area boiled into teas. Since they are holistically balanced, there are no side effects. Herbs used for illness occur in function groups; some herbs fit into more than one function group. Some function groups:

Surface-relieving herbs treat chills, fever, muscle aches, sweatings; these herbs are diaphoretics that induce sweating.

Purging herbs stimulate the gastrointestinal tract for excretion to expel toxins. Clearing heat herbs treat fever conditions, including red face and dry throat.

Fragrant herbs for dissolving wetness are usually acrid, warming, and drying; they are used in cases of food poisoning and other digestive disorders.

Herbs for regulating *Chi* are used for pain in the chest and abdomen.

Herbs for regulating blood are used to stop bleeding or invigorate the blood.

Herbs for removing congestion increase digestive secretions for better digestion.

Many other function groups, including anti-cancer and parasite-destroying herbs exist as well. Many parts of the plant are used: seeds, stem, bark, root, fruits, flowers, leaves, or sometimes the whole plant. Herbs commonly used include:

Mint (*Mentha* sp, haplocalyx) is a surface-relieving herb; leaves are used to treat fever, headaches, rashes, and sore throats. Grow mints in full sun or partial shade in an average soil; water regularly. To prevent invasiveness, place mints, pot and all, in the ground.

Garlic (*Allium sativum*) is used for destroying parasites. The root is used to kill worms, dysentery, and abscesses. It grows easily in full sun in a rich, well-drained soil.

Rose (*Rosa rugosa*) regulates Chi. The flowers are used for irregular menstruation, belching, gastric pain, and poor appetite. This is an easy rose to grow in any soil ion full sun and is very disease resistant. 'Frau Dagmar Hartopp' is a good cultivar for small gardens, with clear pink flowers.

Fuyu persimmon (*Diospyros kaki* 'Fuyu') regulates *Chi*. The fruit is used for hiccoughs, bleeding, hemorrhoids, diarrhea, and dysentery. This is an easy small tree for full sun and provides fantastic fall color. It takes a few years before it fruits.

Joint fir (*Ephedra sinica*) is a surface-relieving herb. The stems are used for fever, headache, lack of sweat, coughing, and wheezing. It will grow in sunny locations in even the poorest of soil. Though slow to get started, it will become established in even the hardest sites in two years; drought tolerant.

Self-heal (*Prunella vulgaris*) is used for clearing heat. Flowers are used to treat enlarged lymph nodes, eye pain, headache, and dizziness. It will grow in any garden soil, in shade or sun. The species is somewhat weedy, so buy a clone selected for pink, white, or magenta flowers.

Madagascar periwinkle (*Catharanthus roseus*) is an anti-cancer herb also used for insomnia and high blood pressure. Grow in full sun or in part shade in hot climates; it needs little care once established. Grow as an annual above Zone 8.

JERRY PARSON, UNIVERSITY OF CALIFORNIA, BERKELEY BOTANICAL GARDEN

Top: Lillium brownii, brown's lily, is used in Chinese medicine.
Center: Crocus is the source of saffron.
Above: Allium sativum, Chinese chives.

SMALL SPACE GARDENS

Many of us have small spaces in which oriental elements can be incorporated in addition to or in place of a full-scale oriental garden. Courtyards are an essential part of oriental gardening, and the elements of the courtyard garden can be easily adapted for use on a patio, balcony, rooftop or small city lot.

The key to developing an effective small-space garden is planning. A larger garden allows the gardener to experiment and move plants around fairly freely, but a small-space garden doesn't afford that opportunity as easily. Planning carefully will assure that the garden achieves an elegant, refined look with every element essential to the overall design.

A small garden can be lush or sparse, depending on the gardener's taste. Whatever the design, it must not look cluttered or it will not be inviting. Plan only one or two focal points, either plants or non-plant elements, and carefully decorate around them. Colors are best kept subdued, with shades of blues, grays and greens dominant. Use a burst of color only as a focal point, such as a red-leaved Japanese maple tucked amidst foliage plants and granite stones. Most importantly, keep the scale of the garden in mind. On a small balcony, use only small containers or one large container planted with diminutive plants. For height in a courtyard, use a vine on a trellis or growing up a wall rather than a tall tree that also takes up a lot of room. Bonsai are often used as focal points, although a small interesting mugo pine in a container will give the illusion of bonsai without the work.

Container Gardens An oriental-style courtyard that has no planting beds can be beautifully graced with a cobalt blue glazed jardiniere containing a berry-laden holly or a rustic cedar box planted with an angular amur maple. Container gardens provide a garden in areas that are unplantable such as on patios, balconies or small courtyard gardens. They offer a chance for creative expression and landscape diversity, hide unattractive features, and even provide special accommodations for tender, fussy plants that need special conditions. The gardener can introduce color changes or change the entire look of the landscape merely by moving containers around. Container gardens are always maintenance-intensive. The plants cannot draw nutrients and moisture from the surrounding soil, so gardeners must be attentive to their needs.

Careful attention to scale and composition allow the hollies, agaves, and grasses in this small garden to form a pleasing whole.

ORIENTAL GARDENS IN COLD CLIMATES

Developing and maintaining a successful Oriental garden in upper midwestern United States or any other cold region presents special challenges. While many of the non-plant items—such as rocks, water features, and sculpture—can be used in any environment, many of the traditional plant materials are not hardy above Zone 6. The Minnesota Landscape Arboretum in Chanhassen, Minnesota is in USDA Zone 4a, where average minimum temperatures are -25 to -30° F. Since many of the plants commonly used in oriental gardens would not survive winter here, we have found substitute plants with similar forms and design aspects that are more cold-tolerant.

Perhaps the most obvious example is Japanese maple (*Acer palmatum*). This beautiful small tree is a mainstay in many oriental gardens, but it is hardy only to Zone 5 at best. In our Japanese garden, we use amur maple (*Acer ginnala*), an attractive multi-stemmed small tree that is also extremely hardy. While not quite as graceful as Japanese maple, amur maple provides fragrant flowers, red-tinged samaras (fruits) in summer, and brilliant red fall color.

Flowering dogwoods (*Cornus florida, C. kousa*), noted for their showy spring displays of white flower bracts, are not hardy here either. Instead, we rely on the native pagoda dogwood (*C. alternifolia*). The distinct horizontal branching habit of this lovely small tree is ideally suited to an oriental setting. Though now as showy in bloom as flowering dogwoods, pagoda dogwood's panicles of small, cream-colored flowers provide floral interest and sweet fragrance in the spring and its foliage turns a nice burgundy-maroon in the fall.

Hardy flowering shrubs are also used in the arboretum's Japanese garden. Star magnolia (*Magnolia stellata*) and Nanking cherry (*Prunus tomentosa*) are both large shrubs that are pruned to smooth, rounded forms. Both produce white flowers in spring. Meyer lilac (*Syringa meyeri*) is used extensively; groups of these small-leaved lilacs are pruned to form undulating organic masses. Hardy azaleas and rhododendrons provide the brightest spots of spring color in our Japanese garden. The deciduous "Northern Lights" series developed by the University of Minnesota are bud hardy to at least -35° F. We also use small-leaved evergreen rhododendrons like as 'PJM' and 'Purple Gem'.

The plant feature that seems to surprise visitors most is a stand of yellow-groove bamboo (*Phyllostachys aureosulcata*) near the garden entrance. This bamboo usually dies in our cold climate each winter, but sends up new green shoots each spring. The leaves tend to stay on the canes through most of the winter, adding visual and aural interest as they rustle in the wind. Near the small tea house, a planting of fernleaf buckthorn (*Rhamnus frangula* 'Aspenifolia') provides an airy texture similar to bamboo.

Given our 45 inches of snow each year, the garden's snow-viewing lantern lives up to its name. The granite lantern's broad, umbrellalike top is often capped with snow for four months straight. Snow also decorates the horizontal branches of the trained Japanese red pines, pagoda dogwoods, and redbuds, adding texture and depth to our winter landscape.

ORIENTAL GARDENS IN WARM CLIMATES

Many regions of the orient are warmer than temperate North America. This means that gardeners in the Southern and Southwest and in the warmer areas of the Pacific Northwest have the opportunity to create some dazzling and authentic effects that are impossible for Northern gardeners.

Among the most effective plants for oriental gardens is the palm. These graceful plants need little care if they are properly sited; what they do need is plenty of sun and water. Among the species commonly used are coconut palm (*Cocos nucifera*) and lady palm (*Rhapis* sp.). Lady palm is also used indoors for traditional bonsailike arrangements. Cycads, among the oldest plants on earth, are wonderful accents in oriental gardens; their huge, ferny leaves undulate slowly, creating the movement that is needed in oriental gardens. Grasses like *Ophiopogon* sp. (mondo grass) will not overwinter north of Zone 7, but are used to great effect in the South. Banana shrubs, particularly when combined with bamboos, are excellent accent plants; their paddle-shaped leaves contrast beautifully with the delicate foliage of the bamboo.

Bamboo is another group of plants where gardeners in warm climates have an advantage. Although a few species of bamboo are hardy in the North, the selection of both tall and groundcover varieties is much fuller in warm zones (see page 152) and most bamboos grow more quickly and lushly in warm regions. However, gardeners must control the plant's invasive tendencies.

Warm-climate gardeners are at a disadvantage when it comes to conifers; several of the best pines do not perform well in warm regions. But many substitutes, like cedars, cypresses, and the exotic podocarpus can fulfill the need for evergreens. Fall color, while never as brilliant as in the North, can be provided by ginkgos, catalpas, and sycamores.

The Japanese Garden at Ganna Walska Lotusland in Santa Barbara, California.

The following Japanese words are often used in reference to gardens

ayasugi, sugi: cryptomeria

biwa: loquat

cha-no-yu: tea ceremony

chi: earth

daimyo: lords of the edo era

dobei: earthern wall

fuji: wisteria

fukki: happiness

fukkiseki: happiness and prosperity rock

go-gyo: Chinese concept of five evolutionary phases of earth, wood, fire, metal, and water

gosho: august place

hinoki: hinoki cypress

ikebana: art of flower arranging

hojo: abbot's quarters

kare: dry

kare-sansui: dry garden

kunseki: master rock

matsu: pine

mire gakure: hide and reveal

misu-gaki: sleeve fence

mizutamari-ishi: water-collecting rock

nashi: pear

nishiki koi: brocaded carp

niwa-shi: garden masters

roji: path

sakura: Japanese cherry

san-sui: mountain and water

seki tei: sand and stone garden

sekka: snow

shakki: borrowed landscape

shime-nawa: ropes around a Shinto sacred area

shion: aster

shiragiku: white chrysanthemum

shishi odoshi: deer scare, bamboo pipe in a stone water basin

shoji: paper doors

shukeiyen: natural garden

tachi-gate: pedastel lantern

take: bamboo

taki: waterfall

ten: heaven

teppo-gaki: pipe fence

tobi-ishi: stepping stones

tsubaki: camellia

tsukubai: water basin

tsutuji: azalea

ume: Japanese apricot

yamazakura: wild cherry

yanagi: willow

yarai-gaki: stockade fence

yatsuhashi: eight bridges

yotsume-gaki: bamboo lattice fence

yuki zuri: snow hanging

yukimi-gata: snow-viewing lantern

Acid soil: Soil with a pH level below 7

Alkaline soil: Soil with a pH level above 7

Annual: A plant whose life cycle comprises a single growing season

Anther: The part of a flower that bears pollen

Axil: The angle formed by a stem and a leaf stalk

Balled-and-burlapped: Describing a plant that is ready for transplanting, with a burlap-wrapped soil ball around its roots

Bare-root: Describing a plant that is ready for transplanting, with no protective soil or burlap covering around its roots

Bipinnate: Having leaflets that are divided into second leaflets

Bract: A modified leaf below a flower, often showy, as in dogwood

Calcaceous: Containing calcium or calcium carbonate (lime), as soil

Cane: A long, often supple, woody stem

Capsule: A dry fruit having more than one cell

Catkin: A long flower cluster comprised of closely spaced, generally small flowers and prominent bracts, as in pussy willows

Chlorosis: A yellowing of the leaves, reflecting a deficiency of chlorophyll

Clay soil: A soil, usually heavy and poorly drained, containing a preponderance of fine particles

Clone: Vegatative produced plants from a single parent plant; clones will not grow true from seed

Columnar: Growing in the shape of column, not spreading

Compost: Decomposed organic matter, usually used to enrich the soil

Container-grown: Grown as a seedling in the container it is to be sold in

Corymb: A flat-topped flower cluster in which flowers open successively from the outside in

Cross-pollination: The transfer of pollen from one plant to another

Cultivar: A variety of plant produced by selective hybridization

Cultivate: To work the soil in order to break it up and/or remove weeds

Cutting: A severed plant stem, usually used for the purposes of propagation

Deadhead: To remove spent blossoms

Deciduous: Losing its leaves at the end of the growing season; nonevergreen

Dicot, Dictotyledon: A plant that bears two or more seed leaves (cotyledons). Most seed plants and most woody plants are cotyledons. See also *Monocotyledon.*

Dieback: Death of part or all of the woody portion of a plant

Dioecious: Having both male and female flowers

Division: The removal of suckers from a parent plant, for the purposes of propagation

Double: In flowers, having an increased number of petals, produced at the expense of other organs

Drupe: A fruit with a fleshy covering over a hard-coated seed

Epiphyte: A plant that grows on another plant rather than in soil; "air plants"

Evergreen: Retaining foliage year-round

Exfoliate: To self-peel, as bark

Fertile: Having the capacity to generate seed

Friable: Ready for cultivation, easily cultivable, as soil

Genus: A group of related species

Germinate: To develop a young plant from seed; to produce a seedling

Glaucous: Blue-hued; covered with a bluish or grayish bloom

Graft: To insert a section of one plant, usually a shoot, into another so that they grow together into a single plant

Habit: A plant's characteristic form of growth

Harden off: To mature sufficiently to withstand winter temperatures

Hardpan: Soil sufficiently clogged with clay or other particles that draining is impossible

Hardwood cutting: Cutting taken from a mature woody stem for the purpose of propagation

Hardy: Able to withstand winter temperatures

Herbaceous: Without woody tissue

Humus: Soil composed of decaying organic matter

Hybrid: A plant produced by crossing two unlike parents

Insecticidal soap: Soap formulated to kill, repel, or inhibit the growth of insect pests

Integrated pest management (IPM): A philosphy of pest management based on the idea of using escalating methods of pest control, beginning with the least damaging; incorporates the selection of resistant varieties, the use of biological and nontoxic controls, and the application of pesticides and herbicides only when absolutely necessary

Invasive: Tending to spread freely and wantonly; weedy

Leaf mold: A form of humus composed of decayed leaves, often used to enrich soil

Leaflets: the parts of a compound leaf

Liana: A fast-growing woody vine; most lianas are tropical

Lime: Calcium carbonate, often added to the soil to reduce acidity

Loam: A generally fertile and well-drained soil, usually containing a significant amount of decomposed organic matter

Lobed: Divided into segments

Microclimate: Climate specific to a small area; may vary significantly from that of surrounding areas

Monocot, Monocotyledon: a plant bearing only one seed leaf (cotyledon), and usually producing little woody tissue. Few, with the exception of palms, become tall trees. Examples of monocots are grasses, lilies, aroids, bromeliads, irises, cannas, and sedges.

Monopodial: Producing indefinite growth and elongation of the stem or rhizome, usually unbranched. Vanda and phalaenopsis orchids are monopodial.

Mulch: An organic or inorganic soil covering, used to maintain soil temperature and moisture and to discourage the growth of weeds

Naturalize: To "escape" from a garden setting and become established in the wild

Neutral soil: Soil having a pH of 7—neither acid nor alkaline

Node: On a plant, the site at which the leaf joins the stem; the area where most rooting activity takes place.

Panicle: A branched raceme

Peat moss: Partially decomposed sphagnum moss, often added to soil to increase moisture retention

Pendulous: Hanging down, drooping (also pendant)

Perennial: A plant that lives for more than one growing season (usually at least three)

Perfect: Having stamens and pistils; bisexual, as a flower

Petal: Part of a flower's corolla, outside of the stamens and pistils, often vividly colored

pH: An expression of soil alkalinity or acidity; the hydrogen ion content of soil

Pioneer: A plant that flourishes in disturbed soil, as after a fire

Pistil: A flower's female reproductive organ

Pods: Dry fruits

Pollen: The spores of a seed-bearing plant

Pollination: The transfer of pollen from one plant to another

Pome: A fleshy fruit

Propagate: To grow new plants from old under controlled conditions

Prostrate: Lying or dragging on the ground.

Prune: To cut back, for the purposes of shaping a plant, encouraging new growth, or controlling size

Pyramidal: Broad on bottom, coming to a pointed top

Raceme: An elongated flower cluster in which the flowers are held on small stalks radiating from a single, larger stalk

Rejuvenation pruning: The practice of cutting all the main stems of a tree back to within one-half inch of the ground during winter dormancy; renewal pruning

Remontant: Able to rebloom one or more times during a single growing season

Renewal pruning: See *Rejuvenation pruning*

Root cutting: A cutting taken from the root of a parent plant for the purpose of propagation

Root pruning: The act of removing a portion of a plant's roots to keep top growth in check

Rootstock: The root of a grafted plant

Runner: A prostrate branch that roots at its joint

Scarify: To sand, scratch, or otherwise disturb the coating of a seed in preparation for its germination

Self-pollination: A plant's ability to fertlize its pistils with its own pollen

Semidouble: Having more than the usual number of petals but with at least some pollen-producing stamens

Semievergreen: Retaining its leaves for most of the winter, or in warm climates

Semihardwood cutting: A cutting taken from a stem that has just begun to develop woody tissue, for the purpose of propagation.

Sepal: The part of a flower that is circularly arranged outside the petals

Serrated: Saw-toothed

Single: In flowers, having only one layer of petals

Softwood cutting: A cutting taken from a green, or immature, stem of a woody plant, for the purpose of propagation

Species: A subgroup of a genus, composed of reproductively similar plants or animals

Specimen: A plant deliberately set by itself to emphasize its ornamental properties

Spreading: Having a horizontally branching habit

Stamen: The male organ of a flower carrying the pollen-bearing anther

Staminoid: A pollenless stamen

Sterile: Unable to generate seed

Stolon: An underground shoot

Stratify: To help seeds overcome dormancy by cleaning and drying them, then maintaining them for a period of time under generally cool and moist conditions

Striations: Fine stripes

Sucker: A shoot growing from the root or base of a woody plant

Tap root: A strong, vertical-growing, central root

Terete: Cylindrical (often tapering)

Topiary: The art of trimming or training plants into decorative three-dimensional shapes

Trifoliate: Having three leaflets

Truss: A flower cluster set at the top of a stem or branch

Understock: The stock or root plant onto which a shoot has been grafted to produce a new plant

Unisexual: Having either stamens or pistils

USDA hardiness zones: Planting zones established by the United States Department of Agriculture, defined by a number of factors, including minimum winter temperatures

Understory plant: A plant whose natural habitat is the forest floor; or one that can be used beneath a larger plant in the garden

Undulated: Wavy

Variegated: Characterized by striping, mottling, or other coloration in addition to the plant's general over-all color

Vascular system: The tissues that conduct water, nutrients, and other elements through plants

Weeping: Having long, drooping branches

Winged: Having winglike appendages.

Winter kill: The dying back of a plant or part of a plant due to harsh winter conditions

Woody: Forming stems that mature to wood

Xeriscaping: Landscaping with the use of drought-tolerant plants, to eliminate the need for supplemental watering

SOURCES Plants for oriental gardens can be purchased at any reputable nursery; some of the sources below specialize in them. Sources for lanterns and sculpture are also included. Inclusion on this list does not imply an endorsement, and many fine sources are not included.

PLANTS

Amberway Gardens
5803 Amberway; St. Louis, MO 63128
314-842-6103
irises; catalogue, $1.00

Bambook Sourcery
666 Magnon Road; Sebastapol, CA 95472
707-823-5866; 707-829-8106 (fax)
bamboo; catalogue, $2.00

Broken Arrow Nursery
13 Broken Arrow Road; Hamden, CT 06518
203-288-1026; 203-287-1035 (fax)
conifers, rhododendron; price list

The Bulb Crate
2560 Deerfield Road; Riverwoods, IL 60015
(847) 317-1417
peonies, iris, lilies, catalogue, $1.00

Kellygreen
6924 Highway 38; Drain, OR 97435
800-477-5676; 503-836-2290 (fax)
Japanese maples (over 100 cultivars)

Lilypons Water Gardens
PO Box 10, Buckeyestown, Maryland 21717; 800-723-7667
PO Box 188; Brookshire, Texas 77423
800-765-5459
PO Box 1130; Thermal, California 92274
800-365-5459
Largest water garden; everything needed to establish a water garden:free catalogue

Matsu-moiji Nursery
Box 11414; Philadelphia, PA 19111
215-722-6286
Japanese maples and pines

Owens Farms
2951 Curve-Nankipoo Road; Ripley, TN 38063
901-635-1588
Japanese maples, Japanese cedar, bonsai; catalogue, $2.00

Shepherd Hill Farm
200 Peekskill Hollow Road; Putnam Valley, NY 10579
914-528-5917; 914-528-8343 (fax)
Japanese maples, rhododendron, conifers

Siskiyou Rare Plant Nursery
2825 Cummings Road; Medford, OR 97501
541-772-6846; 541-772-4917 (fax)
Japanese maples, dwarf conifers, rock garden plants; catalogue, $3.00

Wildwood
14488 Rock Creek Road
Cardon, OH 44024
216-286-3714 (phone and fax)
groundcovers, hostas, catalogue, $1.00

LANTERNS AND ARTIFACTS

Asian Artifacts
1801 Woodbine Place; Oceanside, CA 92054
619-967-3850
lanterns, stone basins, pagodas, bridges, catalog, $2.00

Bamboo Fences
31 Germania Court; Jamaica Plains, MA 02130
617-524-6137; 617-524-6100 (fax)
fences, gates, trellises, sode-gaki

The Brass Baron
10151 Pacific Mesa Blvd, Ste. 104
San Diego, CA 92121
800-536-0987; 800-536-0988 (fax)
Brass fountains and statuary; catalogue

Bridgeworks
306 Lockwood Street; Covington, LA 70433
504-893-7933
Japanese style bridges; catalogue

Dalton Pavilions
20 Commerce Drive; Telford, PA 18969
215-721-1492; 215-721-1501 (fax)
Red cedar gazebos, pagodas; catalogue

Garden Concepts
PO Box 241233; Memphis, TN 38124
901-756-1649; 901-755-4564 (fax)
Wooden garden furniture, made to order

Hermitage Gardens
PO Box 361; Cananstota, NY 13032
315-697-9093; 315-697-8169 (fax)
Japanese-style gardens, pools; catalogue

Nampara Gardens
2004 Gold Course Road
Bayside, CA 95524
707-822-5744
Redwood bridges and lanterns

Stone Forest
PO Box 2840; Santa Fe, NM 87504
505-986-8883; 505-982-2712 (fax)
lanterns, basins, fountains, bamboo

Stonewoods Gallery
Box 35; Tuxedo, NY 10987
800-786-6308; 800-786-6361 (fax)
Inscribed stones; catalogue

Tom Torrens
PO Box 1819; Gig Harbor, WA 98335
206-857-5831; 206-265-2404 (fax)
gongs, bells, lanterns, fountains, catalogue, $2.00.

CONTRIBUTORS

Main Garden
The Japanese Garden of
The Japanese Garden Society of Oregon
611 S.W. Kingston Avenue\
Washington Park
Post office box 3847
Portland, Oregon 97208

Consulting Gardens
Heather O'Hagen
Dr. Sun Yat-Sen Classical Chinese
Garden
578 Carrall Street
Vancouver, British Columbia V6B 2J8
604-689-7133

Henry Painter
Fort Worth Botanic Garden
3220 Botanic Garden Boulevard
Fort Worth, Texas 76107
817-871-7686

Virginia Hayes
Ganna Walska Lotusland
695 Ashley Road
Santa Barbara, California 93108
805-969-3767

Nancy Rose
Minnesota Landscape Arboretum
3675 Arboretum Drive, Box 39
Chanhassen, Minnesota 55317
612-443-2460

Benjamin Chu
Missouri Botanical Garden
PO Box 299
St. Louis, Missouri 63166
314-577-5110

Jerry Parsons
University of California Berkeley
Botanical Garden
Centennial Drive
Berkeley, California 94720
510-643-8040

Roy Forster
VanDusen Botanical Garden
5251 Oak Street
Vancouver, British Columbia V6M
4H1

PHOTO CREDITS

LEAF SHAPES

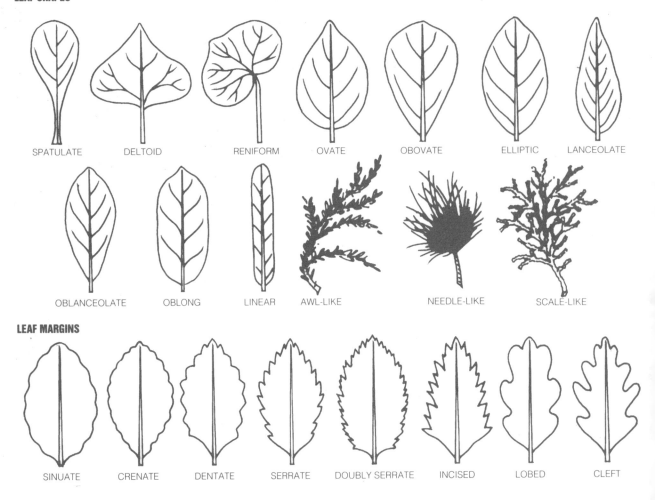

SPATULATE   DELTOID   RENIFORM   OVATE   OBOVATE   ELLIPTIC   LANCEOLATE

OBLANCEOLATE   OBLONG   LINEAR   AWL-LIKE   NEEDLE-LIKE   SCALE-LIKE

LEAF MARGINS

SINUATE   CRENATE   DENTATE   SERRATE   DOUBLY SERRATE   INCISED   LOBED   CLEFT

LEAF ARRANGEMENTS AND STRUCTURES

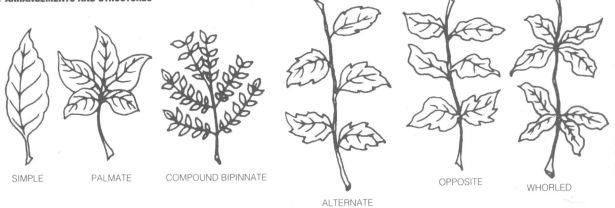

SIMPLE   PALMATE   COMPOUND BIPINNATE   ALTERNATE   OPPOSITE   WHORLED